THE FRONTIER OF CONTROL

Pluto  Press

Carter L. Goodrich

THE FRONTIER OF CONTROL

A Study in British Workshop Politics

Foreword by R.H. Tawney

With a new foreword and additional notes
by Richard Hyman

THIS EDITION PUBLISHED 1975
BY PLUTO PRESS LIMITED
UNIT 10. SPENCER COURT
7 CHALCOT ROAD
LONDON NW1 8LH

FIRST PUBLISHED 1920
BY G. BELL AND SONS LIMITED
LONDON

ISBN 0 902818 69 4 PAPERBACK
ISBN 0 902818 70 8 HARDBACK

FILMSET BY C. NICHOLLS & COMPANY LTD
AND PRINTED IN GREAT BRITAIN
BY REDWOOD BURN LIMITED
TROWBRIDGE & ESHER

COVER AND ADDITIONAL MATERIAL DESIGNED BY
RICHARD HOLLIS GrR

Contents

Foreword to the 1975 edition by Richard Hyman   VII

References to the new foreword   XXXIV

THE FRONTIER OF CONTROL   1
1920 edition (see contents, page v)

Additional notes to the text by Richard Hyman   273

Index to this edition   281

Foreword to the 1975 edition
by Richard Hyman

The Frontier of Control is a remarkable book, written at a remarkable stage in British labour history. In the decade 1910–20, British trade unionism was more clearly on the offensive than in any other period of its development, before or since. Union membership advanced from two and a half million in 1910 to almost eight and a half million in 1920. The number of officially recorded strikes, which had averaged five hundred a year in the previous decade, escalated to three times that number in 1913; and, after a lull caused by the wartime 'industrial truce', rose to a new peak in 1920.

Many of the post-war disputes were major official industry-wide stoppages. At times, the unions' demands included a new type of objective – the control of industry. Labour was forging more powerful organisation: union amalgamations occurred in almost every industry, while workers in key sectors of the economy, the Miners, Railwaymen, and Transport Workers' Federation, were joined together in a Triple Alliance; and there were insistent demands that the Trades Union Congress should be transformed from a loose-knit pressure group and talking shop into a general staff of labour. The new mood was summed up in the slogan 'direct action' – a call to sweep aside the established constitutional procedures wherever these stood in the way of workers' interests and wishes.

Britain in the immediate post-war period was closer to revolution than at any time in modern history. The armed forces were mutinous and indisciplined, frustrated at delays and inequities in demobilisation. For almost a year, the police authorities struggled to contain the spread of aggressive trade unionism in their own ranks. Industrial workers were determined to be repaid for their wartime sufferings. If they were to use their new strength to the full, on whom would the nation's rulers rely? The propertied and privileged classes were understandably alarmed. Even stolid cabinet ministers were haunted by the spectre of Petrograd.[1]

The crisis never came. The established leaders of the trade unions and the Labour Party made fine speeches about winning control of industry, but they shrank from any serious 'challenge to the constitution', and were determined to keep the situation under control. The rank-and-file workers seldom linked their discontent and combativity with explicit revolutionary aims and the small numbers of revolutionaries were disorganised and outmanoeuvred.

Yet talk of workers' control was not simply rhetoric, or the utopian goal of a handful of left-wing activists; it was rooted in significant developments in industrial life. Nineteenth century industry had two contradictory forces: an authoritarian work discipline imposed on the new proletariat, as well as a powerful craft tradition of workshop autonomy and the rule of 'custom and practice'. In the post-war period this craft tradition came under wide-scale attack from new forms of technology, and the application of the utilitarian (and, for the worker, dehumanising and degrading) 'scientific management'. At the same time the spread of union organisation gave workers a means of resistance in areas where authoritarian management was traditional. Hence when Goodrich conducted his research in 1919, the balance of workplace power throughout much of British industry was in a state of flux.

Goodrich recounts in detail the inroads made by workers into the decision-making prerogatives asserted by managements over a wide range of British industries. No other writer, before or since, has provided so comprehensive a survey of the fluid and imprecise borderline between workshop autonomy and managerial authority.[2]

But the book is more than simple description. Goodrich makes a notable contribution to the theory of control in industry. In particular, he makes clear that the forms of workers' control then in evidence were typically reactive or protective in intent, a ns to defend specific material interests rather than an assertion of the principle of industrial democracy as an end in itself. He shows that the boundary between workers' control as a means and as an end is by no means inflexible: actions and trategies which are primarily defensive may spill over into demands for positive control over the direction of industry – an objective then, as now, professed by only a tiny minority of workers. In this respect the book's contemporary relevance is obvious.

While the practice of workers' control has deep historical roots, its relevance for socialist theory was widely recognised only after 1910.[3] Until then, criticism of capitalism focused on the ownership of industry, and on the inequalities that flowed from it, rather than on the structure of control within production itself. Socialism was conventionally defined in terms of nationalisation and state welfare; and the road to it was thought to lead through parliamentary election and legislation. Socialism, it was argued, would radically affect the status of the worker as citizen and as consumer; but few socialists intended a similar transformation in his role as producer.[4] Despite major disagreements on many political issues, such views were common to most members of socialist bodies as diverse as the Fabian Society, the Independent Labour Party (ILP), and the Social-Democratic Federation (SDF).[5]

But in the decade preceding the appearance of *The Frontier of Control* this consensus was increasingly questioned. The first serious challenge was syndicalism, a movement that took its name from the French trade unions – *syndicats*. Its leading theorists rejected all compromise or accommodation with employers, advocated revolutionary violence and sabotage, and called for a general strike as the means to socialism.[6]

In 1910 this doctrine struck a responsive chord in Britain. Wages had failed to keep pace with steadily rising prices since the turn of the century; the newly-formed Labour Party, which achieved an apparent breakthrough in 1906 with the election of 29 MPs, acted as little more than an adjunct to the Liberal government; while the orthodox left-wing alternative, the SDF, made little headway. In this situation, the notion of an *industrially* based socialism held obvious attractions. The most notable convert was Tom Mann, famous as a leader of the 1889 London Dock Strike, and prominent in industrial and political struggles for a quarter of a century.[7] After a decade in Australia and New Zealand, in which he saw how small an impact was made by Labour governments on the conditions of workers' lives, he was convinced that the traditional *political* conception of the road to socialism was futile. Returning to Britain, and inspired by a meeting with some of the French leaders, he played the major part in launching an Industrial Syndicalist movement.

The new movement's doctrines were considerably less precise than those of the French syndicalists. The philosophy of violence was transmuted into a generalised enthusiasm for direct action. Sabotage became 'ca'canny' or going slow, an established element in workshop custom and practice. In effect, what united British syndicalists with their foreign counterparts was disenchantment with parliamentary politics, an emphasis on industrial solidarity, and an aspiration for a general strike. These sentiments proved contagious: while many advanced sections of the new generation of workers were hesitant about volution, they were willing 'syndicalists'. And syndicalism became widely identified as the cause of the growing industrial unrest in the immediate pre-war years. As the government's leading industrial conciliator commented, 'the employment of active propaganda' appeared to be the most important source of conflict.[8]

Syndicalism did influence industrial militancy. The Central Labour College, a marxist breakaway from Ruskin College, adopted the syndicalist approach in its residential and correspondence courses, and was particularly influential in South Wales. There, in 1911, a group of young activists launched an Unofficial Reform Committee and, in the following year, published a telling indictment of the divisive structure of the Miners' Federation, its traditional conciliatory policies, and the subordination of the rank and file to its leadership.[9] Partly as a result, the South Wales district was transformed from one of the most moderate in mining trade unionism to a storm centre of militancy and class consciousness. In Liverpool, in the summer of 1911, Tom Mann led a general transport strike which paralysed the city, and helped spread the unrest to the nation's railways.

Yet labour unrest owed far more to material conditions than to the spread of syndicalist theories. 'It was the mood of syndicalism, not the doctrine, that made headway.'[10] That the syndicalists were able to achieve so close an identification with the eruption was due, in part at least, to the vagueness of their ideas. They 'were generally much more concerned with the burning questions of the day than with the distant future, much more with the methods and tactics of the class struggle than with its ultimate aims. Everybody who was willing to take part in the class struggle, regardless of his organisation or his political views, was welcome in the Syndicalist League.'[11] This flexibility, which was a source of strength during the years of struggle, proved to be a weakness later when the militancy paid off.[12] By 1914, even before the outbreak of war, the 'strike explosion' was obviously subsiding; and the syndicalist movement itself disintegrated. 'Once the industrial unrest was over . . . there was simply no common doctrine or outlook to keep together all these heterogeneous elements.'[13] Some took part in the unofficial Amalgamation Committee movement; others rose to positions of union leadership. Of the ideas of the Syndicalist League little survived but the slogans – of workers' control and direct action.

Wartime conditions generated a new, and more intimate, link between revolutionary theory and industrial militancy. Virtually every union executive responded to the declaration of war with promises of industrial truce. When the government and employers demanded that trade union rules which might interfere with munitions production be suspended, the officials acquiesced. In March 1915 they agreed to abandon the right to strike, to permit the introduction of 'dilutees' (lower-skilled and female labour) on war work, and to relax many of their customary rules; in return the government agreed to restore pre-war practices once hostilities ceased, and to impose (extremely modest) controls over profits in the munitions industries. In July 1915 the terms of this Treasury Agreement received statutory force in the Munitions of War Act.[14]

Shop-floor workers soon felt the effects of their leaders' industrial pacifism: production was often radically transformed; new forms of discipline were applied; new grades of labour, often without a trade union tradition, were introduced; vital protective practices were attacked; and the cost of living surged upwards. In 1915 and 1916, the Munitions Act and the introduction of conscription fostered further grievances. In general, redress could be obtained only through action at workplace level. These were ideal conditions for an upsurge in shop stewards' organisation, which had existed only in vestigial form before the war.

In its origins the rise of the shop stewards was 'a spontaneous movement, arising naturally and inevitably out of the industrial circumstances of the times'.[15] The movement's relations with official trade unionism were ambiguous: many unions recognised stewards for purposes of internal communication, but the rulebooks did not endorse their negotiating functions, and even less their role in leading militant action, sometimes against government as well as employers.

There were two aspects of shop steward activity. The first was to act as a safety-valve for explosive build-ups of workers' grievances. This function received little publicity, but was recognised by perceptive observers of industrial relations: 'Most of the stewards and other workshop representatives were concerned with the countless difficulties which arose in the readjustment of conditions which had to be made in order to adapt the industries of Great Britain to the needs of war . . . Almost every one of these readjustments was a potential source of friction and dispute; and the fact that the vast majority of them were accomplished without trouble shows that the shop stewards played a big part in preventing and settling difficulties as well as in conducting disputes.'[16]

However, it was the second, more militant, aspect of the stewards' activities that caught the headlines and sustained the popular image of the steward as a source of disorder. This was the rise of the shop stewards' *movements* with strong political ties. Beginning in 1915 on the Clyde, Workers' Committees sprang up in many of the main munitions centres to co-ordinate the leading activists in the various factories. On a number of occasions they played a decisive role in directing local struggles.[17] For a brief period towards the end of the war, it even seemed as if the Shop Stewards' and Workers' Committee Movement (SSWCM), set up during 1916–17, would exert a crucial influence on the character of industrial militancy in engineering.

The direction taken by the shop stewards' movement owed a great deal to one organisation: the Socialist Labour Party (SLP). Formed in 1903 as a Clydeside breakaway from the SDF, it took as its central tenet the industrial unionism of the American socialist Daniel de Leon, then being expounded vigorously in Britain and Ireland by James Connolly.[18] The basic principle was that 'they who rule industrially will rule politically'. The predominance of the capitalist class was founded on its economic power; to construct a superior power it was necessary to organise the workers in every factory into revolutionary industrial unions. Such organisation would not only create the basis for a revolutionary general strike; it would also create the structures through which workers could control industry once socialism was established.

Unlike the syndicalists, the SLP did not wholly disavow political action: in a purely industrial struggle, state power might be used decisively in support of the employers. But political action was regarded as subsidiary: once a socialist parliamentary majority was elected its only task would be to dismantle the coercive machinery of state and to dissolve itself. In practice the SLP and the syndicalists differed mainly in their attitudes to the existing institutions of the labour movement: where the syndicalists were committed to a strategy of revolution from within, the SLP advocated 'dual unionism', the formation of 'pure' revolutionary organisations outside and in opposition to the old. Their success was negligible; and their dogmatism and sectarianism ensured that up to the war they remained an insignificant and localised group. But then, under the influence of the wartime struggles, and helped by a tradition of theoretical rigour, their analysis rapidly matured.

Alone of the existing socialist organisations, the SLP had a clear interpretation of the *political* significance of the emergent shop stewards' movement. Those of their activists closest to the shop-floor saw in the spontaneous development of workplace organisation a model for independent working-class institutions which could herald the overthrow of capitalism and direct the new society. The central importance of the shop stewards' committees as independent rank-and-file agencies was defiantly asserted in one of the first manifestoes of the Clyde Workers' Committee, in which SLP members had a key ideological influence: 'we will support the officials just so long as they rightly represent the workers, but we will act independently immediately they misrepresent them. Being composed of delegates from every shop and untrammelled by obsolete rule or law, we claim to represent the true feeling of the workers. We can act immediately according to the merits of the case and the desire of the rank and file.'[19]

The old debate between de Leonites with their blueprints for brand new industrial unions, and syndicalists with schemes for amalgamating existing unions, was seen to be unreal. As powerfully argued by Jack Murphy, the Sheffield engineer who became one of the party's leading theoreticians, the principal task was to unite the workers in the workshop; once this was achieved, the reorganisation of national union structure on industrial lines would follow naturally, but until then the whole question was artificial and premature.[20] For the present, the local workers' committee rather than the industrial union must be the main focus for common action and for the extension of class consciousness. As the war continued, this view of the shop-floor movement was elaborated by the leading industrial members of the SLP until it closely paralleled the theories of Soviet power triumphantly applied, in 1917, by Lenin and the Bolsheviks.

There were however fundamental differences between Bolshevism and the ideology of the Shop Stewards' and Workers' Committee Movement, relating in particular to the questions of state power and the role of the revolutionary party. For the syndicalists, political organisation and action were irrelevant: the bourgeoisie ruled by virtue of their *economic* dominance, and would be overthrown automatically through the development of a superior fighting spirit and industrial organisation on the part of the workers. The SLP were almost as naive: they saw the need to take account of the coercive agencies of the state, but believed that these could readily be neutralised by conventional political means, through propagandist and electoral activity. The notion of an *integrated* structure of capitalist economic-political-cultural domination, requiring a similarly integrated revolutionary challenge, found no place in their analysis. By contrast, the Bolsheviks put the forcible conquest of state power to the fore, and insisted that its achievement demanded a political party which in structure and character differed radically from the traditional social-democratic model.

The success of the Russian revolutionaries had a dramatic impact on their British industrial counterparts. Most of the leading shop steward activists responded to the Soviet appeal for a dialogue with the new Communist International (founded in 1919), and several attended its deliberations in Moscow. They became convinced that many of the principles of Bolshevism were right: not merely because events had proved their efficacy, but also because these principles appeared in many respects to be the logical development of the theoretical position already reached by their own movement.[21] The key figures in the movement were prominent in the formation of the Communist Party in 1920–21 and contributed significantly to its early leadership; the SSWCM itself eventually merged into the Party.[22] But Bolshevisation meant that many of the views once considered central to the movement were dismissed as 'infantilism';[23] and a major casualty was the emphasis on the building of workers' control from the grass roots.

One factor which made it easier for the new leaders of the CP to dilute or abandon their old ideas was the change in their own role in relationship to the rank and file. During the war the shop steward leaders had managed to carry the movement beyond the craft sectionalism and conservatism on which it was largely based, and to give it an offensive character and a broader class orientation. This was possible because 'a subversive potential . . . had always been locked within the craft tradition';[24] but it was a precarious enterprise, which ultimately failed. In 1918 pressure built up among skilled workers for a national strike to obtain special exemption from conscription; and the leaders of the Shop Stewards' Movement, in openly resisting this divisive demand, ruptured their links with the rank and file.

The last major engagement of the wartime movement ended in disaster. In January 1919 the Clyde and Belfast District Committees of the Engineers called a strike for a 40-hour week, protesting against a national agreement which reduced hours to 47. In Glasgow the struggle turned into a general strike; but the government intervened, martial law was declared, the police brutally attacked a mass meeting of strikers, and the leaders were arrested. The strike collapsed and many militants were victimised. In the country as a whole, the period of strong shop-floor organisation came to an abrupt end with the severe disruption of industry following the armistice, and the onset of economic recession at the close of 1920. The most prominent of the wartime stewards were forced to win a new reputation in the 1920s as leaders of the unemployed. Where shop-floor organisation survived it became integrated in, and subordinated to, the official union structures following national agreements with the engineering employers in 1917 and 1919. No wonder many of the wartime militants followed the Russians in elevating the problem of power in society at large above the problem of control at the level of the workplace.

A curious paradox emerged. The slogan of workers' control was initially the virtual prerogative of self-avowed revolutionaries; but after the Bolshevik revolution their commitment to self-management at the point of production was modified or even abandoned. At the same time, the issue was increasingly taken up by those who denied – or at least refused explicitly to assert – revolutionary intent. Of these, the most sophisticated and articulate were the Guild Socialists: a group, initially composed for the most part of academics and similar intellectuals, who first developed their distinctive theories shortly before the outbreak of war. By far the most prominent was G.D.H.Cole, who graduated from Oxford in 1912 and published *The World of Labour* a year later.[25] The Guild Socialists shared the syndicalists' distaste for the orthodox socialist assumption that state ownership was the solution to all social evils. Nationalisation, by eliminating the capitalist profit-maker, might benefit workers as consumers; but if a bureaucratic and authoritarian system of management remained, the workers' status as producers would fail to improve and might even deteriorate. But syndicalism – a 'vague and indefinite movement'[26] – offered an inadequate theoretical basis for an industrially democratic society; in particular the Guild Socialists resisted the syndicalist belief that trade unions should control not merely industry but also the state and indeed the whole of society. Members of society, they insisted, had a variety of distinct interests and functions which could be adequately represented only through a range of separate institutions. The state, constituted on a basis which reflected this plurality, should own industry, but should entrust its management to the workers organised in National Guilds.[27]

The National Guilds League (NGL), formed in 1915 to propagate these ideas among 'advanced' trade unionists, had an influence out of all proportion to its size and social composition. This was largely because, for all their criticisms of the existing structure and policies of the trade union movement, the Guild Socialists assigned to its bargaining activities a central role in the attainment of workers' control. Cole's 1917 analysis indicates how the model society might develop out of the current activity of the labour movement:[28] increasingly effective and self-confident trade unions would successfully erode established managerial prerogatives, in a process of 'encroaching control'; more and more aspects of production would become subject to negotiation; finally the unions, reorganised on a more rational basis, would be strong enough (in key industries at least) to oust the capitalist from detailed management altogether. Instead the employer would pay a lump sum for a specified amount of production, and the union itself would organise the work, appoint supervisors, employ technical experts, and allocate payment among its members. As control intensified, the profits obtained by employers from their 'collective contract' with the unions would be squeezed, until they turned to the state to bale them out through nationalisation. But experience of bureaucratic state management would merely accentuate the struggle for control, until the unions became strong enough to impose Guild Socialism.

Militant and even revolutionary shop stewards were attracted to this scenario since it lent their day-to-day struggles on the shop-floor historic meaning and significance. For example, one of the most influential pamphlets produced by the shop stewards' movement on Clydeside – *Towards Industrial Democracy*, a patently revolutionary tract – reflects strong Guild Socialist influence:[29] the unions, insisted Gallacher and Paton (its authors), must pursue a strategy of encroaching control as 'invaders of our native province of Industry, now in the hands of an arrogant and tyrannical usurper'.

Guild Socialism was also open to a more gradualist interpretation, and it was in this guise that it permeated the official policies of many trade unions, particularly those which had experienced state ownership or wartime government control. Guildsmen like Cole were happy to assist directly in devising trade union plans, such as those cited by Goodrich from the railways and postal service, even when, for the sake of acceptance, the principle of self-management was diluted into various schemes of 'joint control'.

The example to which Goodrich gives special attention is the miners' campaign for public ownership and partial workers' control. The Miners' Federation, which with some 800,000 members was by far the largest union in the country, resolved in 1918 to add the demand for joint control to its established objective of nationalisation; and in January 1919 this was included in a programme of demands submitted to the government. An unsatisfactory response led to a ballot which showed a six to one majority in favour of strike action; and with the Miners ready to call for support from their partners in the Triple Alliance, a major crisis loomed. The government, and in particular Lloyd George, averted the conflict through the 'genius for improvisation' with which it repeatedly outmanoeuvred labour in the turbulent post-war period:[30] the Federation was persuaded to postpone its strike, and participate in a special commission formed to investigate the immediate issue of wages and hours and the more general question of nationalisation.

The Coal Industry Commission was a unique event in British labour history. The chairman, Sir John Sankey, was a judge acceptable to the Miners; of the remaining twelve members the miners directly nominated four and agreed two others with the government;[31] the coal-owners nominated three and a further three were industrialists nominated by the government. Created by special legislation, the Commission had powers to subpoena documents and witnesses; powers which the labour representatives used, in the imposing setting of the House of Lords, to put private ownership on trial. It was a magnificent spectacle, and attracted immense publicity. The three labour intellectuals 'publicly tore the pretensions and performance of the mineowners into such small fragments that no intelligent person could doubt, thereafter, that nationalisation of the mines was bound to come';[32] while the miners' leaders added to the verbal demolition. 'Smillie was the lord high executioner, the judge, the people's man, and in the name of the people had issued orders to the privileged class, which they unwillingly but humbly obeyed.'[33]

The owners' discomfiture was temporary. The King's Robing Room of the House of Lords was not the cockpit of the industrial struggle; the Coal Commission was only a faint echo of the real battle. While the miners' leaders were winning rhetorical triumphs, the government was winning time. At the end of June, the Commissioners presented their various reports, showing a majority in favour of nationalisation. In August Lloyd George, despite a pledge to implement the Sankey recommendations 'in letter and in spirit', rejected nationalisation. Proposals for strike action, with TUC support, now attracted little enthusiasm; the militant mood of early 1919 had been de-fused, and official action on the issue was confined to an ineffectual publicity campaign on the theme 'The Mines for the Nation'. Just over a year later, the government handed back full control of the industry to the owners, and the scene was set for the bitter defeats of the Miners' Federation in the 1920s: the collapse of the Triple Alliance on 'Black Friday', 15 April 1921, and the General Strike and seven months' lock-out in 1926.

In 1920, when *The Frontier of Control* was published, it was still possible to believe in the uninterrupted progress of the workers' movement for rights and status in industry. 'Any history of Trade Unionism that breaks off at the beginning of 1920 halts, not at the end of an epoch, but – we may almost say – at the opening of a new chapter,' wrote the Webbs in the revised edition of their classic study. 'British Trade Unionism, at a moment when it is, both industrially and politically, stronger than ever before, is seething with new ideas and far-reaching aspirations.'[34] They could scarcely have been more mistaken.

The miners' fate merely represents in its starkest form the decline and demoralisation which afflicted the movement as a whole after 1920. The other development to which Goodrich devotes much detailed attention, the 'Building Trades Parliament' or Industrial Council for the Building Industry, proved similarly insubstantial.[35] An attempt, in 1920, to set up self-governing Building Guilds also ended in disaster after two years.[36] Guild Socialism itself crumbled: a section, inspired by the Russian revolution, joined the Communist Party; others, like Cole and Tawney, became increasingly reconciled to orthodox Labour politics. By 1929, Cole himself had followed the Communists in recanting much of his earlier enthusiasm for workers' control – though for diametrically opposite reasons.[37]

It became clear in retrospect that 1920 was indeed the end of an era.

For two generations afterwards, the movement for workers' control appeared to hold little more than historical interest. In the last decade the situation has changed dramatically: 'participation', 'industrial democracy', and 'workers' control' have become part of the small change of social and political discussion. The Labour Party and TUC, both traditionally hostile to the case for workers' control, and committed instead to the hierarchical management structure of nationalised industries, have changed policy significantly.[38] At the same time, various forms of employee involvement in decision-making are being seen by many management theorists as means of reinforcing workers' crumbling commitment to their employing organisations. From a quite different standpoint independent left-wing groups are finding a rapidly growing audience for more revolutionary conceptions of workers' control.

'We are all industrial democrats now,' comment Coates and Topham. 'The term is so general, all-embracing and has such wide appeal that politicians and philosophers of all shades of opinion prefer to pay lip-service to it.'[39] In this respect, the experience of 1910–20 is clearly relevant. 'There is a large body of opinion that is agreed on some extension of workers' control as the next step in trade unionism,' Goodrich records. But 'there is no one break in the long series from Syndicalism to Whitley-ism'.[40]

Syndicalism has already been described; but what was Whitleyism? In 1916, as part of its general planning for post-war 'reconstruction', the government appointed a committee of employers' and union leaders under the chairmanship of J.H.Whitley, Speaker of the House of Commons and member of a mill-owning family. The committee's brief was to make and consider suggestions for securing a permanent improvement in the relations between employers and workmen. It submitted a series of reports, the most famous of which proposed the establishment in each industry of permanent joint bodies of representative employers and union officials.[41]

The Whitley recommendations inspired remarkable enthusiasm. It 'was popularly taken to be a concession of "industrial self-government" to the workers. Actually it conceded nothing. . . It may be said that the compromise reached was to use the phraseology of far-reaching reform, but to confine actual proposals to conservative modifications of the existing practice of industrial negotiation.'[42]

Whitleyism had three separate bases of appeal. For the government, it offered a possible recipe for industrial peace, and at the very least a means by which it could *appear*, without undertaking any serious commitments, to be tackling the labour question. The government welcomed the Whitley proposals and took the initiative, at the beginning of 1919, in convening a National Industrial Conference of several hundred employer and union representatives to consider and make recommendations on industrial relations issues.

For progressive employers, and for trade unionists whose first priority was the restoration of 'orderly' industrial relations, Whitleyism offered a means of containing the disruptive tendencies which the war had unleashed. More collaborative bargaining arrangements would prevent the explosive accumulation of workers' grievances, and would either absorb or exclude the power of the shop stewards whose independent negotiating role was such a threat to established union-employer relations. The notion of 'industrial self-government' was also attractive to trade unionists who sought greater involvement in the control of industry but did not ground this aspiration in any radical political analysis.

For the revolutionaries in the Shop Stewards' Movement, Whitleyism was anathema;[43] but even they had been prepared, in the detailed wartime discussions of control, to qualify their principles and consider schemes for 'joint management'.[44] The Whitley reports clouded the issue further, adding to the pressures to head off and contain any independent and aggressive movement for workers' control.

In the long term, Whitleyism left little mark. Where collective bargaining was already established, both employers and unions soon decided that they had no need for new machinery.[45] Once the post-war industrial crisis had passed its peak, and the danger of revolution had clearly subsided, the government ignored the National Industrial Conference. It fell apart in 1921.[46] But the short-term advantage gained by the government was only too clear: as with the Sankey Commission, 'the same tactics of delay and masterly inactivity were used . . . to placate the working class'.[47] The work of pacification was ably assisted by the established labour leaders – in particular by those with impeccable militant credentials – whose commitment to constitutional procedures, when it came to the crunch, proved stronger than their proclaimed desire to transform the status of the working class. But the ease with which the revolutionary aspects of the struggle for control were contained points to another factor of critical importance: the extent to which vital theoretical questions were fudged or evaded by those in the vanguard of the movement for workers' control.

One such question concerns the relationship between detailed control at the point of production and broader decision-making within society. The main focus of *The Frontier of Control* is on the former, and no doubt an even more extensive range of workplace controls could be documented today. But such controls operate in the context of a number of higher levels of decision-making: first, the detailed terms and conditions of employment; second, the structure and policies of labour force management; third, such other areas of managerial decision as investment programmes, product policy, the organisation and location of production, level of activity, financial arrangements, division of labour and design of jobs; fourth, the character and orientation of ownership and authority in industry; finally, the basic structure and dynamics of society as a whole. Inevitably, control at each lower level of this hierarchy is limited by higher-level structures and policies.

There can be little dispute about the broad features of this larger context. The interlocking inequalities of power and material privilege within our society have been extensively documented.[48] Five per cent of the population own well over half the wealth in Britain. In 1973, half the adult employees earned under £30 for a standard week.[49] By contrast, the privileged receive five- and even six-figure salaries, while disparities in unearned income are immensely greater. Inequalities in earnings parallel other work-related inequalities: in exposure to injury and disease, congeniality of working conditions, hours of work, length of holidays, fringe benefits, promotion prospects, and so on. Variations in the status accoutrements of different occupational positions (most notably, perhaps, the requirement that most manual workers and few others should 'clock in' at work and lose pay if late) reinforce these other inequalities and indicate variations in institutionalised *power* within the workplace, power which existing forms of workers' control may qualify and partially contain but do not overturn. Outside the workplace 'the uninterrupted, albeit modified, dominance of the property-owning classes, in a society which has long been the most highly "proletarianised" in the world, is surely one of the most striking phenomena of modern times'.[50]

In this context, any serious move by workers towards greater control over their working lives challenges those in positions of power and privilege. And since material and political privileges are rarely surrendered voluntarily, a more democratic industry and society are likely to be won only as a result of struggle; which means that those at the rough end of our industrial system need to organise in order to achieve it.

The existence of a privileged class resistant to workers' control is one aspect of the way capitalism's structure and dynamics limit the aspirations of workers to control their lives. Marx argued that the exploitation of workers in nineteenth-century industry should not be attributed primarily to the greed of the capitalist as an individual. Like the miser, he was dedicated to the accumulation of wealth; 'but that which in the miser is a mere idiosyncrasy is, in the capitalist, the effect of the social mechanism, of which he is but one of the wheels. . . Competition makes the immanent laws of capitalist production to be felt by each individual capitalist, as external coercive laws.'[51] Such 'external coercive laws' still operate, and they stem in particular from three features of capitalism. These are the fragmentation which results from an economy geared to commodity production; the fact that workers' ability to labour, and the means of production, are themselves commodities; and the anarchy which pervades the social organisation of production and its fundamental purposes within a capitalist economy.

Marx discusses the 'fetishism of commodities' in a famous section of the opening chapter of *Capital*.[52] A product becomes a commodity when it is produced, not because it is useful or desirable, but in order to be sold. In an economy geared to commodity production, the exchange value of each product is generally known and is relatively stable. Although these exchange values are really the outcome of a network of market relations, of the relationships between people as buyers and sellers, it is generally assumed that the exchange value of a commodity is something fixed and concrete, indeed its most important characteristic. Thus the relation of commodities in the market appears to be more important than the relation of men in production, and 'a definite social relation between men . . . assumes, in their eyes, the fantastic form of a relation between ings'. The market becomes a Frankenstein, an apparently autonomous social agency that comes to dominate men's activity, 'independent of their control and conscious individual action'.

In this way, economic activity becomes dehumanised. The process is carried even further when the 'fetishism of commodities' affects the relations of production themselves. Under capitalism, people's ability to work, and the means of production which their own labour has previously created, become commodities also – wage-labour and capital – and therefore are subject to the same market forces.[53] Instead of being humanely organised, work is dominated by 'external coercive laws'. One important consequence is the extreme division of labour which condemns most workers to narrow, repetitive tasks.

Although many writers discuss this problem, most neglect a vital distinction drawn by Marx between the division of labour within society and the division of labour within the workplace: division of labour in society means specialisation by trade and industry, but each man is his own master and sells what he himself produces. Division of labour within the workshop destroys the independence of the producers and is based instead on 'the sale of the labour-power of several workmen to one capitalist, who applies it as combined labour-power. The division of labour in the workshop implies concentration of the means of production in the hands of one capitalist; the division of labour in society implies their dispersion among many independent producers of commodities.' In the context of capitalism, 'division of labour within the workshop implies the undisputed authority of the capitalist over men, that are but parts of a mechanism that belongs to him'.[54] It is this essentially *coercive* basis of the capitalist division of labour which largely explains the degrading consequences documented by Adam Smith himself, castigated by Marx and by Ruskin, and rediscovered by contemporary social psychologists.

These specific ills are elements in a more general disorder: the anarchy of capitalist production as such. When Marx and Engels spoke of anarchy they normally pointed to the contrast between autocratic control within individual establishments and he absence of any conscious, deliberate co-ordination of the economy as a whole. The notion of anarchy goes deeper, however. It indicates the overriding *dynamic* of capitalist society.[55]

'Accumulate, accumulate! That is Moses and the prophets!' declared Marx.[56] More sombrely, he added that 'past labour overwhelmingly and independently dominates over living labour'.[57] The extraction of profit and the accumulation of capital were built into the structure of the system, pursued as ends in themselves rather than for their possible social value; just as today these same goals, disguised as 'economic growth' and 'technological advance', retain a dynamic apparently independent of human control.

It follows that the organisation and objectives of capitalist industry are structured against the realisation of workers' interests whenever these imply different priorities. This sets rigorous limits to what can be achieved through 'workers' participation' in the absence of a fundamental transformation of capitalist society itself. Unless workers can impose radically different structures of control and forms of productive organisation, their industrial interests are bound to be expressed in ways which are primarily negative and defensive.

As Goodrich makes clear, the exercise of workers' control in the period he describes was predominantly of this character. The same is true today. This reflects a more general feature of workers' industrial organisation: the essential *ambivalence* of trade unionism in relation to the government of industry. For unionism is on the one hand a protest and defence against the economic and human deprivations imposed on workers by capitalist industry; on the other a means of accommodation to the structure of capitalist industry. This in turn reflects the contradictory pressures inherent in trade union organisation and collective bargaining activity: on the one hand they express the basic conflict of interest between employers and employees on matters of pay, conditions and control; on the other they sponsor a stable and compatible bargaining relationship. Hence the curious phenomenon of 'antagonistic co-operation' discerned by many students of industrial relations: the constant interpenetration of conflictual and collaborative aspects of trade unionism.[58] Given this ambivalence neither the oppositional concept of workers' control nor the collaborative notion of participation can be applied without qualification to trade union negotiations and agreements. Collective bargaining institutionalises industrial conflict, generating rules, conditions and procedures which are mutually agreed; the oppositional and independent quality which is intrinsic to the notion of workers' control is in large measure sublimated. But the organisational separateness of the union, and the possibility that disagreement may lead to overt conflict, mean that analysis in terms of participation alone is not appropriate.

To view collective bargaining as a form of industrial democracy – as the Webbs did in their classic study, or as, more recently, Hugh Clegg has done[59] – is to exploit to the limits the ambiguities inherent in the latter notion. As has been argued above, workers within capitalism can at best achieve marginal adjustments to, or at worst acquiesce in, decisions which reflect a structure of power and interests hostile to their own. The currently popular concept of 'joint regulation' indicates that union-employer negotiations focus on the application of rules rather than the direction of company policy. It also diverts attention from the one-sided power structure within which the formally equal and possibly collaborative bargaining takes place.[60]

Unions do win significant material improvements for their members and do impose limits on the arbitrary powers of employers. Yet while ameliorating the *terms* of workers' subordination to management control, they do not and cannot contest the *fact* of this subordination: for to do so would be to challenge the very social order from which trade unions derive their function. Conversely, collective bargaining is a means for sophisticated employers to qualify and contain the workers' own *autonomous* exercise of control, and so to render the problems of labour management more tractable. Wright Mills' familiar description of the trade union function as the 'management of discontent' reflects this tendency.[61]

The exercise of control *over* employees through the processes by which unions win improvements *for* them was one of the key insights of Antonio Gramsci, writing in revolutionary Turin at the time Goodrich was studying the control of industry in Britain. The essence of trade union achievement, Gramsci argued, is the establishment of a form of 'industrial legality'. While 'a great victory for the working class', this achievement nevertheless reflects the continuing preponderance of employer power over that of workers and their organisations. 'Industrial legality has improved the working class's material living conditions, but it is no more than a compromise – a compromise which had to be made and which must be supported until the balance of forces favours the working class.'[62] The development of cohesive and self-confident workplace organisation, able to apply pressure directly at the point of production, is the key to shifting the balance of forces and permitting further inroads into the prerogatives of capital. By contrast, for official trade unionism, order and stability depend on maintaining the established relationships and the established balance of power and the negotiation and re-negotiation of order and stability are central to the trade union function.

Gramsci's description of the Italian scene half a century ago has a familiar ring: 'the union bureaucrat conceives industrial legality as a permanent state of affairs. He too often defends it from the same viewpoint as the proprietor. . . He does not perceive the worker's act of rebellion against capitalist discipline as a rebellion; he perceives only the physical act, which may in itself and for itself be trivial.'[63] Such a disposition on the part of the typical full-time official is not to be explained primarily in terms of corruption by soft living (which is not to say that this never occurs). Nor is the main reason the fact that the official becomes socially and in consequence ideologically divorced from those he represents once he leaves the workplace (though such a tendency has long been recognised).[64] By and large the average union representative, whether lay or full-time, is more progressive in outlook than many of those on whose behalf he acts. The basic problem is one of *function*. The ordinary worker, perpetually subject to the oppression and exploitation of capitalist wage-labour, is always liable to overturn some aspect of the existing 'industrial legality'. The union representative, by contrast, has to 'keep faith' with his negotiating partners, to regard each conflict as a 'problem' to be resolved within a framework defined by the prevailing system. It is precisely at the point where existing structures of industrial domination are under pressure, when the frontier of control is being forced forward, that the potentially conservative role of official trade unionism as defender of industrial legality is most starkly revealed.

The implications of this argument for the analysis of workers' control are threefold. In the first place, where informal work-group controls operate, the trade unions' formal involvement in bargaining over control issues may actually *reduce* the constraints on the dehumanising consequences of capitalist production. The evidence is that relatively informal and spontaneous organisation and activity by workers limit managerial autonomy most effectively primarily because of their *independence* of the employer.[65] This has been the central argument of recent industrial relations analysts, with their emphasis on informal shop-floor trade unionism and the influence of custom and practice. For this very reason it is the activities of the unofficial organisations, rather than official trade unionism, which are shrilly identified as the central industrial relations 'problem'.

By comparison, the role of official trade unionism is far more ambiguous. The enthusiasm shown by managements for productivity bargaining and the 'reform' of procedures in the 1960s, reflects in part an appreciation that they can blunt the disruptive edge of worker controls over such issues as manning, job allocation and work standards by making them the explicit subject of collective bargaining. In this respect, Richard Herding's detailed study of industrial relations in the United States offers important lessons.[67] He shows how union achievements in negotiating contract clauses on 'control' issues relate primarily to the 'rationalisation' of personnel administration or to the regulation of certain forms of inter-worker competition.[67] In both these spheres, the interests of employers and workers run, if not in parallel, then not fundamentally in opposition. But in production – where the employer interest in maximum exploitation conflicts frontally with the workers' interest in humane working conditions – the achievements of 'control bargaining' have been minimal. Indeed, the formal involvement of unions in negotiations on such issues has led to an actual *decline* in the ability of shop-floor trade unionists to control the dehumanising effects of company decisions on production.

Thus what may appear on paper as notable advances in workers' control may represent in fact an erosion and diminution, a reinforcement of the hand of management. In the words of an eminent advocate of such formalisation: 'the paradox, whose truth managements have found it so difficult to accept, is that they can only regain control by sharing it.'[68]

Gramsci's analysis also helps explain the attitudes of trade union officials to workers' control. They have a strong incentive to favour mechanisms which are consistent both with prevailing authority structures within the unions and also with stable bargaining relationships with employers and the state. It is no accident that British labour organisations insist that industrial democracy be exercised through a 'single channel of representation' subordinating workplace institutions to the official union hierarchy.[69] For this would reinforce the authority and status of the official organisation, which might be weakened by workplace-based structures. Just as it is natural for Labour politicians to interpret the socialisation of industry in terms of state management, so it is natural for union officials to conceive industrial democracy in terms of trade union control. Yet the question obviously arises: who controls the controllers? If the unions are assigned a central role in the exercise of workers' control, industrial democracy clearly cannot be isolated from democracy in the unions. It can scarcely be claimed, however, that trade unions are genuinely controlled by their members. Not only do many rulebooks contain highly undemocratic provisions; incumbent leaders in every union are able to manipulate policies and decisions through their disproportionate influence, expertise and control over organisational resources, which are themselves profoundly affected by the structure and character of union-management relations.

The union leaders favour 'officialised' control for another reason: it does not challenge in any fundamental way capitalist relations of production or those who benefit from them. On this point the Labour Party Working Party, chaired by one of the leading left-wing union secretaries was uncompromising: 'We believe that the extension of industrial democracy is important both because of its likely beneficial effect on the well-being of individual workers and because of the contribution it can make to the overall efficiency of industry by removing many of the existing obstacles to a genuine collective effort in industry by both management and workers. Both factors urge us in the same direction, and we do not choose between them. They are of equal weight.'[70] Yet such comfortably collaborative perspectives beg the crucial question: if industrial democracy means imposing radically new goals and strategies, and suppressing the power and privilege of those currently occupying dominant positions, what sense does it make to speak of 'a genuinely collective effort in industry by both management and workers'? The ideology of Whitleyism recurs, and so do its limitations: those who regard industrial democracy as a mere extension of existing union-employer collaboration will attempt to contain the movement for workers' control, to prevent it undermining the stable role of trade unionism as a permanent mediator between wage-labour and capital. Potential agencies of self-management will be threatened with asphyxiation by the existing agencies of collective bargaining.

This points to a third and more general implication of Gramsci's analysis. When the stability of industrial relations is threatened, union officials may well react in ways which *restrict* rank-and-file self-activity. For several decades, suspicion and hostility towards membership initiative and unofficial organisation was a built-in reflex of most union leaders in Britain. Recent years have seen the emergence of leaders who insist that the membership has the right of direct involvement in union decision-making, and who are prepared to associate themselves openly with the idea of workers' control. Yet even in such favourable circumstances, the relationship between union leaders and their members' militancy retains elements of the older, more authoritarian pattern. One example may suffice.[71] Huw Beynon, in his study of the Ford car assembly plants at Halewood, documents the intervention of Jack Jones and Hugh Scanlon (leaders respectively of the Transport and General Workers and the Engineers) to settle the 1971 company-wide strike. Their intervention, over the heads of shop-stewards organisation, virtually shattered the sophisticated, militant and responsive system of shop-floor representation that existed at the time. Does this merely prove a lack of sincerity or goodwill on the part of the officials concerned? It is important to seek a *structural* explanation which relates their actions to the situation in which they operate. One of the main union negotiators hinted at such an explanation. 'Once you've been a full-time official you realise that certain things are part of an agreement which the Executive have committed the union to and you are empowered to carry out. You're obliged to follow it. It's out of your hands as it were. You know, it's the system I suppose. The system we work to. It's like everything else, you've got to give some order to it.'[72]

'The system we work to' – the words of a radical union official, sympathetic to the goal of workers' control – illustrates the problem succinctly. Even among unofficial worker representatives, the pressures towards accommodation can be strong. Cole's comments on the situation in the 1914–18 period have already been quoted: 'the shop stewards played a big part in preventing and settling difficulties as well as in conducting disputes.' Today, when the image of the shop steward as a 'trouble-maker' is equally widespread, informed opinion can again describe him as 'an accepted, reasonable, and even moderating influence; more of a lubricant than an irritant'.[73] Permanent officials, being far more detached from the direct experiences of the rank-and-file worker, are still more strongly committed to the prevailing limits of 'industrial legality'; and in consequence, official trade unionism is necessarily an ambiguous ally of the cause of workers' control. At certain points, and particularly at times of grass-roots offensive, even the best and most honest official will feel constrained to suppress forms of self-activity which from the standpoint of workers' control are healthy and desirable, and indeed an essential part of the forward movement. This was the ultimate lesson of 1919–20. It is even more relevant today.

Carter Lyman Goodrich was born in Plainfield, New Jersey, in 1897, and studied for his bachelor's degree at the liberal arts college of Amherst, Massachusetts. His versatile talents were well suited to the broad-based Amherst curriculum. Initially his major interest was in the arts; he edited a literary magazine, *The Amherst Monthly*, and developed a close and lasting friendship with Robert Frost, whose poetry had recently achieved national acclaim and who was then attached to the Amherst faculty. But he later specialised in economics. On graduating in 1918 the College awarded him a fellowship which financed his studies in Britain. Here his research on control in industry was guided by Henry Clay, who until his appointment as Fellow of New College Oxford in 1919 was involved in the formulation of government labour policy, and by R.H.Tawney, closely involved with the unions and the Guild Socialist movement. The outcome of these studies was *The Frontier of Control*, completed at the end of 1919.

After returning to America, Goodrich completed his postgraduate studies at the University of Chicago. In 1921 he successfully submitted *The Frontier of Control* as his PhD dissertation, and in this form it was published in the United States.[74] His concern with the struggle for dignity and autonomy in work continued. He became associated with the Bureau of Industrial Research, a body formed to assist the trade union movement. (Arthur Gleason, a fellow-American whose research on British labour coincided with that of Goodrich, was also attached to the Bureau.) This led Goodrich to a close involvement with the United Mine Workers in Pennsylvania and in particular with John Brophy, one of the leading 'progressives' in American trade unionism. One of the outcomes of this period was *The Miners' Freedom*, a book in which Goodrich probes further into problems of control.[75] A further travelling fellowship allowed him to spend a year in Australia, where he studied the impact of migration patterns on the character of the labour movement.

After teaching posts at Amherst and the University of Michigan, Carter Goodrich became Professor of Economics at Columbia University in 1931. He remained there until 1963, when he moved to the University of Pittsburgh to become Mellon Professor of History and of Economics. From the 1930s he became increasingly involved in research in economic history, and in particular the role of government in the development of transportation. His long investigations in this field resulted in what are commonly regarded as two of his outstanding publications, *Government Promotion of American Canals and Railroads* and *Canals and American Development*.[76] In addition to his work in university teaching, research and administration, Goodrich was actively involved in the work of the International Labour Organisation (serving as chairman of its governing body during the war years) and the United Nations. It was his strong conviction that the insights derived from the study of economic history could illuminate current programmes of economic development. He was Director of one of the first United Nations technical assistance missions, to Bolivia in 1952, and took part in other missions in Latin America and Vietnam. He was in Mexico City when he died in 1971.

The Frontier of Control was the first of many varied publications in Carter Goodrich's long academic career, and it would be surprising if he subsequently regarded it as his most significant book. Nevertheless, it is a crucial document for anyone seeking to understand either past or contemporary relations in industry. Much that was written on labour questions in that turbulent period of transition half a century ago was shallow and superficial, and has sunk into deserved obscurity. But *The Frontier of Control* has stood the test of time; and though long out of print and almost inaccessible, it has in recent years acquired the reputation of a classic. This reputation is, for the most part, second-hand. It can only be enhanced as the present reprint makes the book again widely available.

The book is a work of scholarship, and the author's personal preferences are kept firmly in the background. Even so, there is clear evidence of his humane sympathy towards the efforts of workers to carve out an area of liberty and dignity within an often oppressive industrial system. This concern is made explicit in his later work, *The Miners' Freedom*. 'It is often said,' he wrote there, 'that modern society has chosen efficiency in production rather than richness in working life.' But, he insists, 'society makes no choices as such, and the countless individual decisions out of which have come mass production as efficient as that at Ford's and jobs as dull as those at Ford's have most of them been made without the slightest reference to the quality of the working life that would result . . . They are made on the basis of figures of output and cost and profit for the immediate business in the immediate future.'[77] Turning to the evidence of worker resistance to these new forms of 'scientific' dehumanisation, he argues 'that the issues raised by this new producer's protest are vitally important – for men are alive (or should be) even during working hours – and that the issue of the quality of the working life is too important to be left to chance. My argument is not that we have always chosen badly but that we have not chosen at all, and that we should find ways of forcing this issue into consideration, not in sentimental regrets after the event, but in the actual industrial decisions themselves.'[78]

It is clear from this eloquent plea that the analysis of control is not only a topic for academics but, more importantly, a burning problem for organised workers themselves. Goodrich shows the need to make positive and directive the workers' control which is at present mainly negative and defensive. His argument is that the character of industrial organisation and work experience, and hence people's social lives and relationships as a whole, are the outcome of a mass of separate decisions and strategies of individual capitalists, each pursuing the profitability of their own companies. This is, quite literally, economic anarchy. Today, as this anarchy threatens to destroy the whole environment and humanity itself, the need to impose some collective human control becomes ever more urgent. As workers, both manual and white-collar, struggle against forms of work organisation which exploit and dehumanise in new and more sophisticated ways, the creative potential of the working class becomes increasingly obvious.

It is by no means inevitable that this potential will be fully realised; indeed the obstacles are immense. Workers' control, as a comprehensive system of positive social direction, implies not merely an economic but also a political and cultural confrontation with those who currently shape our lives. When Goodrich wrote, this challenge seemed so immense that it intimidated many who, within their own spheres, were worthy defenders of workers' interests. The same is true today. Inside every worker there is a human being striving to get out: but for freedom to be won requires clear understanding, resolute determination, and effective organisation. *The Frontier of Control* helps us appreciate that all three are both necessary and possible.

References to the new foreword

1. Such fears are illustrated by W.A.Orton, *Labour in Transition*, Phillip Allan, 1920. A more recent assessment of the revolutionary possibilities is given by Walter Kendall, *The Revolutionary Movement in Britain*, Weidenfeld and Nicolson, 1969. For a fascinating insight into the fears of government ministers see Thomas Jones, *Whitehall Diaries*, Vol.I, Oxford University Press, 1969, pp.96–103. Jones, who was private secretary to Lloyd George (then Prime Minister) reports a widespread belief that a major industrial dispute would lead to sabotage and insurrection. 'There are large groups preparing for Soviet government', reported the Minister of Labour; since the police and army were of doubtful reliability, the most effective solution was apparently to arm the stockbrokers.

2. Studies of American industrial relations which cover somewhat similar ground are the monumental work by S.H.Slichter, J.J.Healy and E.R.Livernash, *The Impact of Collective Bargaining on Management*, Brookings, 1960; and Richard Herding, *Job Control and Union Structure*, Rotterdam University Press, 1972.

3. Elements of this theory can be traced back at least to the Owenite movement of the 1830s. For the historical development of the theory of workers' control see Ken Coates and Tony Topham, *Workers' Control*, Panther, 1970 (originally published as *Industrial Democracy in Great Britain*, MacGibbon and Kee, 1968).

4. The most obvious exception was William Morris (1834–96) and other members of his Socialist League (especially the anarchistically inclined). But they were untypical of the main development of socialist organisation in Britain.

5. The SDF, the main 'marxist' organisation in Britain, merged in 1911 with dissident ILP branches to form the British Socialist Party.

6. For an illuminating contemporary analysis of French syndicalism and its influence in Britain see G.D.H.Cole, *The World of Labour*, Bell, 1913 (the 1919 edition is reprinted by Harvester Press, 1973).

7. Tom Mann (1856–1941), President of the Dockers' Union, founder of the Workers' Union, Secretary of the Engineers, socialist and later Communist. For an autobiographical account see *Tom Mann's Memoirs*, Labour Publishing Company, 1923 (reprinted MacGibbon and Kee, 1967). A brief appraisal of Mann's career is given in the introduction to the reprint of his first pamphlet, *What a Compulsory 8 Hour Day Means to the Workers* (1886), Pluto Press, 1972.

8. G.R.(Lord) Askwith, *Industrial Problems and Disputes,* John Murray, 1920, p.294 (reprinted Harvester Press, 1974).

9. This manifesto, *The Miners' Next Step,* (reprinted by Pluto Press, 1973) was to achieve fame (or notoriety) far beyond the South Wales coalfield.

10. John Lovell, *Stevedores and Dockers,* Macmillan, 1969, p.156.

11. B. Pribicevic, *The Shop Stewards' Movement and Workers' Control,* Blackwell, 1959, p.17.

12. The specific grievances of railwaymen and miners, whose national disputes compelled government intervention, were at least partially resolved: in the one case by the establishment of Conciliation Boards on which union officials, long refused recognition by the railway companies, could participate; in the other by the Coal Mines (Minimum Wage) Act of 1912, which conceded the demand for a guaranteed basic rate of pay, albeit on a district rather than a national basis. (For details see P.S.Bagwell, *The Railwaymen,* Allen and Unwin, 1963; R.Page Arnot, *The Miners: Years of Struggle,* Allen and Unwin, 1953; E.H.Phelps Brown, *The Growth of British Industrial Relations,* Macmillan, 1959.) Among the mass of hitherto unorganised 'general labour', where struggles contributed greatly to the strike figures, the mushroom growth of general unionism led to the creation of collective bargaining institutions, and often to substantial improvements in conditions. Across the economy as a whole, the decline in real wages was halted, and after 1912 they rose significantly.

13. Pribicevic, *op cit,* p.18.

14. For details see G.D.H.Cole, *Trade Unionism and Munitions,* Clarendon Press, 1923.

15. G.D.H.Cole, *Workshop Organisation,* Clarendon Press, 1923, p.1 (reprinted Hutchinson, 1973).

16. *ibid,* pp.3–4.

17. The spread of the movement was assisted by the 'deportation' of many of the Clydeside leaders to other munitions centres in 1916, when the government intervened to smash the Clyde Workers' Committee. See James Hinton, *The First Shop Stewards' Movement,* Allen and Unwin, 1973.

18. Connolly (1868–1916), the most famous of Irish socialists, spent several years at the turn of the century in the United States; his *Socialism Made Easy* achieved widespread circulation. For an interesting account of the development of the SLP see J.T.Murphy, *Preparing for Power,* 1934 (reprinted Pluto Press, 1973).

19. Hinton, *op cit,* p.119.

20. J.T.Murphy (1888–1966) was involved in the amalgamation movement before the war, joined the SLP, played a key role in working for SLP participation in the formation of the Communist Party, of which he was a leading member until he resigned in 1932. His wartime ideas were eloquently expressed in the pamphlet *The Workers' Committee* (1917), reprinted by Pluto Press, 1973.

21. Walter Kendall, in *The Revolutionary Movement in Britain,* presents Communism as an alien strain which choked the more fertile native revolutionary tradition. For a critique of this interpretation see the review by James

Hinton in the *Bulletin of the Society for the Study of Labour History*, Autumn 1969.

22. The CP derived most of its initial membership from the British Socialist Party, but the most important national leaders in the early years came from the SLP. The latter split over the issue of joining the new party.

23. A term deriving from Lenin's polemic, *'Left-Wing' Communism: an Infantile Disorder*. In later years, many of the founders of the CP exaggerated the 'immaturity' of their previous theories, and in the process suppressed some of the valuable insights of the shop stewards' movement. Partly because their primary concern was with the conquest of state power and the creation of a new state machine controlled by the working class, the attitude of the Bolsheviks to workers' control at enterprise and industry level was ambivalent. 'We shall reduce the role of state officials to that of simply carrying out our instructions as responsible, revocable, modestly paid "foremen and accountants",' wrote Lenin in *State and Revolution*. 'This is our proletarian task, this is what we can and must start with in accomplishing the proletarian revolution' (*Selected Works*, Lawrence and Wishart, 1968, p.298). Lenin was also one of the first to appreciate the revolutionary role of the spontaneously created factory committees and soviets; but he viewed them essentially as oppositional instruments – as agents of workers' control *against* capitalist management – rather than as potential agencies of *self*-management. And after the revolution of November 1917 the principle of management from above – shorn, it is true, of some of its repressive features – continued; workplace organisation remained confined to limited and largely defensive functions, protecting workers against bureaucratic distortions within the state and against the managers and experts of bourgeois origins on whom the Bolsheviks felt obliged to rely. Lenin made clear on the eve of the revolution his restricted conception of workers' control: 'the country-wide, all-embracing, most precise and most conscientious *accounting* of the production and distribution of goods' ('Can the Bolsheviks Retain State Power?', *ibid*, p.374; Lenin's emphasis). The enormous problems confronted by the infant Soviet state reinforced this lukewarm attitude towards self-management, and helps explain why political revolution was not carried through into a revolution in authority relations in industry. The initial decision on strategic priorities facilitated the subsequent process of bureaucratic distortion and – as economic difficulties intensified – erosion of the institutions of even negative workers' control, culminating in the dictatorial labour discipline of the Stalin era. One consequence has been the long history of confusion and equivocation in the official Communist movement on the question of workers' control.

24. Hinton, *op cit*, p.337.

25. Cole (1889–1959) wrote voluminously. Among his most important works on Guild Socialism were *Self-Government in Industry*, Bell, 1917 (reprinted by Hutchinson, 1972) and *Guild Socialism Re-stated*, Parsons, 1920. For an intellectual biography see L.P.Carpenter, *G.D.H.Cole*, Cambridge University Press, 1973; and for a study of Guild Socialism see S.T.Glass, *The Responsible Society*, Longmans, 1966.

26. *The World of Labour*, p.55.

27. The Guilds were to develop out of existing trade unions, restructured on industrial lines. The name reflects a romantic and mediaevalist tendency, particularly evident in the early Guild Socialist literature.

28. *Self-Government in Industry*. Cole's emphasis altered significantly over time, and the conceptions held within the NGL also varied.

29. The pamphlet, written in 1917, is reprinted as an appendix to *Workshop Organisation*. William Gallacher (1881–1965) was chairman of the Clyde Workers' Committee; unlike most of its leaders he was a member of the British Socialist Party. His susceptibility to Guild Socialism had weakened by 1919, when with J.R.Campbell he wrote *Direct Action* (reprinted by Pluto Press, 1972), and was disavowed entirely when he became one of the prominent founders of the CP. (Goodrich spells Gallacher's name incorrectly throughout much of the book). John H. Paton, an ILP member and shop steward, was the most prominent manual worker active in the NGL. He launched its journal *The Guildsman* and became a full-time organiser in 1919, but died the following year.

30. See Charles Loch Mowat, *Britain Between the Wars*, Methuen, 1955, pp.30–6.

31. The Miners nominated three of their leading officials together with a sympathetic economist, Sir Leo Chiozza Money, MP. The officials were Robert Smillie, Herbert Smith and Frank Hodges, respectively President, Vice-President and Secretary. Smillie (1857–1940), a socialist when virtually all miners' union officials were Liberals, was President of the Scottish Miners' Federation from 1894 to 1918, and national President from 1912 to 1921. Despite his well-established militant reputation he was far from being a revolutionary; in the post-war period in particular he repeatedly shrank from direct confrontation with the Lloyd George government. Growing criticism within the Federation led to his resignation in 1921. Smith (1862–1938) was President of the Yorkshire Miners' Association from 1906, national Vice-President from 1917 and President from 1922 to 1929. Hodges (1887–1947), one of the young South Wales syndicalist militants, rose rapidly to become Secretary of the national Federation in 1918. In 1921, when the mine-owners (who had been given back control of the industry by the government) demanded the abrogation of the principle of a national standard wage, Hodges hinted at a possible compromise; he was disowned by his executive, and his reputation never recovered. He was obliged to resign his position on election to Parliament in 1924. His subsequent career lent some credence to accusations of treachery. The two other Labour members of the Commission were Sidney Webb and R.H.Tawney. Webb (1859–1947), with his wife Beatrice (1858–1943), chief ideologist of the Fabian Society, famous for his writings on trade unionism, minister in the Labour governments of 1924 and 1929–31, was particularly influential within the labour movement in the immediate post-war years. Tawney (1880–1962), best known academically for his *Religion and the Rise of Capitalism*, was a Guild Socialist whose political views were most fully expressed in *The Acquisitive Society*, Bell, 1921 (reprinted by Fontana, 1961) and *Equality*, Unwin, 1931 (reprinted by Allen and Unwin, 1964).

32. Margaret Cole, *The Story of Fabian Socialism*, Heinemann, 1961, p.175.

33. Arthur Gleason, *What the Workers Want*, Harcourt, Brace and Howe, 1920, p.49.

34. Sidney and Beatrice Webb, *The History of Trade Unionism*, Longmans, 1920, p.704.

35. Malcolm Sparkes, whose initiative was primarily responsible for the formation of the Industrial Council, was a Quaker and a Guild Socialist; Thomas Foster was also influenced by Guild Socialism. The Foster Report's vision of 'the whole of the building industry being welded together into one great self-governing democracy of organised public service' was little more than the dream of a few unrepresentative employers. As Hilton comments, 'it was unreasonably idealistic to believe that the employers were ready for what amounted to industrial suicide... Though the Council lingered on until 1924 before being wound up, it never looked like having great influence on the course of events within the industry.' (W.S.Hilton, *Industrial Relations in Construction*, Pergamon, 1968, p.114).

36. Various Guilds were set up during this period, but those in building were the most significant; here, too, Malcolm Sparkes was one of the main initiators. Enthusiasm for such utopian exercises came primarily from those whose attachment to Guild Socialism was ethical rather than political; but those who, like Cole, were sceptical nevertheless felt obliged to give their support. For an account see Cole, *A Century of Co-operation*, Co-operative Union, 1944, Ch.17.

37. See Cole, *The Next Ten Years in British Social and Economic Policy*, Macmillan, 1929, Ch.8.

38. See for example, TUC, *Interim Report on Industrial Democracy*, 1973, and Labour Party, *The Community and the Company*, 1974.

39. Ken Coates and Tony Topham, *The New Unionism*, Peter Owen, 1972, pp.39–40.

40. See below, pp.6–7.

41. *Interim Report on Joint Standing Industrial Councils*, Cd.8606, 1917.

42. Henry Clay, *The Problem of Industrial Relations*, Macmillan, 1929, pp.150–2. Clay (1883–1954) interrupted his academic career towards the end of the war to work in the Ministry of Labour.

43. A clear critique of Whitleyism was developed in a pamphlet by J.T.Murphy, *Compromise of Independence*, Sheffield Workers' Committee, 1918.

44. See the studies by Pribicevic and Hinton, and see also the Clyde Dilution Agreement reproduced by Goodrich in Chapter 14. The position of the Guild Socialists was in this respect far more equivocal: Cole even acted as secretary to the trade union side of the National Industrial Conference, an involvement scarcely consistent with his frequently declared opposition to such collaborative exercises.

45. Joint Industrial Councils were, in fact, set up principally where trade unionism was comparatively weak, and in particular in the public sector.

46. For an account of the Conference (by a fervent enthusiast of industrial collaboration) see Rodger Charles, *The Development of Industrial Relations in Britain 1911-39,* Hutchinson, 1973.

47. Mowat, *Britain Between the Wars,* p.36.

48. For comprehensive summaries see John Urry and John Wakeford, eds., *Power in Britain,* Heinemann, 1973; and Dorothy Wedderburn, ed., *Poverty, Inequality and Class Structure,* Cambridge University Press, 1974.

49. 'New Earnings Survey 1973', *Department of Employment Gazette,* October 1973.

50. Peter Worsley, 'The Distribution of Power in Industrial Society' in Urry and Wakeford, eds., *op cit,* p.253. The intimate connection between economic power and the institutions of political control – which helps explain the persistence of massive inequalities in the face of at least vaguely egalitarian social values – has been convincingly demonstrated by Ralph Miliband, *The State in Capitalist Society,* Weidenfeld and Nicolson, 1969.

51. Karl Marx, *Capital,* Vol.I (1867), Lawrence and Wishart, 1959, p.592.

52. See the lucid commentary by Norman Geras, 'Marx and the Critique of Political Economy' in Robin Blackburn, ed., *Ideology in Social Science,* Fontana, 1972.

53. See Marx, 'Wage Labour and Capital' in Karl Marx and Friedrich Engels, *Selected Works,* Lawrence and Wishart, 1958.

54. *Capital,* Vol.I, p.355.

55. This double sense of 'anarchy' is clearly analysed by Robin Blackburn in 'The New Capitalism' in *Ideology in Social Science.* It follows that the notion of economic rationality has two levels of meaning: within the perspectives of capitalism, the mere planning and co-ordination of the *means* of economic life; from a socialist perspective, the conscious collective determination of its *ends*.

56. *Capital,* Vol.I, p.595.

57. *ibid,* Vol.III, Lawrence and Wishart, 1962, p.391.

58. For an elaboration of this point see Richard Hyman, *Marxism and the Sociology of Trade Unionism,* Pluto Press, 1971.

59. Sidney and Beatrice Webb, *Industrial Democracy,* Longmans, 1897; H.A.Clegg, *Industrial Democracy and Nationalisation,* Blackwell, 1951 and *A New Approach to Industrial Democracy,* Blackwell, 1963. For a powerful critique of the latter see Paul Blumberg, *Industrial Democracy: the Sociology of Participation,* Constable, 1968.

60. For a more detailed discussion of these points see Richard Hyman, *Strikes,* Fontana, 1972; Alan Fox, *Man Mismanagement,* Hutchinson, 1974.

61. C. Wright Mills, *The New Men of Power,* Harcourt, Brace, 1948.

62. A.Gramsci, *Soviets in Italy,* Institute for Workers' Control, 1969, p.15.

63. *ibid,* p.17. For more recent discussions of the incorporating pressures on union representatives see V.L.Allen, *Militant Trade Unionism,* Merlin, 1966; and Hyman, *Marxism and the Sociology of Trade Unionism.*

64. The Webbs noted, in their *History* (p.469) that once an official left the shop floor 'the former vivid sense of the privations and subjections of the artisan's life gradually fades from his mind; and he begins more and more to regard all complaints as perverse and unreasonable'. In *The Workers' Committee* (pp.13–14), J.T.Murphy pointed out that 'a man in the workshop . . . feels every change; the workshop atmosphere is his atmosphere; the conditions under which he labours are primary; his trade union constitution is secondary, and sometimes even more remote. But let the same man get into office. Those things which were once primary are now secondary. He becomes buried in the constitution, and of necessity looks from a new point of view on those things which he has ceased to feel acutely.'

65. The strength of spontaneous and immediate shop-floor organisation derives from the employers' dependence on workers' active co-operation, ingenuity and initiative. The massive economic power attached to the ownership of capital and the imposing prerogatives and authority of the employer (backed by the legal sanctions underwriting capitalist employment relations), are not sufficient to *compel* workers to carry out all the functions required for the smooth operation of a modern industrial organisation. A thoroughly disaffected workforce can find a thousand ways to sabotage management's objectives; and this is all the easier the more sophisticated the work process or the more strategic the role of the particular work group. Capitalist industry can only function because of a constant process of give-and-take at the point of production, in which the agents of management concede part of their formal prerogatives in order to gain a measure of goodwill from the workforce.

This spontaneous potential for disruption ensures that the employer is *compelled* to surrender a portion of control, and also that this most primitive level of collective worker organisation cannot 'sell out' or become incorporated in the same manner as higher-level union representatives. But at the same time, the primitive and sectional character of worker control at the point of production means that *in itself* it can never overturn capitalist production relations and establish self-management.

66. *Job Control and Union Structure*.

67. The 'seniority' principle in the United States is a good example.

68. Allan Flanders, *Collective Bargaining: Prescription for Change*, Faber, 1967, p.32. This much-quoted comment needs supplementing by noting that those with whom managements share control in formal collective agreements are not the same as those from whom they regain it.

69. This principle was particularly strongly asserted by the Labour Party Working Party report on *Industrial Democracy*, 1967.

70. *ibid*, p.17.

71. For a more detailed discussion see Richard Hyman, 'Workers' Control and Revolutionary Theory: an Appraisal of the Publications of the Institute for Workers' Control' in Ralph Miliband and John Saville, eds., *Socialist Register 1974*, Merlin.

72. Huw Beynon, *Working for Ford*, Penguin, 1973, p.300.

73. *Donovan Report*, p.29 (quoting W.E.J.McCarthy, *The Role of Shop*

Stewards in British Industrial Relations, HMSO, 1967, p.56).

74. Harcourt, Brace and Company, 1921.

75. *The Miner's Freedom: A Study of the Working Life in a Changing Industry*, Marshall Jones, 1925.

76. Columbia University Press, 1960 and 1961.

77. *The Miners' Freedom*, pp.5–6.

78. *ibid*, p.11.

The University of Chicago

THE FRONTIER OF CONTROL

A Study in British Workshop Politics

A DISSERTATION

SUBMITTED TO THE FACULTY
OF THE GRADUATE SCHOOL OF ARTS AND LITERATURE
IN CANDIDACY FOR THE DEGREE OF
DOCTOR OF PHILOSOPHY

DEPARTMENT OF POLITICAL ECONOMY

BY

CARTER LYMAN GOODRICH

NEW YORK
HARCOURT, BRACE AND COMPANY
1921

THE QUINN & BODEN COMPANY
RAHWAY, N. J.

ACKNOWLEDGMENTS

For the fun I have had in doing this job, my two heaviest obligations are to Amherst College—for sending me to England to study—and to Mr. Henry Clay—for directing my work here.

The trip was made possible by the award of the Roswell Dwight Hitchcock Fellowship to which the Trustees of Amherst College voted a special addition. My personal debts to the college and to the men working with President Meiklejohn there are too many and too great to mention here. It is Professor Walton H. Hamilton, however, to whose teaching I owe my start in labor problems and to whose planning I owe this special opportunity.

To Mr. Henry Clay, late of the Ministry of Labour and now Fellow of New College, Oxford, I am indebted both for suggesting a job that "wanted doing" and for giving me almost day-to-day counsel and guidance in the doing of it. Without the many kindnesses of Mr. Clay and his friends, I could hardly have begun to find my way about in an investigation of the current British situation.

Mr. G. D. H. Cole and his associates of the Labour Research Department were good enough

ACKNOWLEDGMENTS

to give me access to their useful collection of trade union journals, constitutions, rules, etc. and to help me in other ways. Mr. R. H. Tawney, Mr. Arthur Gleason and Mr. Robert W. Bruère have very kindly read my manuscript and made valuable suggestions.

Finally I feel warmly grateful to a large number of people in various parts of Great Britain—employers and workers, managers, foremen, trade union secretaries, tutorial movement students and tutors, government officials and "rebel" shop stewards—for the readiness and courtesy with which they have taken time from their immediate and practical concerns with industry to answer the questions of an outsider and an American.

C. L. G.

LONDON,
December 1, 1919.

CONTENTS

PAGE

ACKNOWLEDGMENTS

FOREWORD BY R. H. TAWNEY

INTRODUCTION: THE DEMAND FOR CONTROL . . 3

THE EXTENT OF CONTROL:

SECTION

I—Control 51

II—The Frontier of Control 56

III—Employment 63

IV—Unemployment 72

V—"The Right to a Trade" 92

VI—"The Right to Sack" 104

VII—Promotion 111

VIII—The Choice of Foremen 117

IX—The Organization of Foremen . . 126

X—The Standard of Foremanship . . 135

XI—Special Managerial Functions . . 146

XII—Methods of Payment 161

XIII—Technique: Restriction and Restrictions 176

XIV—Technique: Consultation over Changes . 186

XV—Technique: Insistence on Improvements 202

XVI—Technique: Suggestions and Inventions 217

XVII—Trade Policy: Joint Action . . . 223

XVIII—Trade Policy: Workers' Demands . . 241

XIX—The Extent of Control 253

NOTE ON SOURCES 267

INDEX 273

FOREWORD

By R. H. TAWNEY

IT is a commonplace that during the past six years the discussion of industrial and social problems has shifted its center. Prior to the war students and reformers were principally occupied with questions of poverty. To-day their main interest appears to be the government of industry. An increasing number of trade unionists regard poverty as a symptom of a more deeply rooted malady which they would describe as industrial autocracy and demand "control." Anxious to establish some *modus vivendi* which may promise industrial peace, employers consider the concession of a workshop committee or an industrial council. The Government gives the movement its official blessing and has taken steps through the Ministry of Labor to propagate the proposals of Mr. Whitley's Committee. That "control" should stand to different sections of opinion for quite different types of industrial structure was only to be expected. But the necessity of meeting some demand for which that is now the accepted name is generally admitted. The formulation of a "Constitution for Industry" is conducted with something of the same energy as that which past generations have given to the discussion of a Constitution for the State.

The change of angle is interesting. No doubt it is all to the good that the task of reorganizing industry should be recognized for what it is—a particular case of the general problem of constitutional government. But if it has been useful to show that recent industrial movements have "self-government" as their genus, it is no less important now to be clear as to their species. The formulation of programs of "joint control," such as—to give only one example—that advanced by the Miners' Federation, the demand for "industrial democracy," the analogies drawn between representative institutions in industry and in politics—these things have been invaluable in broadening horizons and in opening windows through which new ideas could pass. But the emphasis needed to compel attention to the significance of a point of view which till recently was unfamiliar has by now, it may be suggested, done its work. The new field for investigation and practice has been mapped out. What is needed to-day is to give precision to its content and to test general propositions in the light of particular facts. "Control" is the most ambiguous and least self-explanatory of formulæ. The aspirations behind it may be genuine enough. But unless it is to remain a mere aspiration, it must be related much more closely than has been done hitherto to the actual conditions of industrial organization and to the realities of human psychology. We must know how much control is wanted, and control over what, and through whóm ít is to be exercised. We must decide whether the demand is the passing result of abnormal economic conditions, produced by the war and seized upon by theorists as a basis for premature generalizations, or whether it represents a movement which is so fundamental and permanent that any future scheme of industrial relationships, unless it is to be built upon sand, must take account of it.

The first condition of answering these questions is an impartial survey of the actual facts as they exist to-day. Mr. Carter Goodrich's book supplies it. He is concerned not with theory, but with practice. His object is not to propound any doctrine, to suggest any reforms or to formulate a judgment as to the merits or demerits of any features in the industrial system. It is simply to offer the materials without the possession of which these exercises, however exhilarating, are apt to be sterile. He has set himself the question: —"How much control over industry do the rank and file of those who work in it, and their organizations, in fact exercise?" He answers it by an analysis of industrial relationships, of the rules enforced by trade unions and employers' associations, of the varying conditions which together constitute "the custom of the trade" in each particular industry, and of the changes in all of these which took place during the war.

Such a study of "The Frontier of Control" is indispensable to the formation of any reasonable judgment upon the larger issues which the phrase suggests. Mr. Goodrich is well qualified to provide it. He has made a careful investigation of such aspects of British industrial organization as are relevant to his subject. Residence in Great Britain has familiarized him with the atmosphere in which its industrial politics are carried on. He has mixed with members of Whitley Councils and Boards of Control, Trade Boards and Royal Commissions, trade unions and employers' associations. He knows what men of business like Mr. Foster and Mr. Malcolm Sparkes hope for the building industries and the views on mining of leading members of the Miners' Federation. To the economic perplexities and agitations of a foreign country he brings the wide background of a student of economics and a dash of charming skepticism which to one heated by the somewhat feverish temperature of British industry during the last two years, is as refreshing as the ice at the close of an American dinner.

Mr. Goodrich has shown admirable self-restraint in allowing the facts to speak for themselves, and in resisting the temptation to enlarge upon their moral. With regard to certain broad questions, however, his book encourages the reader to attempt the generalizations which the author withholds. It suggests, in the first place, that the sharp division ordinarily drawn between the sphere of "management" and that of "labor" is an abstraction which does less than justice to the complexity of the facts. If it is broadly true that in modern industry the function of the former is direction and of the latter the execution of orders transmitted to it, the line between them, nevertheless, fluctuates widely from industry to industry. It varies, for one thing, quite irrespective of any deliberate effort on the part of the workers to move it, with the nature of the work which is being carried on. There are certain occupations in which an absolute separation between the planning and the performance of work is, for technical reasons, impracticable. A group of miners who are cutting and filling coal are "working" hard enough. But very little coal will be cut, and the risks of their trade will be enormously increased, unless they display some of the qualities of scientific knowledge, prevision and initiative which are usually associated with the word "management." What is true of miners is true, in different degrees, of men on a building job or in the transport trades. They must exercise considerable discretion in their work because, unless they do, the work does not get done, and no amount of supervision can compensate for the absence of it. It is not, it may be suggested, a mere chance that workers in these industries should have taken the initiative in the movement for "control." They demand more of it, because the very nature of their work compels them to exercise something of it already.

In industries such as these the character of the work pushes the frontier of the workmen's control further into the employer's territory than is the case in—say—a cotton mill or a locomotive shop. But the degree to which workers exercise in some industries functions and powers reserved in others for the management does not depend merely upon economic conditions. It is also, of course, the result of conscious effort, which is not the less significant because till recently it took the form of specific claims to be consulted upon particular matters incidental to the wage contract and was not related to any general social philosophy. The organization of sufficient power to assert those claims effectively is the history of trade unionism. Of its result in establishing or failing to establish them, Mr. Goodrich's book is the best account known to me. The reader can judge from it how much "control" had in practice been secured by workmen up to 1919. If he compares the position with that which obtained fifty years ago he will see that long before the movement for "self-government in industry" had become explicit, the line between "management" and "labor" had been, in fact, redrawn. On one point, apprenticeship and the entry to a trade, the effective power of the workers appears for obvious reasons to have diminished. On all the rest it has enormously increased. As Mr. Goodrich's survey shows, the intensive development of trade unionism has been even more remarkable than its extensive growth in membership. On the whole group of questions, in particular, suggested by the word "discipline," it is every year more and more succeeding in the establishment of the same claims as it made effective thirty years ago with regard to wages and hours.

In the light of the facts presented by Mr. Goodrich it is a question whether the conventional description of industrial organization given in most economic text-books does not require a somewhat radical revision. The picture of "the employer" achieving economic progress by "substituting" one "factor of production" for another may have been adequate to the early days of the factory system. What the present study brings out is the vital importance at every point of a condition which is apt to be lightly touched upon or omitted altogether, the condition of corporate consent on the part of the workers. How vital that condition is is one of the discoveries of the past five years. It was emphasized first by the events of the war, which revealed how little reality there was in the common assumption that the settlement of the larger questions of industrial organization was a matter for the employer and the employer alone. It became necessary to reorganize industry for the purpose of increasing production or of economizing materials. The condition of carrying out the reorganization effectively was the consent of all engaged in the industry. Consent could be obtained only by a formal recognition of the fact that the representative of the workers had a right to be consulted with regard to questions of policy and management, because they possessed *de facto* the power to frustrate the required changes or to make them effective. Hence, as Mr. Goodrich points out, the creation of representative organs, such as the Textile Control Boards, through which the views of the workers on these matters could be expressed. When, as in the textile trades, that representative machinery worked effectively, the emergency was met with comparatively little difficulty. When, as in the engineering trades, the policy pursued was to force drastic innovations upon workers who were not consulted with regard to them, the result was endless friction. The moral suggested by the situation since the armistice in the building and coal-mining industries—to mention no others—and emphasized by Mr. Foster's Committee, by Mr. Justice Sankey, and by the report on dock labor of Lord Shaw's Court of Inquiry, is the same. It is that, as matters now stand, the first condition of economic progress is such a change in the position of the workers as will throw on to the side of increased efficiency the public opinion which is at present skeptical both of the objects for which it is urged and of the methods by which it is sought to attain it.

The truth is that, with the pushing forward of the "frontier" through the process described by Mr. Goodrich, the conditions of industrial efficiency have changed. In no very remote past discipline could be imposed upon workers from above, under pain of dismissal, which meant in the last resort, however hateful it may be to confess it, by an appeal to hunger and fear. "Members of this Court," states Lord Shaw's report, "can recall a period when men, gathered at the dock gates, fought fiercely for a tally which, when obtained, might only enable them to obtain one hour's work, and so limit their earnings for the day to 4d." Workmen were conscious of individual grievances, but they had not formulated an interpretation of their position in general terms, and the willingness of the personnel of industry to co-operate in production without raising fundamental questions as to its constitution and government could be taken for granted. To-day that assumption is possible only to the very short-sighted. As the present study shows, the effect of the piecemeal advances made by trade unionism has been to effect, in the aggregate, a radical redistribution of authority between the parties engaged in industry, which results, in extreme cases, in something like a balance of power. To discuss how that situation is to be resolved, whether by a frontal attack on trade unionism, such as appears to be favored by the more naïve and irresponsible section of opinion in the United States, or by giving it a vested interest in the continuance of profit-making through schemes of profit-sharing and representation on directorates, or by a partnership between a trade unionism undertaking responsibility for the maintenance of professional standards and the consumer for whom industry is carried on, does not fall within the scope of Mr. Goodrich's book. But a reasonable consideration of these large and burning issues will be materially assisted by the clearness and impartiality with which he has set forth the precise facts of the existing situation.

R. H. TAWNEY.

INTRODUCTION

THE DEMAND FOR CONTROL

"In the past workmen have thought that if they could secure higher wages and better conditions they would be content. Employers have thought that if they granted these things the workers ought to be contented. Wages and conditions have been improved; but the discontent and the unrest have not disappeared." So far the quotation might be from almost any American business man. But the place was the King's Robing Room of the British House of Lords, and the speaker was a veteran trade union leader, Mr. William Straker, presenting the case of the Miners' Federation before the Coal Commission which was sitting in judgment on Great Britain's key industry.° Mr. Straker went on:—"Many good people have come to the conclusion that working people are so unreasonable that it is useless trying to satisfy them. The fact is that the unrest is deeper than pounds, shillings and pence, necessary as they are. The root of the matter is the straining of the spirit of man to be free."

In the name of this "deeper" unrest, the Miners' Federation was demanding a bold scheme of *workers' control*. And the "deeper" unrest itself—or at least the unrest which is concerned more with discipline and management than with wages—is often spoken of as the *demand for control*. The main business of this book is to discuss the facts of the present extent of workers' control in British industry; the purpose of the introduction is to indicate the significant setting of these facts in the human terms of the demand for control. Control is important only because people want it.

But how many workers do want control, and how much control do they want? No answer can pretend to be definite. Control is a slogan in several vigorous propagandist programs. Control has more than once been a definite issue both in the active conflicts and the formulated policies of the labor movement. But even for this conscious and organized demand, no accurate count of heads can be made. And for the much more significant estimate of the underlying demand for control—the desires of individual workers for the simpler things that are grouped as control, and the restlessnesses for which the word control is an attempted rationalization—it is possible only to offer a few clues for further study.

Control is the central idea of various propagandist isms. The Syndicalist cry of 1911— "The Mines for the Miners"—has died out, but the idea of workers' control remains. "Complete control of industry by the working-class organizations," is the slogan of the Marxian Industrial Unionists.[1] Control of industry by guilds of producers co-operating with a democratized state representing the people as consumers, is the subtler syndicalism [2] of the Guild Socialists. And the cries of "complete control" and "encroaching control" of these groups of theorists are echoed more and more faintly through various grades of opinion to the "share in control" and "voice in control" [3] offered in the Whitley Councils. The thoroughgoing disciples of either of the two complete gospels of control—Marxian Industrial Unionism and Guild Socialism—are a tiny minority. The Socialist Labor Party, the chief organization of the former, has about two thousand members, but this number included the ablest of the leaders of the shop stewards' movement, and the movement served as a channel for the doctrine. The Central Labor College, which "promises to be candid but not impartial" and preaches an uncompromising revolutionary orthodoxy, reaches through its correspondence and other courses perhaps ten thousand students a year—chiefly among the members of the National

[1] G. D. H. Cole, *An Introduction to Trade Unionism*, pp. 97, 98.
[2] *Cf.* the footnote on p. 37 of Cole's *Self-Government in Industry*.
[3] The corresponding Americanisms are "management-sharing" and "voice in management."

Union of Railwaymen and the South Wales
Miners' Federation. The Guild Socialists, too,
are insignificant in enrolled members. The National Guilds League, their propagandist body, has
less than a thousand members. This figure is,
however, little indication of the actual number
who accept more or less fully the guild idea and
little indication of the actual influence of this small
group—composed as it is largely of able and pro-
lific writers and of the younger trade union
officials. The working-class circulation of Mr.
Cole's books, his personal influence as adviser to
the labor movement, and the obvious guildsman's
hand in documents such as the Miners' Bill for
Nationalization [4] and the Foster Report to the
Building Trades Parliament [5]—are suggestions of
this. One shrewd observer declared that:—

"The Guild Socialist propaganda has gone as far in
the trade union movement in two years as the State
Socialist propaganda had gone in twenty years."

In addition to these elaborate and definite
theories of control there is a large body of opinion that is agreed on some extension of workers'
control as the next step in trade unionism. No
trade union leader would admit that he wanted
less control than the minimum offered in the
Whitley Councils scheme—which is itself some indication of the spread of the control doctrine.

[4] See below, p. 12.
[5] See below, p. 86.

THE DEMAND FOR CONTROL

There is no one break in the long series from
Syndicalism to Whitleyism, and the widespread
acceptance of the latter in middle-class thinking is
a hint of the driving force of the more drastic
doctrines. Next possibly to "nationalization,"
"control" is the most talked-of word among trade
union theorists.

The control issue, moreover, has passed from
labor theory into labor activity and declared policy. Its most spectacular expression was in that
revolt against or within trade unionism known as
the Shop Stewards' Movement.[6] This, it is true,
was many things besides an expression of the demand for control. *It began largely as a protest
against the special helplessness of the trade union
leaders before the special war-time problems.* The
cost of living was rising sharply, dilution was
threatening the wage standard of the skilled engineers,[7] the number of war-time restrictions was
multiplying. Meanwhile the trade union leaders
were bound not to lead strikes—first by the "industrial truce" agreed upon at the beginning of
the war, later by the anti-strike provisions of the
Munitions Act. The unrest broke out in spontaneous and unauthorized strikes. The movement
found leaders in the shop stewards or trade union
representatives from within the various shops,

[6] G. D. H. Cole, *Introduction to Trade Unionism*, pp. 53-58.
[7] See below, pp. 100 and 189.

men whose position before the war had meant little more than collecting dues for the union.[8] The issues were concrete and immediate. The first of these strikes was the "Tuppenny Strike" for a long-delayed wage increase on the Clyde in January, 1915. The strike committee of stewards elected from the various works organized permanently as the Clyde Workers' Committee and this simple type of structure was copied by other districts. The movement at Sheffield broke out when a certain skilled engineer was drafted into the army. And so through the other engineering centers. The movement was first and most simply the workers' attempt by whatever means came handy to get the immediate concessions which their official machinery was failing to win. *It became in part, however, a revolt against officialism in general.* This in fact furnished the chief dogma of the movement—"the vesting of control of policy in the rank and file"—and its common name, the "Rank and File Movement." "Refer grievances to the rank and file," and "Get a move on in the shop before reporting to official sources," are rules from the Sheffield Shop Stewards' Manual. *The movement was largely a breaking away from the cumbrous structure of engineering trade unionism.* "We organize for power," wrote the

[8] Ministry of Labour, *Works Committees*, pp. 2-10. See Note on Sources.

chief spokesman of the movement,[9] "and yet we find the workers in the workshop divided not only amongst a score of branches but a score of unions." *Shop* vs. *branch* and *industry* vs. *craft*, were the two issues of organization. The trade union branch in engineering is based on the residence, not the working-place, of the members. Men who work side by side may be scattered among a number of branches. But grievances arise in particular shops. Therefore "Direct Representation from the Workshops to the Committees" is the first of the "Principles" on the member's card of the Sheffield Workers' Committee. In the second place, the industry is organized in a score or more of separate and often competing trade unions.[10] Jealousy frequently runs high between craft and craft and higher between skilled and unskilled. The shop stewards' movement took in all grades of labor and was in effect an amalgamation from below. "Work always for the solidarity of *all* the workers," is the last rule from the Shop Stewards' Manual. The movement was, then, a double attempt to fit the structure of the labor movement to the structure of the industrial unit.

So much for the motives other than the demand

---

[9] J. T. Murphy, *The Workers' Committee.* See Note on Sources.
[10] Eight of these unions, including the Amalgamated Society of Engineers, have just voted to unite.

for control. The movement won its chief support
by appeals to simple and very practical war-time
issues; its chief effect may possibly be in the field
of trade union structure. But its connections
with the demand for workers' control are close
and highly significant. Whatever the rank and
file wanted, the conspicuous leaders were out for
control. This is evident in all the propaganda of
the movement. The first of the "Objects" on the
Sheffield member's card was "To obtain an ever-
increasing Control of Workshop Conditions." It
is evident in such by-products of the movement as
the Clyde Dilution Scheme [11] and the Gallecher-
Paton memorandum on collective contract.[12] But
it is clearest of all in the actual seizures of power
by the shop stewards and in the way the leaders
played on each particular grievance and played
up each particular issue to swell the general demand for control. Several instances of shop
steward tactics are given in Section X. The use
of a particular blacksmith's objection to the boss's
watching his fire to establish a general refusal
to be watched at work is a minor but typical case.[13]
Moreover the very changes in structure themselves
were often argued on control grounds: fit your
organization to industry to make it fit to control
industry. The shop stewards' movement was a

[11] See below, pp. 197-201.
[12] See below, p. 173.
[13] See below, p. 138.

genuine movement towards the control of industry. And as an object-lesson in control it has become a stimulus to further demands. The powers won by the shop stewards are being used up and down the country as a text for vigorous propaganda. The shop stewards' control was decidedly *contagious control* [14]; its actual extent may be easily underrated by an outsider. It was recorded in no formal agreements. It rested on the war shortage of labor and was abruptly checked in the period of unemployment that followed the end of the war. The full story has nowhere been put together, and the evidence must be pieced out from the accounts of the shop stewards themselves and from employers' tales of "what they had to put up with during the war," but it is clear that the movement was enormously powerful throughout the great engineering centers and that it has spread to other industries, and it is clear that in certain works the shop stewards exercised the greatest degree of control ever held by British workers in modern industry. *The shop stewards' movement was both an expression of the demand for control and an incitement to further demands.*

But the demand for control is by no means confined to "rebel" trade unionism. The demand that among the engineers broke through the union machinery has in other unions found its outlet in

[14] See below, Section XIX.

official programs. Its expressions in official trade union policy have been less picturesque than the unofficial outbreak, but they are no less significant. Two of the greatest trade unions, the Miners' Federation with its 800,000 members and the National Union of Railwaymen with its 450,-000, have not only accepted the principle of control but have put forward specific schemes of control as serious parts of their programs. At the annual conference of the Miners on July 9, 1918, the following resolution was carried:—

"That in the opinion of this conference the time has arrived in the history of the coal mining industry when it is clearly in the national interests to transfer the entire industry from private ownership and control to State ownership with *joint control and administration by the workmen and the State*" (italics mine).

"The workmen should have some directive power in the industry in which they are engaged," said Mr. Frank Hodges in urging the resolution. "I do not believe that nationalization will do any good for anybody, unless it is accompanied by an effective form of working-class control." Another leader declared:—"We have the brains amongst the miners to work the mines." The sense of this resolution was embodied in a Mines Nationalization Bill [15] which was drafted early in 1919 and

[15] See below, Note on Sources.

presented to the Coal Commission. Under this
scheme the industry would be administered, under
a Minister of Mines, by a National Council made
up of ten Government nominees and ten men
chosen by the Miners' Federation and by a series
of subordinate District and Pit Councils on each
of which one half of the members should be directly elected by the workers affected. The system
of control outlined in the majority report of the
Coal Commission, known as the Sankey Scheme,[16]
differs from this in the important particular that
on each of these boards the workers are given
slightly less than half of the places. The representatives of the Miners nevertheless accepted the
Sankey Report with minor reservations. After
the Government rejected it, it was endorsed by an
overwhelming majority at the Trades Union Congress at Glasgow and is now the subject of vigorous propaganda on the part of the entire trade
union movement.

The National Union of Railwaymen was first
committed to a control policy by the following
resolution passed by a National Conference of
District Councils early in 1917 :—

"That this Conference, seeing that the Railways are
being controlled by the State for the benefit of the
nation during the war, is of opinion that they should
not revert to private ownership afterwards. Further,

[16] See below, Note on Sources.

we believe that national welfare demands that they should be acquired by the State to be jointly controlled and managed by the State and representatives of the N.U.R.''

Mr. Bellamy in his President's address that year declared:—

"Whether nationalization or [state] control be decided upon, it ought to be made unmistakably clear that neither system will be acceptable to railwaymen unless we are given a share in the management.''○

A special conference in November, 1917, voted by a majority of 74 to 1:—

"That there should be equal representation, both national and local, for this union upon the management of all railways in the United Kingdom.''

In March, 1918, the Executive at a special meeting adopted a control scheme similar to that of the Miners and providing for a National Board of Control, half of whose members should be elected by the House of Commons and half by the railway trade unions. The scheme is now under negotiation with the Prime Minister and the Minister of Transport. The Government's counter offer seems to be an improvement in the Conciliation Board machinery—to allow for the hearing of grievances over discipline—and a small minority of places for the union on the Railway Executive Committee.○

The Miners and Railwaymen, then, have put control schemes into their official programs and have pressed them in their actual bargaining. The other unions have no such detailed proposals as parts of their serious immediate policy, but it would be easy to fill a book with statements from trade union journals and from responsible trade union officials that the control of industry is their "ultimate aim." The Postal and Telegraph Clerks,[17] whose leaders are all National Guildsmen, are definitely committed to a control policy. The following bit from a correspondent's letter is a fair sample of the tone of their official publication:—

"I am out for a Postal Guild; so is Francis. He wouldn't be worth a dime . . . if he wasn't."

But it is unnecessary to go down the list of individual unions to discover commitments of the trade union movement to the idea of control. The issue came before the Trades Union Congress at Glasgow in September, 1919. Mr. Bromley of the Locomotive Engineers moved a resolution favoring workers' control of industry to end exploitation. The motion was carried unanimously and with some enthusiasm. Control has become an official and avowed aim of the whole labor movement.

[17] Now a part of the new Union of Post Office Workers.

How much this commitment really means is another matter. A resolution carried unanimously and without debate at a Congress whose real interest was in the hot fight over "Direct Action" is hardly evidence of immediate responsible policy. But together with the other commitments to control, it *is* a significant sign of the times. It is at least a sign of the phenomenally rapid growth of the demand for control. In 1907, the leaders of the railwaymen declared in all honesty that they had no intention of having anything to do with discipline. In 1919, the railway unions are negotiating on the basis of a demand for half control of the entire management. This is partly a matter of the increased power of the union; a union's strength may be roughly gauged by the issues on which it fights. But it is largely a matter of a change in the ideas of the trade union movement. The demand for "control of industry" in so many words is a new thing or possibly the revival of a long-forgotten thing. Bits of what would now be called control have long been fought for and often won by the trade unions—of that this whole book is evidence. But the conscious demand is a new and significant phenomenon. The very vocabulary of control is new. It had hardly been heard before Mr. Tom Mann [18] stumped England

[18] A leader in the great dock strike of 1889, mass orator to three continents, now General Secretary of the Amalgamated Society of Engineers.

in 1911. All the movements discussed have started since that time. Eight years of propaganda at the most and a new and revolutionary idea officially accepted by the trade union movement.

The resolution indicates one more thing—that there is within trade unionism practically no active opposition to the idea of control. There is no doubt at all of the truth of Mr. Cole's claim in the *Introduction of Trade Unionism* that the theorists of control are in line with the immediate tendencies of the "younger active trade unionists." But just here must be made the first serious discount of the force of the demand. Younger active trade unionists are by any count a mere handful. The percentage of members interested in general policy is small in any union. "I sometimes feel," said Mr. Hodges, "that there is a great mountain of indifference even in the Mining Movement." Younger active trade unions are perhaps also a minority. Few unions have both the power and the desire to push forward programs of control. Many must be written off almost completely in any calculation of the demand. The great cotton unions have hardly been touched by the control propaganda. The aristocratic monopolists of the old crafts discussed in Section XIX make no part of the new demand. The women's unions have showed little effective demand for control—so far at least dilution by woman labor has been also a dilution of the demand for control. All this is not to minimize the demand. Control has been genuinely fought for in trade union activity. The idea of control has officially captured the trade union movement. But to say that the trade union movement is committed to control by a resolution passed unanimously at Glasgow is not to say that control is actively demanded by each of the five and a quarter million trade unionists represented at the Congress. Nor is it to say that every trade union represented will fight for control. Trade unionism is no such coherent and united force.

Nor is control so simple and definite a thing. The word is a slogan and a convenient general term. But in actual reference to the facts of industry it breaks up into a bewildering variety of rights and claims—as the rest of the book will show. Control is no "simple central objective," no one clear-cut thing which people either know they want or know they don't want. The demand cannot be put glibly into a single phrase or a single resolution—too many diverse motives are blended and crossed in the strivings of many workers for the complicated set of things called control.

The demand for control is not the unified expression of some single specific impulse. If it were, it might be easier to separate it from the other strands of motive in industrial life. But instead, the elements of the demand must be hunted for in the whole jungle of the reactions of workers to the industrial situation. It is a hunt for facts that can neither be classified sharply nor weighed accurately. "It is essential," says the report of the Garton Foundation,[19] "to disentangle as far as possible the economic and non-economic factors." That would be hard enough, but would lead only to the edge of the problem of distinguishing among the non-economic factors. It is a study to which there is no end, but even the most tentative beginning may fill in some of the human content of the phrases of control. What are some of the wants and feelings on which the propaganda is based?

A start might be made by setting down a few general heads under which to group the workers' feelings about industry. The worker's interests in industry are roughly these:—

(1) How much he gets—Wages, etc.

(2) What it's for—The Object of the Work.

(3) How he's treated—Freedom and Authority.

(4) What he actually does—Workmanship.

To put these down in a row is not to pretend that

[19] See Note on Sources.

they are equal or even sharply distinct, but the classification will serve as a tool in the examination and comparison of some of the elements in the demand for control. The first two sets of interests are concerned with the *consumption* of the products of industry, the others with the conditions of *production*. The third and fourth interests fit closely the issues of discipline and management which are the frontier of control. The first and second apparently bear less directly on the personal and technical organization of production. But no serious study could ignore the cross-relationships between all four sets of motives.

How much the worker gets—in wages, hours of leisure, etc.—is of course the chief field of trade union activity.[20] The immediate bargain for hours and wages is ruled out of the subsequent descriptions of the extent of control. But most of the complicated forms of control are themselves merely elaborate safeguards of the standard of living. Most of the control already won by the workers is *control as a bulwark of wages*. The checkweighman is there to see that wages are

[20] The annual official *Reports on Strikes and Lockouts* give figures of the numbers of workpeople involved in disputes and a classification of the disputes according to the issues involved. According to these, 64 per cent of the workpeople out in the years 1901-13 were out over question of wages and hours. See Note on Sources.

not nibbled away by fraud.[21] Apprenticeship and similar restrictions are frankly for purposes of wage monopoly.[22] The constitution of the Amalgamated Society of Engineers talks of the "vested interest" in craft rights. Consultation over changes in technique is mainly an outgrowth of the piece-rate bargain.[23] It is only a slight exaggeration to say that all present forms of workers' control, except those that secure the rudiments of decency in discipline, are by-products of the wages-and-hours struggle.

The wage element is the dominant factor in present-day control. But what are its bearings on the demands for more control? There are at least three widely different interrelations to be noticed. The first and most talked-of is opposition. The average workman, it is often said, is interested in "mere wages." [24] He cares nothing about control; he doesn't want to run things. What he wants is to draw his pay regularly and get away as quickly as possible. Nor is this merely an

[21] Section XI.
[22] Section V.
[23] Section XIV.
[24] I do not intend the phrase " mere wages " to carry any moral stigma. It is not argued that it is sordid or immoral to want wages and short hours and a steady job, and gloriously moral to want control and personal dignity and an interesting task. Nor is it argued that it is natural and healthy for men to want money and decent ventilation, but unnatural and sentimental for them to desire freedom and joy in work. The question is not what people *should* want but the sufficiently difficult one of what people *do* want.

employer's view of working-class psychology. I
heard it also from an impatient leader of shop
stewards who said that most workmen were "not
interested beyond wages and hours" and that
therefore he "had no intention of waiting for the
majority." It is true that the wage and control
movements are sometimes in competition, and no
doubt on a straight vote between wages and control wages would still win.

But it is a great mistake to suppose that the
two interests are always or even usually in opposition. The short-run economic interest—what R.
F. Hoxie called the demand for "more now"—is
indifferent to control movements. The longer-run
economic demands—which take shape in the planning of drastic changes in the distribution of
wealth—may on the other hand be found greatly
strengthening the demand for workers' control.
In fact, the latter form a major part of the driving force of current control movements. The shop
stewards are emphatic on this point. "What we
want," a Sheffield leader told me promptly, "is
the product of the industry, and"—after hesitat-
ing a moment—"conditions," by which he meant
chiefly protection from trade diseases. Mr. Frank
Hodges of the Miners has been perhaps the
clearest of all labor leaders in his insistence on
the need for control as an "avenue for great"--
and non-economic—"longings." Yet he too de-

clares that the control demand is mainly one for satisfactions outside working hours:—

"Workers' control is a means, and not an end. Work in the modern industrial world is unpleasant for the majority of workers. They will find their expression as human beings outside the working hours. . . . Control they will use to get efficient management and machinery. . . . Control they wish to save them from the waste and insecurity and long hours of the present system . . . which leaves no secure and creative leisure. . . . But control will never of itself be an answer to the instincts thwarted by standardized machine industry. The answer will be found outside working hours." [25]

The demand for high pay may strengthen the demand for control. The desire for sure pay—for security against unemployment—is even nearer the surface of control schemes. This is in fact the chief immediate appeal to the workers of such an elaborate plan of control as the Foster Report.[26] Indeed, several working-class students have told me that the desire for security is the chief factor in the demand for control. Both security and high wages might conceivably be won without workers' control, but the demands for them furnish much of the impetus of current movements toward control.

[25] Quoted by Arthur Gleason, *What the Workers Want.*
[26] See below, p. 86. And *cf.* all of Section IV.

There is still a third interrelation between the wage motive and the "non-economic factors" in the demand for control. What starts as a wage demand may easily—often unconsciously—be colored by an admixture of other motives. The clearest case is the transition in motive from *wages* to *workmanship* to be discussed in Section XV. Every demand on the part of the Miners for improved technique has had as its basis the effect of bad management on piece-work earnings. The first and obvious motive was wages. Yet a large part of the feeling with which I have heard individual miners talk about needed improvements was clearly—whether they knew it or not—a sheer workmanlike disgust at inefficiency. And at the Miners' Conference on output committees, held in November, 1916, the Yorkshire leader, Mr. Herbert Smith, declared:—

"I say it has nothing to do with it . . . whether a man gets 15 shillings or 20 shillings . . . opportunity must be given . . . to get as many tubs as possible."

The strictly economic motives, then, are found both opposing and greatly strengthening, and occasionally even passing bodily over into, the non-economic factors in the demand for control. Clearly they are not the whole demand, but any estimate of the future of the demand is worthless

if it does not consider on which side their great
weight is likely to fall.

Certain of the motives centering around the
object for which the work is done or the purpose
for which the product is to be used—*what it's for*
and *for whose benefit*—have a bearing on control.
The good economic man, it is true, in an imper-
sonal economic system cares for none of these
things. But actual workers sometimes do. The
patriotic motive made a difference in war-time production. Moreover workers sometimes refuse to
do certain pieces of work because they disagree
with the purposes of it:—the Sailors' Union during the war would not carry delegates to the
Stockholm International Labor Conference;○
more recently certain trade unionists have refused
to make munitions for the Russian Campaign.○
More to the present point is the extent to which the
control demand is fortified by the objection to
working for private profit. The *organization* of
industry is right enough as it is, one shop steward
told me, what we want is to eliminate private
ownership. The Foster Report names as one of
four causes of restriction of output, "the disin-
clination of the workmen to make unlimited profit
for private employers." "We don't want to work
any longer for private profit," was the burden of
the Miners' case before the Coal Commission.

That this was more than a wage matter and clearly bound up with state socialist or community feeling, comes out clearly in a passage in the cross-examination of Mr. Straker of the Northumberland Miners by Mr. Cooper of the Northumberland Coalowners:—

"*Mr. Straker.* . . . . He [the miner] objects to those profits being collected by any few individuals.

Mr. Cooper. What possible difference can it make to him whether the profits are collected by few or many, or by a neutral body like the State, so long as he gets his fair share?

Mr. Straker. Because he is realizing now that he is a citizen of the State."

The feeling is evidently in part that the status of "public servant" is somehow honorable in itself. It is no accident that the two strongest official trade union movements toward control—those of the Miners' Federation and the National Union of Railwaymen—are for "nationalization *and* joint control." There is no doubt that the older socialist feeling is a powerful element in the control demand. One careful working class student, in defining the essence of the demand for control, said that it was: "To serve the community, not a man and a class." The blending is not logically necessary. Socialist Utopias have been planned with no thought of workers' control. The interest in what happens to the product of industry does not necessarily involve an interest in the internal control of the production. But in the ideas of the British labor movement, at least, these two sets of motives are inextricably mingled. When Mr. Straker says that the miner must "feel that the industry *is being run by him* in order to produce coal *for the use of the community,*" it would be hard for him to say where the one motive ends and the other begins.

How the worker is treated—what sort of authority he is under, how much freedom he is allowed, how much authority he has—on these questions the demand for control becomes most nearly a demand for *control for control's sake.* "The conflict of interests between employers and employed in private industry has two aspects," writes Mr. Henry Clay in the *Observer,* "the purely economic aspect of wages, and the moral aspect of subordination to discipline." There is no lack of testimony to the importance of the discipline aspect in present-day labor feeling. Self-respect, status, independence, personal freedom, personal dignity,—a whole propaganda literature and a whole set of commentaries on labor have been written around these terms. And the roots of this sort of feeling run far back into the older trade unionism. Trade union membership, says the constitution of the Friendly Society of Iron-

founderș"enables men to exhibit the principle of
self-respect which, if duly exercised, will in its
turn command the respect of others, thereby plac-
ing a man in that position where he may demand
that he should be treated as a factor in any
arrangement involving his services, and not as
though he was a mere human machine." A recent account of a dispute carried on by the shop
stewards at a Cowes aircraft factory runs in almost the same terms:—

"A mass-meeting of all sections made it quite clear
that they were going to insist that any attempt to treat
any group of men without regard to their feelings or
self-respect would be treated as a challenge to all the
unions."

Lord Robert Cecil put the case to the House of
Commons in the phrases of political theory:—

"What is really the position of the wage-earner in
most industries? He is paid so much wages. He is a
mere item. He has to carry out a certain industrial
policy on which he has never been consulted, and with
which he has no power of dealing at all. He is not
really a free, self-governing man in industrial matters.
. . . It [this feeling] is really at the bottom of this
claim for nationalization."

Professor Edwin Cannan put the same claim into
homelier language in his testimony before the
Coal Commission:—

"It is all right to work *with* anyone; what is disagreeable is to feel too distinctly that you are working *under* someone. You suffer from this feeling when you are told to do what you know, or think you know, to be the wrong thing, and also when you are told to do the right thing in a disagreeable manner."

Dr. Cannan's shrewd analysis makes a good beginning for an attempt to separate out the elements of the freedom-authority demand. The most conspicuous is surely the objection to being told in a disagreeable manner, to being told the wrong way. It is just this that the Welsh colliers and the railwaymen and the other workers described in Section X are "quick to resent." *Being told the wrong way* is almost an exact translation of "alleged harassing conduct of a foreman," and the great number of disputes on this head is a sign of the strength of the feeling. The aircraft-workers already quoted were demanding "the right to work under a manager who will realize that men are men inside the shop, and not servile slaves." Similar evidence of the intensity of this resentment against harsh discipline may be taken from a writer whose sympathies are entirely on the employers' side. The author of *The Man-Power of the Nation* [27] is warning foremen of "The Pitfalls of the Promoted":—

[27] See Note on Sources.

"Domination, even when veneered by a display of sympathy, tends to active guardianship of privileges cherished by the worker and the exercise of that willfulness which finds expression too often in an enforcement of selfish rights. In fact, were one to probe deeply into the basal cause of many disputes in works, it would be found that in a large number of cases a little thoughtfulness and tact on the part of the foreman would have nipped the trouble in the bud."

There is no doubt at all that irritation at "petty tyranny or constant bullying" is "at the bottom of some of the bitterest strikes."

All these hot protests against particular abuses of authority are perhaps not yet a demand for control. There is certainly a distinction between the resentment *against being controlled in a certain way* and the resentment *against being controlled at all*. But even more significant than the distinction is the fact that the one passes so readily over into the other. The objection to being "messed about" by an unusually fussy foreman becomes an objection to being "messed about" by any sort of supervision. The fierce resentment against illtreatment by a particular "gaffer" or boss crystallizes into the general phrases "sack the gaffer" or "eliminate the bosses." Resentment at being given orders in a disagreeable manner becomes, as Cannan suggests, the general resentment at feeling too distinctly under orders at all.

Much of the touchiness of the workers toward the display of authority comes very near to resentment against all control. "The British attitude," said the secretary of a powerful employers' association, "is this:— I know how to do my job and won't be told how." "Policing" is pretty generally resented. And sometimes the objection is put rigorously into practice, as in the case of the Scottish miners who refuse to work while the overman is in their stall [28] or of the Clyde blacksmiths who would not let their managing director watch their fires.[29] All this is not the demand for control in the sense of an explicit theory of opposition to authority and only a small minority of the workers hold any such complete theory. But this resentment may easily be the "makings" of such a demand. One of the shop stewards declared vehemently:—

"People talk as if the demand for control was something that had to be created among the workers by a slow process, *but it's there already!*"

He must surely have meant, however, that it was "there" in the shape of a latent resentment that might be focused on this or that particular issue, not "there" as a fully conscious program. There is some evidence, too, of the workings of this process by which irritation with certain orders be-

[28] See below, p. 137.
[29] See below, p. 138.

comes a resentment against all control. A Yorkshire carpenter gave me a theory to account for
the war-time increase in the control demand which
illustrates this in detail:—Work before the war
went along much the same way from year to
year, and few new orders had to be given. There
was nothing to make the workers especially conscious that they were under control. The rapid
war changes made necessary a sudden stream of
novel and disturbing and often conflicting orders.
All this made the workers feel themselves more
distinctly bossed, and therefore ready to think
in terms of opposition to control. The intellectual
history of one of the prominent Clyde shop
stewards has run a somewhat similar course. Before he had any particular social theories he used
to resent being watched at his work. When the
manager brought guests through the shop he used
to switch off the power and walk away from his
machine—"bad enough to have to work in a factory anyhow without being put on exhibition doing it!" It was this sensitiveness to all subordination which became the basis for his later revolutionary theories; and it is this, he claims, which is
the real driving force in the minds of the leaders
of the extremist movements. The sensitiveness of
those who always "feel too distinctly" that they
are under someone is very near the core of the
conscious theories of control. The feeling of

servility in subordination to the employer's authority is the leading note in shop steward propaganda. This is what makes the bitterness that runs through Mr. J. T. Murphy's pamphlets:—

"Why are men and women servile to directors, managers, and foremen? Why do men dodge behind machines and in lavatories to smoke while the employers can and do stroll through the shops smoking cigars? . . . Why do men and women work long hours and show all the characteristics of subjection to the employers if the latter do not possess a power over them? . . . The workers show all the characteristics of a subject people when in contact with the employers." [30]

Mr. Straker is a labor leader of quite different temper, but the same feeling of resentment that the worker should be "merely at the will or direction of another being" [31] appears again and again in his testimony before the Coal Commission. The following passage is typical:—

"*Q.* I notice that you lay considerable stress in your précis upon this idea that under the pre-war system the workmen were in what they called a servile position: do you really seriously put that forward?

Mr. Straker. I do. . . . It is always a servile position when men are almost entirely under the control of another." [32]

[30] *Compromise or Independence?* See Note on Sources.
[31] Coal Commission Evidence, Question 23116. See Note on Sources.
[32] Questions 23433, 23434.

A resentment against the whole system of control in industry, a resentment constantly fed by irritation at particular cases of clumsily-exercised control, is a genuine and distinct factor in the demands of labor.

It may still be pointed out that all this is merely a negative resentment *against* control and not specifically a positive demand *for* control. This distinction may seem like an attempt to cut between things never separated in practice, but it is not merely a quibble. The desire to be let alone, to be free from the irksomeness of control by others, is not identical with the desire to co-operate actively in the work of controlling. The "will to be responsible for oneself" does not automatically resolve itself into the will to take part in representative government. The question of how far and under what conditions the one passes over into the other is a highly important practical point. Men might be ungovernable by authority without being thereby ready to govern themselves.

The demand for personal freedom within industry is not identical with the demand for political power within industry; the one begins as a desire for no government, the other is a desire for a share in self-government. How much of the latter is there in the present-day control demand? Clearly it is a less vocal part. The roots and beginnings of the control demand are in the felt irksomeness of the present system of control, not in a conscious desire for a new field of activity. I heard a group of Derbyshire miners thrashing out the problem. "Supervision is nauseous." On that they heartily agreed. "But supervision is necessary." Yes, if only for safety. Then one of the men suggested that there might be another sort of supervision—"amicable discipline" he called it—in which the supervisors should be elected by and responsible to the workers. It is apparently in some such way as this that the positive demand arises. Mr. Frank Hodges is almost alone in putting the demand for responsibility—for the "daily exercise of directive ability" —in the forefront of the claim for control. Little direct evidence of the reality of this demand can be taken from industry itself. What interest the ordinary workman may have had in running things or in managing men has had to be satisfied outside of industry if at all. Evidence from the few firms that have experimented with the "devolution of managerial functions" is conflicting. Some report an almost pathetic pleasure over consultation on very minor matters,[33] some a real interest in general policy, some a refusal to take responsibility. Perhaps a better judgment of the interest of workers in "running things" might be formed from a study of their organizing activities outside

[33] *Cf.*, p. 191.

the workshop,—the Trade Union Movement itself,
with the remarkable series of experiments and
failures and successes in devising forms of
organization which make (or should make)
the two great books of the Webbs books for the
political scientist; the Co-operative Movement,
with what D. F. Schloss called "its power to pro-
mote the organization upon democratic lines of
the working classes by the working classes"; the
Dissenting Chapels, in regard to which Mrs. Webb
wrote of "the debt which English democracy
owes to the magnificent training given by Protes-
tant Dissent in the art of self-government;" the
national and local work of the Labor Party; and
so on. The question runs beyond the scope of the
present study. The extent and range of working
class organizations may be put on one side, the
poor attendance at trade union meetings [34] and the
low percentage of votes cast on important trade
union ballots on the other. Some organizing interest is surely "there," in the shop steward's
phrase; the important question is really whether
or not it will be turned inwards upon industry itself.

These demands that bear directly upon the question of authority are of the highest importance
in a study of the control problem. *Control* is a

[34] "To get an attendance of 70 to 100 out of a branch membership of 300 to 1000 is a sign of stirring times, or of unemployment," says Mr. J. T. Murphy.

political [35] word. The demands previously studied
are not primarily political; they are concerned
with the control of industry not as an end but as
a possible means, and they might conceivably be
satisfied without changes in workshop politics.
But the "political" demands now under discussion are concerned more nearly with control for
its own sake; their chance of satisfaction depends
directly [36] upon the type of industrial government.
These "political" demands may be phrased as
*the demand not to be controlled disagreeably, the
demand not to be controlled at all,* and *the demand
to take a hand in controlling.* The first runs
through all trade union activity. The second is
less widespread. The conscious general resentment is vastly less than the sum of particular irri-
tations, but it is the powerful driving passion of
the control agitation. The third—the desire for
a share in the job of running things—is real but
less immediate.

The force of these freedom demands is hard
to measure. Apparently they run as an under-
current in many of labor's campaigns on other
issues. It is impossible to judge the extent to
which a vague and uneasy sense of oppression

[35] " Political," that is, in the wide sense of concerned with authority relationships; not " political " in the narrow sense of
relating to the authority of the State of territorial unit.

[36] Except in so far as the organizing interest is drawn off into
non-industrial channels.

adds to the bitterness and determination with which apparently trivial disputes are fought. It is by now a commonplace [37] to say that the occasion or formulated issue of a strike, as of a war, is only a part of its cause or of the emotions that are called out; surely a part of the emotion that gathers around any industrial struggle is that of servant against master. It is in this sense that Mr. Straker calls "the straining of the will of man to be free" the root cause of labor unrest. And it is the linking of this feeling with the economic motive that makes "wage-slavery" a powerful phase for propagandists to conjure with.

These political factors are rightly thought of as the essential part .of the demand for control. Possibly they are not the strongest part of the demand, but they are the part least likely to be diverted from the issue of the government of industry. They are the core of the demand; the other motives may in various circumstances be added unto it.

The worker's interests in the work itself—in *what he actually does,* in the technical processes of industry—have also important bearings on the control problem. Cannan's analysis of the resentment against control includes both "political" and

[37] Thanks in part to the work of the late Carleton Parker.

technical factors. The "feeling when you are told to do what you know, or think you know, to be the wrong thing," is surely a workmanlike distaste for inefficiency. The technical interests are often grouped under the one term *workmanship* [38]; it is safer to discuss them simply as *interests in the job.*

The interest usually mentioned first under this head is *craftsmanship,* the feeling of the individual craftsman toward his own particular bit of skilled technique. And the first thing that is usually said about it is that it is dead or at least dying out.[39] Certainly the long run effects of the transition from handicraft to modern machine industry bear heavily in that direction. "In the technique of handicraft the central fact is always the individual workman." On the other hand, "the share of the operative workman in the machine industry is (typically) that of an attendant, an assistant, whose duty it is to keep pace with the machine process and to help out with workmanlike manipulation at points where the machine process is incomplete."[40] Crafts and craftsmanship are clearly going down together

[38] *Cf.* especially Thornstein Veblen, *The Instinct of Workmanship.*

[39] "The worst indictment of capitalism," one ex-joiner told me with unexpected bitterness.

[40] *The Instinct of Workmanship,* pp. 234, 306. The last two chapters of the book are a discussion of the institutional bearings of this technological change.

before the advance of fool-proof machinery and standardized industry.

But it is much too early to count off craftsmanship as a genuine force in industry. Nor is it strictly true to say that it survives only in the tiny remaining handicrafts or only in the trades mentioned in Section XIX under the topic of "old craft control." Even in the great industry there are occasional indications of craftsmanship —though no propagandist movement is finding it worth while to bring together evidence on the point. The best signs of it are in fact those that come out incidentally in the course of discussions on other subjects—such as the use by a certain skilled joiner of his own dexterous hands as the basis for his social theories,[41] the use by an engineering trades official of "cutting a micrometer scale" as the type of something that required real skill, or the following passage on rate-fixing from the Ministry of Labor's report on *Works Committees*:—

"A discussion that starts about the price of a job often finishes by two men staking their reputations as craftsmen and their experience as workmen that they are absolutely right."

I have even heard an engineering shop steward confess to a certain pride in the skill of the craft whose special privileges he was attacking.

[41] "Human hands too valuable " to be used for "donkey work."

Craftsmanship is still a force, though a diminishing one. In relation to the control demand it cuts two ways. It is a conservative factor in the resistance of the old crafts against "encroachments" upon their ancient forms of control.[42] It moreover is an element in stiffening the demand not to be controlled. The true craftsmen will stand very little supervision in regard to his own technique. The glass bottle maker will not work under a manager who is not trained as a glass bottle hand. "I know how to do my job and won't be told how"—this was quoted as almost the central element in the demand not to be controlled. Pride in craft skill may often make a part of that independence which resists irksome control.

But craftsmanship seems to cut just the other way in relation to the positive side of the control demand. The old craft unions are completely indifferent to the newer "political" demands. The craftsman may be quick to resent interference with his own work, but he is not likely to bother about organizing activities very far outside that work. "The artist, the craftsman, the scholar and the scientist have one overpowering desire; to be let alone," writes Mr. Arthur Gleason. "They haven't the slightest wish to run anything or anybody, to manage, to 'know the commercial side,' to market the product or to control the raw

[42] See below, Section XIX.

material.'' It is true that some of the control propaganda—notably that of one school of Guild Socialists—runs in terms of a return to craftsmanship; but the immediate program of workers' control is a program of opportunities for political activity within large-scale industry. If Professor Wallas°is at all right in making ''concentration on what he can see and touch'' the essential characteristic of the craftsman,[43] it is no use for National Guildsmen to talk arts and crafts and at the same time to point to the Miners' Federation of Great Britain and the National Union of Railwaymen as promising steps ''Towards National Guilds.'' Craftsmanship has no direct connection with representative government. By its concentration on the immediate and highly individual skill it runs counter to the general organizing interest which makes up the positive side of the demand to exercise control, but by the very pride in that individual skill it stiffens the refusal to be controlled.

So much for the relation of craftsmanship to control. But the chances of interest in the work for the work's sake do not end with individual manual craftsmanship. The enthusiastic managing director of a great engineering firm may have as keen an interest in the process of production as any Swiss wood carver. Large-scale ''social pro-

[43] Graham Wallas, *The Great Society*, p. 4.

duction" has to a great extent taken the place of individual production. With it have come a set of interests in the technique of group-organization as well as in the technique of individual work. *Collective workmanship* might serve as a general term for them, but the interests covered would run from an interest in the routing of work in a particular shop to an interest in the governing and lay-out of great industrial enterprises. Some of these feelings—that of the individual inventor,[44] for example, or the pride in a great industry,[45] or the queer generalized pride in being "practical men"[46] and "industrialists"—bear only indirectly on the demand for control. At least one interest, the pride in a particular firm's workmanship—Wedgwood's in the Potteries is one of a few cases—may run counter to the control demands. But certain of these interests in collective work appear directly as part of the control demand.

The most conspicuous of these is the demand for *the right to make suggestions* about the conduct of the work. Of the reality of this interest there is abundant evidence.[47]   A foreman in one of

[44] But *cf.*, pp. 217-219.

[45] But note the use of the pride in " the industry as a national service " in the Building Trades Parliament.

[46] It would be amusing to count the number of times this phrase is used, both by employers and workers, in a year's crop of arbitration proceedings and blue books on labor problems.

[47] See Section XVI.

the National Factories [48] was telling me how the management had encouraged suggestions both from the foremen's and the workers' committees. "It isn't only the big wages," he declared emphatically. "The men like to have their ideas taken up." In discussing the demand for control with a group of Derbyshire miners, I found—to my surprise—that this was the issue on which they showed the greatest interest. One man got up and declared:—

"There isn't a man in this room who hasn't time and again made suggestions and been told he was paid not to think but to work."

The evening turned into a sort of testimony meeting in which the men related different specific suggestions that they had made, and the next noon the colliery blacksmith stopped me on the road to explain to me how he thought his company might use compressed air more efficiently, and so on. This interest in making suggestions—and the strong feeling that the chance to make them is blocked under the present type of industrial government—are real factors in the demand for control.

The interest in making suggestions, moreover, can hardly be separated from the interest in seeing those suggestions put into force. It is in fact

[48] Munition plants run directly by the Government.

only a special form of a general interest in the running of modern industry. Various traces of an interest in the technical efficiency of industry may be found in labor feeling. There is at least a certain negative interest, a disgust with various sorts of inefficiency. Evidence is hard to collect since, as a building trades union official remarked, most of the discussions of workmen on a job about the inefficiency of their employers can find no outlet in the form of suggestions.[49] One of the Derbyshire miners just quoted talked of being "told to do the silliest things imaginable." A Clyde shop steward told me that a disgust with the inefficiencies of management was always there for the agitator to "play on"—evidence the more interesting because the object of the agitation was certainly not to stir up technical interest. How widespread this sense of irritation with inefficiencies in organization may be, it is impossible to say. Its clearest expression is in the complaints of the Miners, enforced by trade union power, against inefficiencies in the arrangements for haulage, etc.[50] Nor does this interest always remain merely negative. There are even cases of the urging of positive changes in organization. This is shown in the elaborate schemes of the

[49] See Section XVI for the results in a few cases where an outlet has been provided.
[50] See Section XV.

Post Office Workers for extending the financial side of the postal service, of which one of their leaders speaks as follows:—

"The workers want to take part in the administration of the Department. For years past they have proffered suggestions whereby the public could be better served and the services more efficiently organized and managed, but they have been turned down."

It is shown in the detailed suggestions on the technique of the industry presented to the Coal Commission by the Miners' Federation. What Justice Sankey called the Miners' "higher ambition of taking their due share and interest in the direction of the industry," is, as he realized, of great significance. It marks the appearance of the managing and planning interest as a definite factor in the control demand.

Workmanship in this most general sense is an idea that has run through part of the propaganda of workers' control ever since the agitation of 1911. One of Mr. Mann's followers declared that year:—

"I for one believe we have yet to see good work, and that will be when work is made pleasant and attractive, well organized by capable men, who will have been elected by their mates. . . . I understand Syndicalism is to use some of its efforts at making the worker take a vital interest in the industry he is connected with, thereby preparing him for the democratic control of the industrial community of the future.''

The most comprehensive statement of the workmanship part of the demand—and one that adds to it the demand for knowledge about large-scale industry—is given in Mr. Straker's testimony before the Coal Commission on March 13, 1919:—

"Any administration of the mines, under nationalization, must not leave the worker in the position of a mere wage-earner, whose whole energies are directed by the will of another. He must have a share in the management of the industry in which he is engaged, and understand all about the purpose and destination of the product he is producing; he must know both the productive and the commercial side of the industry. He must feel that the industry is being run by him in order to produce coal for the use of the community, instead of profit for a few people. He would thus feel the responsibility which would rest upon him as a citizen, and direct his energies for the common good.

This ideal cannot be reached all at once, owing to the way in which private ownership has deliberately kept the worker in ignorance regarding the industry; but as that knowledge which has been denied him grows, as it will do under nationalization, he will take his rightful place as a man. Only then will labor unrest, which is the present hope of the world, disappear.''

This explicit plea for the chance of workmanship is the demand of a few. When Mr. Ben Turner, the veteran leader of the Textile Workers, put the question at the Trades Union Congress:—"Why shouldn't they sing at their work?" the cheers were more out of pleasure in his personality than from any very definite notion of work that might be worth singing about. The *Right of Workmanship* is not carried as a motto on the street banners of the labor movement.

These various interests in the job tie back to all the other factors of the control demand. A striking case of the substitution of the *workmanship* for the *wage* motive has already been mentioned. The last statement quoted from Mr. Straker's evidence is one of many that show the blending of the public service and workmanship interests. The relations between the freedom and workmanship demands are even more central to the control problem. Craftsmanship has already been spoken of as strengthening the objection to being controlled, and surely all forms of workmanship fortify what Mr. Cole calls "the natural impulse we all feel to push aside anyone whom we see doing badly what we can do better." The feeling of inferiority which deepens the bitterness of the agitation for control is in part a feeling of *functional inferiority*. It is impossible to separate the "organizing interest" spoken of as the positive side of the "political" demand from the interests in organizing industry just discussed.

In fact it is just where the two are one that the control demand is the clearest. The general interest in organization becomes directly important for control only when it is turned to the organizing of *industry*; the general interests in industry become directly important for control only as they become *organizing* interests. In a list of the nucleus elements of the demand for control—those elements, that is, that can hardly be diverted from the issue of the control of industry—it is necessary to put with the "political" factors of the *determination of workers not to be run* and their *desire to run things* the "workmanship" addition *that it is industry that workers want to run.* This is indeed implied in the quotation which began this introduction. Mr. Straker, it is true, states the demand in terms of "the straining of the will of men to be free;" but he has more than once explained that he means by that not merely a negative freedom but a positive freedom, a freedom to do something. The content of his idea of freedom is in fact workmanship. It would, I think, be fair to his position to rephrase it as follows:—

Wages and conditions are not enough. They have been improved and the unrest is still strong. Mere negative freedom from harsh discipline is not enough. That the Northumberland Miners have long been able to secure and the unrest is still strong. The root of the

matter is a demand for a positive freedom of responsi-
bility and self-expression.

But such a clear-cut claim for control is the claim of a tiny minority. Most of the driving force of the movement comes from other motives, and no single statement can pretend to express all the confused strivings that make up the total demand. The whole of this introduction makes only a beginning at describing its complexity. The actual demand for control is a tangle of half-expressed and shifting and richly varied desires. That is, it is a human phenomenon.

It is a dogma in the somewhat Early Christian faith of the Clyde shop stewards that "the ferment creates its own organization." It is at least "ferment" that makes "organization" interesting. And it is the ferment of the demand for control that makes worth while a patient study of the present extent of control.

A STUDY IN BRITISH WORKSHOP POLITICS

I

CONTROL

THERE is a theory current that the employer does and should exercise something that is known as "complete executive control" over industry. There are other theories current that the organized workers should—sooner or later, and more or less completely—take over "the control of industry." Workshop politics are forcing themselves into first place in social politics, and the workshop conflict represented by these ideas is perhaps the most significant fact in the social politics of the day. This study is an attempt to make a record of the present stage of the conflict in Great Britain in terms of the questions:—*What is the present extent, and what are the boundaries, of workers' control? How much control of industry do the British workers now exercise?*

But "control" over what?. The term is used by the contestants in the struggle in an undefined but somewhat specialized sense. When one of the coal-owners on the Coal Commission asked one of the Miners' Executive what they meant when they said they wanted control, and the answer was:—"We mean just what you mean when you say we must not have control," they were using a term an outsider might well try to define for himself.

"Complete executive control" might mean, among other things, that the employer "by his absolute knowledge and mere motion" provides capital, decides what to produce and how to produce it, provides any sort of place to work, hires whom he likes, pays his hands any wages by any system, works them any number of hours he likes, drives them by any method and with any degree of supervision, promotes, fines, or dismisses them for any cause, trains any hand for any job, dictates every process in the minutest detail—and does all this and more "subject to change without notice." But the most cursory acquaintance with industry or a glance at a few typical collective agreements shows that the employer [1] has no such

---

[1] The use of the phrase "the employer" is not meant to imply that all employers are alike either in personality or in their position in industry. But the differences between employers, great as they are, are comparatively unimportant in the present connection since they are not usually expressed in differences of the *extent* of control they leave to their employees. The popular distinction between "good" and "bad" employer is of no use for the present purpose,—except in so far as the "bad" employer may arouse his employees to devise means of controlling him, or as the "good" employer may also happen to believe, in Mr. Seebohm Rowntree's phrase, in "giving as much control as he can instead of as little as he must."

control as this. The real question is how much less does he mean by "complete executive control." There is after all such a thing as a trade union and, as Professor Commons°says, "If it cannot prevent the employer from doing as he pleases at some point or other, it is something besides a trade union." But the question is, *which points?* What matters have been recognized as subjects for consultation, at least, rather than employer's fiat?

First and most obviously, *wages and hours*. The "wage bargain" has always been in the eyes of the law a bargain between equals. The primary function of the trade union has been to restore to this contract some degree of real equality. These are of course the questions on which the workers now exercise their most important share of control.

In the second place, some of the more obvious physical "conditions of employment"—ventilation, sanitary arrangements, and works conveniences generally—have also long been subject both to collective bargaining and Factory Act legislation.

Neither of these things, though, is control in the sense that either a fighting employer or a propagandist of "workers' control" would use the term. An employer's control over industry is not destroyed by the fact that he has to buy labor with much the same equality in bargaining that he buys other factors in production. And matters of toilets and air space and welfare work are after all not vital to absolute power over the actual organization of production.

The question of "control" arises beyond the immediate contract of so many hours or so many pieces of work for so much pay, and beyond the obvious physical "conditions of employment," in the debatable ground where regulating the "conditions of employment" appears from another point of view to be actual sharing in the organization of industry. The object of the present study is to find out how much control the workers have over matters that are

(1) Less immediate to the "wage bargain" itself than Rates of Wages and Hours of Labor.

(2) More immediate to the "actual business of production" than Ventilation, etc.

What degree of control do the trade unions exercise over the relations of man to man in industry— the employment and discipline relationships; and over the relations of man to the work itself— to the plans, processes, and technique of industry? How much say have the workers over what the boot manufacturers once called "the internal economy of the workshop and the manipulation of the workman by the employer?"

The first and obvious answer is—directly and explicitly, very little. A longer and more critical answer requires study and analysis of collective agreements and arbitration awards, of trade union regulations, of jealously guarded shop practices and customs of the trades, of the issues of strikes, and of the demands of the revolutionary minority.

In theory trade union rules rarely extend beyond the "conditions of employment" in the sense of the famous definition of the Webbs of a trade union as "a continuous association of wage-earners for the purpose of maintaining or improving the conditions of their employment." [2] But it is at least worth a study of such "conditions" as the non-unionist, apprenticeship and demarcation questions; the various expedients for meeting unemployment; discipline, dismissals and the handling of grievances; promotion and the choice and authority of foremen; methods and payment and the measurement of results; restrictions on technique; consultation over change in technique and over trade policy, etc., to determine to what extent they involve, in fact if not in form, trade union

      (1) interference with
      (2) consultation over
      (3) direction of

the actual organization of industry.

[2] *History of Trade Unionism,* p. 1. See Note on Sources.

II

THE FRONTIER OF CONTROL

"WORKERS' control" is, I suppose, often trans-
lated as "interfering with the employer's business." A definite notion of the meaning attached
to the latter phrase would be of use in finding the
fighting frontier of control. Where does the
issue come into the open? At what point does
the employer say—beyond this there shall be no
discussion, the rest is my business alone? The
line is a hard one to draw; the issues are rarely
thought out in the abstract and rarely presented
dramatically. The real frontier, like most lines in
industry, is more a matter of accepted custom
than of precisely stated principle. In a few instances, however, there have been definite attempts to stake out the boundary, evidently as
results of disputes in which the principle became
explicit.

There are for example a number of collective
agreements [1] that attempt to define the "Authority
of Employers" in such terms as these:—

"Each employer shall conduct his business in any
way he may think advantageous in all details of man-

[1] *Report on Collective Agreements.* See Note on Sources.

agement, not infringing on the individual liberty of the workman or these rules.'' (Liverpool Carpenters and Joiners.)

"Each employer shall have the power to conduct his business in any way he may think advantageous in the matter of letting work, taking apprentices, using machinery and implements, and in all details of management not infringing these rules." (Birmingham Bricklayers.)

"That Dressers shall not interfere in any way whatever with the management of workshops." (Scottish Steel Dressers.)

"The right of the Association to organize its equipment and to regulate its labor with a view to the lowest cost of production." (Bradford Dyers Association.)

The most famous of these declarations of the employers' authority was the Engineering Trades Agreement signed in 1898 after a great and unsuccessful strike. This declared under the head of "General Principle of Freedom to Employers in the Management of their Works," that:—

"The Federated Employers, while disavowing any intention of interfering with the proper functions of Trade Unions, will admit no interference with the management of their business. . . . Employers are responsible for the work turned out by their machine tools, and shall have full discretion to appoint the men they consider suitable to work them, and determine the conditions under which such machine tools shall be worked."

In addition to these attempts to define positively the borderline of control there are a number of agreements which define it negatively by setting aside questions which are not matters for discussion. Certain questions, they say, are questions for bargaining or arbitration; certain questions are vital and reserved to the employer. It is worth while to mention a few of these *non-justiciable questions of industry*. The Pottery arbitration agreement which preceded the present Joint Industrial Council ruled out the two questions of "Good from Oven" (deduction from wages for broken pots) and "Limitation of Apprentices." A Liverpool Dockers agreement provides "that the Union shall not interfere with the methods of working cargo on ships or quay." Leicester Boot and Shoe arbitration arrangements provide that "no Board shall interfere with the right of an employer to make reasonable regulations for time-keeping and the preservation of order in his factory or workshop." The last rule of a pioneer Works Committee in the woollen industry reads:

"It is understood and agreed that it is the business of the management, and is not the business of the Conference to deal with:—

    (a) The allocation of work to particular sets of drawing.

    (b) The allocation of winders to particular machines."

More typical, however, are provisions such as the following:—

"Questions of discipline and management not to be interfered with." (London Motor Bus Employees.)

Under questions to be discussed:—"Differences relating to general conditions of labor (not being questions of discipline and management)." (London County Council Tramways.)

Arbitration on "any question other than one which he [the arbitrator] shall decide to relate to management and discipline." (Bobbin Turners, etc., at Garton and Coverholme.)

The phrase "discipline and management" has been made most prominent by its appearance in the remarkable succession of railway crises. During the "all-grades movement" of 1907,° which turned on the issue of union recognition, Mr. Robert Bell, the Secretary of the Railway Servants,° was "on all occasions most emphatic in denying that it was the desire of the men's executive committee to interfere with the discipline of the railway staffs," while Lord Claud Hamilton (who wanted his men "to be free and independent as subjects of a Constitutional Monarch") and other railway directors were firm in their "absolute refusal to allow the society to interfere in our domestic relations with our staff." The Concilia-

tion Boards, set up in that year as Mr. Lloyd
George's solution of the difficulty, were expressly
limited to the consideration of "rates of wages
and hours of labor." By the time of the railway
strike of 1911, the attitude of the men was changed.
When their leaders testified before the Royal
Commission of that year, they were no longer
willing to repeat the absolute denial of an interest
in discipline. Mr. J. H. Thomas in fact argued
that, "the common sense of two parties meeting
in a representative capacity is more likely to arrive
at a right decision than through one side's taking
up the attitude that it is purely a question for
them to determine. . . . The men are distinctly of
opinion that all questions ought to be discussed
and settled by the Board." The Commission, however, reported that "with their great responsibilities the companies cannot and should not be expected to permit any intervention between them
and their men on the subjects of discipline and
management;" and by the 1911 scheme, although
the companies are to receive deputations on "any
questions affecting the contractual relations between the company and its employees," the
Boards themselves are limited to consideration of
"rates of wages, hours of labor, or conditions of
service, other than matters of management and
discipline." Since that time the last clause has
been the storm center of the industry, and the dis-

satisfaction with it is now expressed in a demand for nationalization with joint control by the workers and the State.

"Discipline and management," then, has often summed up the issue of control. The phrase would perhaps most often be used by an employer to describe the issues over which he would refuse to share control. And, from the other side, the president of the National Union of Railwaymen declares that, "it is in the fierce questions of discipline and management," that his union has found its soul.

But when one has said that discipline and management are the crux of the control problem, one is not very far along. The phrase almost disappears under analysis. The specific issues that have come under what the *Railway Review*°calls "the symbols D and M" include such things as dismissals, promotions, classification of employees, a doubtful safety regulation, etc. The Steel Dressers agreement quoted above goes on to include under the reservations to management the allocation of work between classes of workmen. The Engineering agreement put in the same category the selection, training, and employment of operatives and the right to pay according to ability. And in 1907 the *Railway Gazette*°even argued that if wages and hours were "fixed by two different bodies" (*i.e.* by negotiation with a union) an impossible "duality of management would arise!" But all these questions have of course been subjects for collective bargaining in other trades.

On the other hand, there are many cases of what an outsider would surely call consultation over "management" into which the disturbing word or idea never enters. The employment manager for an employers' association told me, for example, that various works committees in his trade found themselves discussing such matters as the reason why on a given morning there was no work ready for the piece workers. If anyone had suggested that that was a question of "management," of the actual arranging of production, the employers would doubtless have closed the discussion. But to everybody concerned it seemed merely the question of how to make sure that the piece workers should find work at starting time.

Discipline and management, then, are convenient terms for the frontier of control. But that frontier must be looked for as a shifting line in a great mass of regulations in regard to which the question of control may never have arisen. The material in this section, then, is interesting only as indicating a few of the cases in which the issue of control has been fought consciously, in which the frontier of management has seemed to its defenders a hard chalk line.

III

EMPLOYMENT

THE employer is sometimes spoken of as the man who finds jobs for workers. But to what extent do the trade unions determine which jobs are found for which workers? To what extent do the trade unions possess what D. F. Schloss called the "power of rejecting as fellow workers persons who appear to them to be undesirable companions?"

An obvious limitation on the employer's control under this head is the tendency of any strong union to reject non-unionists as fellow-workers. The employer's right and practice of keeping union members out and employing only non-unionists has practically gone by the board in Great Britain, if not in America. The issue now, where there is an issue, is whether the employer shall be permitted to employ any but unionists. The natural intensity of feeling on this point is best expressed by a comparison made by the shrewd secretary of an employers' association of the non-unionist to the conscientious objector, or by the following extract from a form letter drafted by a

Railwaymen's district council to be sent to the wives of non-unionists:—

"Dear Madam,

Do you know your husband is in receipt of a War Bonus, which the members of the N. U. R. have worked and paid for, and he has done nothing except to act like the young birds in a nest and take what others have struggled hard to get?"

It is difficult to measure the exact extent to which union membership has become a necessary condition of employment. Two or three great industries, certain skilled trades within other industries, and a few old crafts are practically "blackleg-proof." [1] Coal-mining is the nearest approach to a completely-unionized great industry. The Miners' Federation of Great Britain claims just under 99% of the underground workers, excluding officials, and 95% of the surface workers; and of the remainder many are organized in other unions.[2] In certain collieries the management itself collects the union dues by deducting from the men's pay and receives a percentage for its pains; and there are even instances of successful strikes against the employment of men in arrears to the union. In cotton there is practically no opening for the non-unionist on the spinning side

[1] "Blackleg" is the British trade unionist's equivalent for the American trade unionist's expression "scab."
[2] Coal Commission Evidence, Question 23635 *et seq.*

of the industry, at least in Lancashire, and very little in weaving. The Boilermakers have long claimed 95% organization and the other skilled shipbuilding unions are in practically the same position. The remarkable growth of the National Union of Railwaymen and the Railway Clerks' Association○has made the railways stand very high in percentage of unionists. In the wool industry the Dyers claim a 100% organization, and their agreement with the Bradford Dyers' Association provides that "any employee ceasing to be a member of any of the Unions shall be required by the Association to resume membership of one or other of the Unions." The Huddersfield Dyers and the Bradford Woolcombers○work under similar arrangements. Such old crafts as the Glass Bottle Makers, Flint Glass Makers and Hand Papermakers○are almost completely unionized, as well as such small skilled sections of larger industries as the Stuff Pressers (wool), Lithographic Printers, Calico Printers and Tape Sizers (cotton)○ Other industries—probably most industries—vary widely in this regard from district to district or from shop to shop. In the Manchester district, for example, the painters have a closed-shop agreement (though only with the organized employers) and the other building trades are pushing for it; in many parts of the country these trades are very imperfectly organized. In engineering, with a high total percentage of union membership, the enforcement of the closed shop condition varies entirely with the strength in the various works of a given town. In printing, although the union compositors refuse to work except in "fair houses" (*i.e.* all-union), rival "rat houses" continue to flourish; and the London Society of Compositors wages a continual campaign to make sure that all public contracts go to the former class of firms. In many industries, of course, and particularly in the distributive trades, there are hardly the beginnings of compulsory unionism.

From the point of view of our question about control, this enforcing of union membership is interesting chiefly as a basis for extensions of control to issues more closely bound up with the actual processes of production. The same is true of the custom of using the trade unions as employment exchanges. This is usually merely a matter of obvious convenience to both parties, without any thought of control. The man out of work goes to his union office to sign the "call book" and draw his out-of-work pay; the employer naturally sends there to find him. The union secretary will probably boast that his office is a better employment agency for his own trade than the public one—or possibly fear or despise the public exchanges as blackleg agencies—but that is about all it comes to.

More interesting, however, are cases where the union, in the interest of fairness between its members or for other reasons, makes some regulation as to which men shall be hired first. The "Rules Governing Calls" of the London Society of Compositors provide:—

"All calls for workmen received at the Society House shall be given to the members whose names appear first on the list. . . . "

"Employers, overseers, or their agents may choose workmen from the list irrespective of the position in which their names appear on the book; but the members so chosen may, if they think fit, refuse such employment, unless of those present they are first in order on the book."

The workman may look for work on his own account, but "any member intercepting, in the street or elsewhere, a messenger with a call that is intended for the Secretary, shall be dealt with by the Committee as they may determine."

Many unions advise, and in some cases require, their members to consult the union secretary before applying for a job in order to make sure that conditions are "fair." An adaptation of this principle is the claim of the Sailors' and Firemen's Union, denied in 1911 but granted for the duration of the war with the setting up in 1914 of the National Maritime Board, that representatives of the union "be present when men sign on."

The rules of this Maritime Board also established the principle of "a single source of supply jointly controlled by employers and employed." An important further extension of control is the requirement that the employer must hire exclusively through the union or at least give the union first chance to provide a man. The agreement in the China Furniture trade—where the employers and employed combine to keep up prices—provides:—

"The Operatives' Association shall undertake to provide at all times for a due supply of efficient workpeople, so that the business of Members of the [Manufacturers'] Association may in no way be hindered. Should the supply of workmen fall below the number required, the Wages Board shall at once take into consideration the best way of remedying the evil."

The Bradford Dyers' Association agreement of July 1, 1914, reads:—

"The Association[3] shall on the engagement of employees first make application to the unions to supply the employees required. The unions shall supply employees with the least possible delay, and if the unions do not supply employees satisfactory to the Association within 24 hours of receipt of a requisition in writing from the Association, the latter shall be free to engage persons who are not members of the unions, but such

[3] A trust not an association of independent firms.

persons shall be required by the Association forthwith to become members of one or other of the unions.''

This last system, together with the method of collective piece work provided for by the same agreement, has an interesting by-product in trade union responsibility for technique. The members of the National Society of Dyers are supposed to be able to perform all the processes of the trade; if, however, their secretary has to send to an employer a man who has had no experience in the particular process for which he is wanted, he sends at the same time a note to the shop steward [4] so that the others will "pull him through.''

The Stuff Pressers, a small and highly skilled craft within the wool industry, are by far the most striking example of trade union regulation of employment. With them the " staffing of shops" is entirely the function of the union. The method is described by a member in the *Organizer* of April, 1918:—

"The success of the union is further demonstrated by its methods of dealing with trade depression and slackness of shops. The experience gained in this direction during the past ten years has been invaluable. . . . To-day the Pressers' Society has a travelling man power, a

[4] " Shop steward " as used here means merely a representative of organized workers within a particular shop or works. The term is most widely used in the engineering industry; " constable " and " father of the chapel " are parallel terms in printing. The " shop stewards' movement " has already been discussed.

small but efficient body of skilled men who are ready
to respond to any call that the demand might make.
This mobile reserve has contributed largely to the solution of the unemployment problem [in an industry of
marked fluctuations in trade] . . . The method of choosing men is usually by the request for volunteers from the
shops.   If the voluntary principle is ineffective, the
shop resorts to the ancient method of 'picking out of
the bag'. . . . The success of the scheme can be gauged
from the fact that the Society has not had an unemployed
member for nearly five years.''

It is worth noting, in reference to the relation
of 100% unionism to other forms of control, that
the writer goes on to say that, ''the principle of
the mobility of labor . . . owes its success to
the fact that the Society is practically blackleg
proof.'' This is, I am sure, the instance of most
complete actual control over the finding of jobs.
In this case it apparently grew up without any
conscious theory, certainly without any public
propaganda.   The theorists of control, however,
have not completely neglected the possibilities of
the control of labor supply as a basis for the
control of industry.   The Engineering and Shipbuilding Draughtsmen, whose journal talks much
of ''status'' and ''control,'' voted in March, 1919,
to secure for their Association, as soon as possible,
a monopoly over employment quite consciously
as a ''new and formidable engine of control.''
And Messrs. Gallecher and Paton, of the Clyde en-

gineering shop stewards, in their *Memorandum on Workshop Control,* suggest for their District Committee both the "skilful manipulation" of labor supply as a weapon for immediate fighting purposes and the ultimate function under full workers' control of "the effective and economical distribution of labor."

IV

UNEMPLOYMENT

THE last paragraph of the preceding section shows how the problem of employment becomes the problem of unemployment. Here we might well expect to find real trade union attempts at the organization of industry, for the question is of much more pressing importance to the union than to the employer. The difference in immediate economic interest is this:—the employer is interested in finding men for jobs; the union is interested in finding jobs for men—interests "identical" only in busy seasons. In fact the employer's bargaining power increases directly with the size of the "reserve army" of unemployed. In slack seasons the unions are faced with this danger to their standard as well as the necessity of supporting their own members "on the funds." This is only another way of saying that the fear of unemployment is a ruling motive both for the individual workman and for his trade organizations. "Want or uncertainty of employment for the industrial classes," is still what William Thompson called it in 1830—a "master-evil of society as now constituted."

The principle expressed in most trade union attempts to meet the problem is a simple one—that no one should have more work than he needs until all have as much as they need. "They want to *ration employment* so that all will have their proper share." (*Strike Bulletin,* Clyde, February 8, 1919.)

The simplest arrangements, usually found in the less important trades, are those for the *sharing of work*. The Webbs give us the most primitive instance the "Turnway Societies" of Thames watermen for regulating the "turns" of work. The London Corn Porters provide for equalization of work by "rotation of gangs." A reflection of quarrels under this head is the following agreement reached by the tailors after the strike of 1892:—In reference to the trade union rule that provides that "during slack seasons a fair equitable division of trade should be compulsory in all shops," the employers, after stipulating that this did not necessarily mean "distribution of the work in turns," stated that "we fully recognize that the work ought to be fairly shared during the slack season in harmony with the above, and we urge upon our members throughout the country to carry these principles into effect." And in 1903 the Scottish Master Tailors stated, "that in quiet seasons they used their own discretion as at all other times in giving the work to such work people as they consider best capable of turning it out; but the principle of job about shall be recognized." Perhaps the most drastic regulation is that enforced by the highly monopolistic Yorkshire Glass Bottle Makers:—

"In the event of any furnace being out for repair, slack trade or stopped from any other cause, the workmen shall be allowed, so far as practicable, to share work—provided, nevertheless, that after a furnace has been out for four months the master can discharge the surplus workmen."

Many restrictions against *overtime* are based partly on this principle. The general question of overtime, in its important bearings on the standard of leisure and the payment of extra wages, is beyond the present inquiry; but so far as it bears on the equalization of work, it is of interest here. The weakly-organized Garment Workers, who are subject to busy seasons of constant overtime and slack seasons of wholesale dismissals, are pressing for the complete abolition of overtime as a means of forcing the employers to take steps to prevent or minimize seasonal fluctuations. A 1919 agreement in the Making-up Clothing trade in London provides for avoidance of overtime. The same principle is evident in a Boilermakers' agreement covering the South Wales ports:—

"No member . . . shall work more than one whole night or two half turns as overtime, in addition to the usual working days . . . in any one week, *whilst competent men are idle in the port,* except on finishing jobs which can be completed in not exceeding three hours' labor. If more overtime be required on particular jobs, *such overtime must be given to the unemployed members in the town"* (italics mine).

A rule proposed by the Manchester building trades unions puts the demand briefly :—

"No overtime to be worked in any branch of the Building Industry whilst any men in that branch of the industry and district are unemployed."

Organized *short time* is the most familiar palliative for unemployment. There is, says Professor Bowley (*An Elementary Manual of Statistics,* p. 151), "a group of industries in which certainly more than two million persons are employed, in which it is the custom to regulate the working week in relation to the demand for the product, employing nearly the same number of persons in good trade and in bad, but working short time when the market becomes overstocked . . . Coal-mining is the most conspicuous industry of this group. The textile trades (cotton, wool, and others) organize employment with a similar result; short time is worked, or the work is spread out among the operatives, when the demand is slack; but the great number of those employed in moderately busy times draw some wages nearly every week.'' The ''pound stint'' was a similar pre-war expedient in pottery. In most cases these arrangements are based on the convenience of the employers as well as of the employed or on tacitly-accepted ''custom of the trade,'' rather than on trade union insistence. They are interesting for the present purpose as the basis of experience from which have come two conscious movements toward control,—the one toward the use of short time against reductions of pay on account of over-production, best illustrated by the ''Miners' Four Days'' and the great cotton dispute of 1878 (see Section XVIII below); the other the extensive propaganda for shortening hours to absorb the unemployed. The last idea has been behind many of the demands for shorter hours made since Mr. Tom Mann's speaking tour in 1911. The Miners' claim for the six hour day was urged partly on this ground; and the ''40-hour movement'' in engineering, which boiled over in the Clyde and Belfast strikes early in 1919 and is simmering in the other districts, is based on this theory. ''They have come into the strike to abolish unemployment,'' said the Clyde *Strike Bulletin*. This is an item in the current propaganda of the shop stewards' movement, though one at least of its leaders thinks that, even after they had won their

30 or 40-hour week and absorbed the present crop of unemployed, they would "never have to go back." The most workmanlike attempt to write into an actual agreement this notion of reducing hours to meet unemployment is in the proposed new rules for the Coventry district of the engineering industry:—

"When the unemployed list reaches 2½% [of the union membership], the above hours shall be reduced by one hour per week, and if 5% of unemployment is reached the hours shall be reduced by 2½ hours per week. If more than 5% are at any time unemployed, the unions reserve the right to take any reduction of hours they consider necessary."

It is no longer true that, as the Webbs stated in 1897, "wisely or unwisely, the Trade Unions have tacitly accepted the principle that the capitalist can only be expected to find them wages so long as he can find them work." In a number of trades, there has been a movement toward forcing the employer to make it his business to regularize work or, failing that, to "make unemployment [that is, the maintenance of the unemployed] a charge on the industry." In its simplest form this is merely an objection on the part of a number of trade unions to the practice of keeping their members waiting without pay at the employer's convenience on the chance that work may be found for them. The demands put forward in October, 1919, by the National Union of Railwaymen and the Transport Workers Federation°on behalf of the coal-tippers include the provision:—

"All men shall be paid waiting time at the rate of 2/6d. per man per hour or part of an hour in all cases."

Various unions have been able to establish the principle of *guaranteed time,*—that is, that if a worker is hired at all he must be assured a full day's or week's work or, failing that, full pay for the period. The Manchester Carters won in 1911 an agreement that "all carters employed at or before 9 a. m. shall be paid a day's pay." The Boot and Shoe agreement of February 13, 1919, contains an elaborate stipulation that with certain exceptions, "where operatives attend at the factories on the instruction of the employers . . . work shall be found for them for at least half a day . . . or they shall be paid . . . at not less than the minimum or agreed wage rate." A rule proposed by the Manchester building trades unions reads:—

"Six hours per day shall be the minimum time paid to men who attend on the job up to 9 a.m. and remain on the job during the day, or until told by the management they may leave."

The Compositors on the London newspapers have daily guarantees of at least two galleys (approximately 7 hours' work). The Glass Bottle Makers have a guaranteed weekly rate or, in some districts, the guarantee of enough metal to allow them to make the weekly rate. Of the other old crafts, the Hand Papermakers are guaranteed "six days' custom" and the Flint Glass Makers "eleven moves a week" (33 hours). Finally, the first item in the terms of settlement with the National Union of Railwaymen in March, 1919, reads :—

"The standard week's wages, exclusive of any overtime or Sunday duty, to be guaranteed to all employees who are available for duty throughout the week."

Guaranteed time by the day or week has been a definite part of trade union policy. A further extension of the idea is guaranteed time all the year round. This is what is meant by the phrase "unemployment a charge on the industry" which Mr. R. Williams (*The First Year's Working of the Liverpool Docks Scheme*) explains as follows :—

"If a reserve of labor is required by any industry, then that industry should maintain that reserve not only when working, but also when it is unavoidably unemployed."

The idea does not necessarily involve any element of workers' control. Mr. Williams was writing from the viewpoint of a government official, and in at least one case responsibility toward its unemployed has been assumed by a powerful trust. The Bradford Dyers' Association agreed in 1907, "that to the men displaced from any cause whatever during the year the Association shall pay an amount equal to and in addition to that paid under their out-of-work benefit by the Society." But the most important experiment in this direction—that of the Cotton Control Board during the war—was much more to the present point. It involved both partial trade union responsibility for the policy of the scheme and complete trade union responsibility for administration of the unemployment benefit. The lack of shipping, due to the submarine campaign and the diversion of tonnage to war purposes, had caused an acute shortage of raw cotton and widespread unemployment in the industry. The Cotton Control Board, with representatives of the Board of Trade, the cotton merchants and manufacturers, and the cotton trade unions, was established in June, 1917, with broad powers to deal with the emergency. There were two main problems to be considered:—the allocation to the various manufacturers of their share of the limited supply of material, and the provision for the maintenance of the unavoidably unemployed. The first problem was dealt with by fixing the purchase price of raw cotton and by allowing manufacturers to run only certain percentages of their machinery. To meet the unemployment problem, a fund was created by a levy upon the manufacturers who exceeded their percentage of machines; this fund was used as unemployment pay under principles laid down by the Control Board; its actual administration, both to union members and to the few non-unionists, was left solely (with the trifling exception of a few outlying villages) to the trade unions. For a part of the first year of the Control Board's work and during the sharpest crisis, the industry ran on what was called the "rota" system—work for four weeks and the fifth week a holiday with pay provided by this levy upon the industry; this was finally given up in order that the surplus labor might be drained off to the making of munitions; but the general policy of making necessary unemployment a charge on the industry was maintained throughout the war. The importance of the work of the Cotton Control Board as a case in which trade union representatives shared, at least nominally, in the determining of trade policy will be discussed in Section XVIII. Its importance for the present subject lies not only in its actual steps for meeting unemployment but in the partial control by the workers in planning those steps and in their complete control over a part of the administration.

It will be noticed, however, that even the most

elaborate of these expedients, except perhaps the
little flying squadron of Stuff Pressers, are directed toward the end, not of decreasing irregu-
larity of employment but merely of distributing
more equally the incidence of its hardships. If
there is any effect on the reducing of the fluctuations themselves, it is only the indirect but important one of making it worth the employer's while
to plan to that end. In general the problems of
"business cycles" and the like have been left as
obviously beyond the reach of what little control
the trade unions have secured over industry.

It is the more interesting, then, to examine the
few instances in which the trade unions have taken
a part or an interest in attempts at the regularizing of employment as distinct from the mere
mitigation of the evils of unemployment. Attempts
to regularize employment may be divided into
those which begin from the end of regularizing
the supply of labor and those which begin from
the end of regularizing the demand for labor.
The history of the attempts in the former direction falls largely outside the scope of the present
study. The trade unions have played little part
in it, and most organized schemes of this sort are
attempts to secure for unskilled workers the sort
of regularity of employment which trade union
"limitation of numbers" (which will be discussed
in the next section) in part secures for certain

skilled workers. *De-casualization,* the policy
which Mr. (now Sir) W. H. Beveridge defined [1]
as follows:—"that all the irregular men for each
group of similar employers should be taken on
from a common center or Exchange, and that this
Exchange should so far as possible concentrate
employment upon the smallest number that will
suffice for the work of the group as a whole,"
was an invention of reformers from outside industry, as an attempt primarily to solve the
problem of irregular dock labor. The most
famous attempts at putting it into practice,
those which substituted some degree of regularization for the hideous scramble for work at the
London Docks, [2] made no provision for trade
union activity. More recent attempts, however,
have used the trade unions at least in a sort of
junior partnership. The Liverpool Docks Scheme,
an attempt to reduce the necessary surplus of dock
labor to the minimum by a system of registration
of workers and central clearing houses and call-
stands, [3] was started in 1913 as a government undertaking, but from the first provided for a joint
committee of employers and trade union representatives to supervise its working, and one of the
rules was to the effect that:—

[1] *Unemployment: a Problem of Industry,* p. 201.
[2] *Ibid.,* pp. 81-95.
[3] For details, see R. Williams, *The First Year's Working of the Liverpool Docks Scheme.*

"Employers shall issue a Registration Card to any man who produces his Dockers Union Membership Card stamped by the Branch Office to which he belongs."

It is clear, however, that this degree of control was given to the trade union in order to secure its co-operation with the scheme and does not represent real initiative on the part of the workers to prevent unemployment. In fact the government official who carried out the scheme speaks of the initial "diffidence" of both employers and employed and tells the story of a strike of dock laborers against the scheme.

Similar schemes are now in force in a number of other ports and in some cases involve much more positive trade union activity. In many of the ports where all men employed are union members registration is left in the hands of the union as agents for the Port Labor Joint Committee—in some cases union badges are even used as the tallies. And, although there has been in certain ports trade union opposition, a number of trade union leaders, notably Mr. Ernest Bevin of the Bristol Dockers, have themselves been active in the devising of the schemes to lessen unemployment. The trade unions, then, have played at least an acquiescent and in some cases an active part in certain attempts to regularize the supply of labor.

On the other question, the attempt to regularize the demand for labor, the trade unions have again assumed only a slight degree of control. There are occasional instances of joint attempts to solve particular problems of shortage of work. It is not at all uncommon for a trade union official in the course of his ordinary work to discuss with an employer ways and means of avoiding a stoppage of work that will throw his members out of employment. Similar matters are occasionally discussed by works committees. The Ministry of Labor's report on *Works Committees* [a] speaks of committees of building trades shop stewards which "may make representations to, or be consulted by, the employer on questions such as the proper allocation of work in order that sufficient inside operations may be reserved for wet weather" (p. 40), and of a works committee in a shipbuilding yard which considered among other matters, " unemployment questions—e.g., the purchase by the firm of an old vessel so as to employ idle men, and subscription to an unemployed fund" (p. 95).

These of course are minor and immediate expedients and the great question of trade fluctuations is naturally almost untouched by trade union activity. Political Labor, with which this inquiry has little to do, has given some attention to the

[a] See Note on Sources.

carefully thought out suggestion of Professor Bowley, taken up by Mr. and Mrs. Webb and embodied in the Minority Report of the Poor Law Commission (1908) and in "Labor and the New Social Order," of spraying work from a public reservoir to counteract trade fluctuations. An expression of this policy in trade union activity has been the strenuous protest by the trade unions affected against the wholesale discharge from National Factories and Dockyards since the armistice, on the ground that the Government should convert the establishments to some sort of useful work in a time of unemployment.

An ambitious recent project attempts to combine the four principles just discussed:—unemployment a charge on the industry, trade union administration of unemployment pay so provided, regularization of the supply of labor, and regularization of the demand for labor—in a single scheme intended to be carried out jointly by employers and employed in a great industry. The Joint Industrial Council for the Building Industry had placed in its constitution the "Prevention of Unemployment" as one of its objects. It had appointed a sub-committeee to consider the more efficient organization of the industry. At the annual meeting of the Council, held August 14 and 15, 1919, this Committee presented a report—known as the "Foster Report" from Mr. Thomas Foster, the

chairman, a master-decorator of Burnley—on
"Organized Public Service in the Building Industry,"[5] a document which was signed by all the
workers on the Committee and three of the employers, five employers dissenting. The report
was debated at length and, after a definitely hostile
amendment had been voted down, was referred
back to the same Committee for reconsideration
and elaboration. The Report covers a wide range
of subjects which will be referred to in later sections—the problem of unemployment, however,
takes first place in the arrangement of the report
and apparently in the minds of its supporters
from the operatives' side. "Fear of unemployment" is stated as the first cause of restriction
of output. The remedies may be quoted under the
headings given above. In charging necessary unemployment to the expense of the industry and in
entrusting the trade unions with administering
the benefit, the report follows the practice of the
Cotton Control Board. The significant passages
are as follows:—

"15. When all other methods of providing steady
and adequate employment for the operatives have been
exhausted, then the Industry is faced with the question
of its responsibility towards its employees during possible periods of unemployment. We are convinced that
the overhanging fear of unemployment must be finally

[5] See Note on Sources.

removed before the operative can be expected whole-heartedly to give of his best. . . .

17.— We further recommend that in cases of unavoidable unemployment, the maintenance of its unemployed members shall be undertaken by the Industry through its Employment Committees, and that the necessary revenue shall be raised by means of a fixed percentage on the wages bill, and paid weekly to the Employment Committee by each employer on the joint certificate of himself and a shop steward or other accredited trade union representative.

19.— While the collection of this revenue should be carried out by the Employment Committees, the payments should be made by periodical refund to the trade unions, who would thus become an important integral part of the official machinery and would distribute the unemployment pay in accordance with the regulations prescribed by the Industrial Council and its Committees."

The question of regularizing the supply of labor, which was at the same time being incidentally considered by the Resettlement Committee of the same Council, was touched on as follows:—

"42.— It is obvious that the important improvements we have outlined will tend to make service in the Industry more attractive; and while the interests of the public service emphatically demand the enrollment of every member who can be trained and utilized in the Building Industry, we fully recognize that indiscriminate enrollment must be prevented by careful regulation.

43.— We therefore recommend that the development

of the Industry should be kept under constant review by the Employment Committees, and that these Committees should periodically notify the trade unions as to the number of new members that may apply for registration under the Employment Scheme, after a suitable trade test or evidence of previous service in the Industry.

16.— . . . The machinery for filling vacancies already exists in the trade union organization and should be developed to the greatest possible extent, in order to supplement the State Employment Exchanges so far as the Building Industry is concerned."

The most elaborate and far-reaching proposals have to do with the regularization of demand, by the planning of public work to counteract trade depressions and by dove-tailing with other industries to counteract seasonal unemployment. The report reads as follows:—

"9.— . . . We consider it essential that the whole productive capacity of the Industry should be continuously engaged and absorbed, and that a regular flow of contracts should replace the old haphazard alternations of congestion and stagnation.

It is well known that the proportion of public to private work is very considerable and that it is well within the powers of Public Authorities to speed up or to delay contracts. We therefore recommend:—

    (a) That the Industrial Council shall set up a permanent committee entitled the Building Trades Central Employment Committee, with the necessary clerical staff.

(b) That each Regional Council shall similarly set up a Building Trades Regional Employment Committee.

(c) That each Local or Area Council shall similarly set up a Building Trades Area Employment Committee.

(d) That each Committee shall consist of an equal number of employers and operatives with one architect appointed by the local professional Association of Architects or by the Royal Institute of British Architects as may be most appropriate.

10.— The first duty of these Committees would be to regularize the demand for building:—

(a) at the approach of slack periods, by accelerating new building enterprises, both public and private, with the co-operation of architects and local authorities;

(b) conversely, at periods of congestion, by advising building owners to postpone the construction of such works as are not of an urgent character. . . .

13.— . . . The difficulty of providing employment during wet and bad seasons has yet to be faced. We feel that a certain amount of investigation is still needed in this direction, and venture to suggest that the Building Trades Industrial Council should approach the representatives of other industries with a view to investigating the possibility of 'dove-tailing' or seasonal interchange of labor.

There would appear to be a large volume of national and private work which could be undertaken when the Industry itself could not usefully employ all its available labor, for example:—

(a) Afforestation.
(b) Road-making.
(c) The preparation of sites for housing schemes.
(d) Demolition of unsanitary or condemned areas in preparation for improvements."

The Foster Report is of course only in the discussion stage; it is, however, of great interest as the most elaborate plan for joint action against unemployment being seriously debated by employers and employed. In the field of already accomplished fact, the instances of any degree of workers' control over unemployment problems are of two sorts. There are first the numerous rules by which the trade unions exert pressure upon employers to distribute work equally and to plan against unemployment. Of these the principle of *guaranteed time* is the furthest development. In the second place there have been the exercise by trade unions of administrative functions in connection with jointly controlled attempts to meet the problem of unemployment. Of these the Cotton Control Board and the Dock Clearing House schemes are the only important examples.

V

" THE RIGHT TO A TRADE "

THE trade union control studied in the preceding sections dealt almost entirely with th. quantitative regulation of employment or with the condition of union membership. There still remain the qualitative restrictions on employment—the attempts of the unions to say what class of workman shall be set to do a particular sort of job.

Apprenticeship—the limiting of work in a particular trade or on a particular process to men who have served a specified term of years as learners of the trade—is the most talked-of restriction of this nature. But perhaps the most important thing to say about it is how little of it there really is. Even in 1897, the Webbs emphasized this by the following table (*Industrial Democracy,* p. 473, footnote) :—

(1) Membership of Trade Unions actually enforcing apprenticeship regulations.... 90,000
(2) Membership of Trade Unions nominally retaining apprenticeship regulations, but effectively open 500,000

(3) Membership of Trade Unions having no
   apprenticeship regulations:—
   a. Transport workers and
      laborers 250,000
   b. Textile, mining, and
      other occupations ... 650,000   900,000
                                     ——————
                                     1,490,000

A few moments' figuring will show that their
argument now holds *a fortiori;* that the proportion
of the trade union movement in class (3) is at the
present time much greater than when the Webbs
wrote. Class (3) (a) in 1915 would have included
under transport workers (738,000) and common
labor (including builders' laborers—789,000) more
than a million and a quarter workers. Adding to
this the 857,000 engaged in mining, the 258,000
shop assistants, clerks, and employees of public
authorities and the 500,000 in the textile industry
(from which, however, a few minor sections should
be subtracted) the figures come to 2,850,000 without any attempt to study the smaller trades; and
a detailed investigation would surely show that
many more than three million out of the 4,126,793
members reported in 1915 were in unions not even
claiming apprenticeship regulations. Even this
fails to weight the figure sufficiently, since it is
precisely in general labor and women's labor that
trade unionism has grown most rapidly since 1915.

Fully as striking for the purpose is the break-down of what was left of apprenticeship in the trades classified by the Webbs under (2). The numbers of trade unionists in these trades is now greater, but the importance of apprenticeship in them has greatly dwindled. The Webbs spoke then of the " complete collapse" of apprentice-ship regulations in engineering—a phrase which unfortunately leaves little room for describing the changes both before and during the war by which the industry was invaded by dilutees who were taught one process alone and were used on repeti-tion work.

Apprenticeship, then, is no longer of first-class importance in the greater industries; [1] but it is still worth while to notice what degree of control it involves. This is of two sorts—the limitation of numbers and a certain command over technique and training in technique. The first is no doubt the more important object of the regulations; limitation of entry means monopoly and there-fore high wages and some security of employment, and a much more considerable basis for control than even the compulsory trade unionism referred to in the third section. The power of the Stuff Pressers rests largely on the regulation which

---

[1] An incidental indication of this is the fact that the word "apprenticeship" does not appear in the index of G. D. H. Cole's *Introduction to Trade Unionism*.

limits apprentices to a proportion of one to ten journeymen, though even in this extreme case the union finds it sometimes necessary to admit men who have not served their time. This is of interest for this inquiry merely in so far as it becomes a means for securing further control—for our purpose it is more interesting to study the few instances in which apprenticeship means some control by the union over the education of the worker in his trade.

Probably every trade that retains apprenticeship retains some degree of control over the training of apprentices, if only, as with the Glasgow Bakers, to the extent "that the Operatives' Committee have power to make inquiry so as to ascertain that the apprentice is not an underpaid journeyman." Often, however, this means a certain control over the actual training the apprentice receives—if not positive control in the sense of directing the training, at least negative control in the sense of effective complaint when the employer fails too signally to give the apprentices a full chance to learn the trade. The Power Loom Overlookers○(wool), for example, will fight the issue of the proper training of an apprentice. The monthly form which the "father of the chapel" (the printers' shop steward) fills out for his union contains a space for reporting a failure to give apprentices a fair chance to learn the trade. In

one old-fashioned monopoly craft, in which the
employing side admits that "the unions have
earned supremacy over the question," the union
exhorts its members to "intelligently study the
handicraft" and claims in dignified language the
right to protest against the choice of unfit apprentices, which in practice means a veto power on
their selection. The handful of "potters' painters," the most skilled workers in the potting industry, claimed and won the right to fill the latest
vacancy in their craft. Much more striking is the
rule of the Britannia Metal Smiths, one of the tiny
archaic unions of the Sheffield light trades, which
requires:—

"That every boy on completing his apprenticeship
shall be reported upon by the men working at the firm
as to his abilities, before he is accepted by the Trade.
If it be found that the said boy is incompetent as a workman, the Committee shall institute an enquiry and, if
possible ascertain the cause, and take the necessary steps
to prevent a similar misfortune."

There are several instances of joint control
over apprenticeship. An extract from an arbitrator's award, dated 1909, shows the situation
among the Bookbinders:—

"It being further agreed by the employers . . . that
the apprentices be trained not merely in a sub-section

but in a branch. Evidence was given me as to the
technical training of apprentices at technical classes and
as to the desire of the employers to co-operate with the
societies in encouraging and improving the apprentices'
training."

The 1916. report of the London Society of Compositors welcomes the adoption of a joint scheme
"for the better education of the printer's apprentice" with the following remarks:—

"The training of apprentices has long been regarded
as a matter of supreme importance both to the Society
and to the trade at large . . . The apprentice is not
only the journeyman of the future; he is the trade
unionist of the future. Our effort, then, should be to
make him a better printer and a better man, and therefore a better member."

Since the Joint Industrial Council of the building
industry announced that one of its objects was
"to arrange for adequate technical training for
the members of the industry," there has been some
activity in planning toward that end. One scheme,
originated by Mr. Frank Woods, a Bolton builder,
and already approved by the Joint Council for the
North Western Area, provides an elaborate plan
of training under supervision of a committee representing (1) the employers' association, (2) the
unions, (3) the Education Authority, and (4) the
Juvenile Employment Committee of the Ministry
of Labor, which shall deal both with the selection

of apprentices and with complaints either as to
their misconduct or as to the employer's failure
to teach the trade. "Those employers who shirk
their duties and do not train apprentices will have
to be dealt with," the argument runs; but "I am
strongly against State interference. I would
rather trust to joint control and joint action to
remedy this defect."

The claim of a craft union to some control over
training in the technique of the craft is only one
manifestation of its feeling that, as a body of men
possessing a special skill, it possesses a certain
"right to a trade" comparable, and in fact com-
pared in the constitution of the Amalgamated
Society of Engineers,[2] to the right belonging to the
holder of a doctor's diploma. This "right" involves two principles (1) that the tradesman shall
be asked to do only his own sort of work and (2)
that no other workman shall do the tradesman's
sort of work. The first principle has been somewhat obscured by the sharp conflict over apprenticeship, demarcation, and dilution, which involve
the second issue; but it is worth noticing as indicating the background of the second claim. Even
in as loosely-organized an industry as pottery, the
union will usually back a man who refuses to do
work other than that for which he was hired.

[2] Which corresponds roughly to the International Association
of Machinists.

The *demarcation*[3] issue, both because of its
practical importance to the organization of the
trade union world and because the principle of the
right to a trade is most plainly seen when two
rights to a trade meet head on, is usually taken as
the illustration of this right. Two trades claim a
monopoly of a particular job—*e.g.* "the whole of
the fitting up and repairing of the Downton
pumps"—based on what is for all intents and purposes a property right to their "means of living."
The fierceness with which these disputes are
fought cannot entirely be explained on the basis
of wages, though there is always the fear that the
job will go to the union with the lower rate. "The
whole question from our point of view is one of
wages," said Mr. George Barnes, then Secretary
of the Engineers, in 1897; but the apparently
reasonable suggestion that the issue be solved by
setting a rate for the disputed job and letting the
employer choose a man from either or any union
does not seem to solve the difficulty. It leaves untouched the fear of unemployment, which "gives
most of the bitterness to the troublesome demarcation disputes among the different crafts,"[4] and
also whatever may be left of the old feeling of
craft-right and the craftsman's distaste for seeing

[3] The familiar American term is "jurisdictional dispute."
[4] Sidney Webb, *The Restoration of Trade Union Conditions*,
p. 69.

somebody else do what he is trained to do. The issue is by no means a settled one—one former trade union official even said that "the trade union movement spends a third of its energy on demarcation"—but it may be left at one side in this discussion. Disputes over demarcation are not an extension of workers' control but a division of it, and they are to the point merely as making explicit the feeling of a craft's prescriptive "right to earn its bread without the interference of outsiders," which is at the base of many of the regulations of the more exclusive trades.

Dilution—or the replacing of skilled men by less skilled men or women—is at the moment an even more serious problem. It will be considered again in the sections on "Technique," but the objection to dilution is worth mentioning here as exhibiting again the feeling of the right to the trade. This is a case not of craft against craft but of craft against unskilled and woman labor, and the same fear of an inrush of numbers into the trade and the consequent danger of unemployment is even more strongly marked. "Do I feel that the man on the next machine is competing for my job!" writes Mr. J. T. Murphy.[5] " Do I feel that the vast army who have entered into industry will soon be scrambling with me at the works gates for a job in order to obtain the means of a livelihood?

[5] *The Workers' Committee*, p. 1.

My attitude towards the dilution of labor will obviously be different to the man who is not likely to be subject to such an experience." Limitation of entry is in part, as was suggested in the last section, an attempt to bulwark the workers already in the trade against unemployment. It is in those terms that Mr. Bradshaw, the secretary of the National Federation of Building Trades Operatives, argues [6] against an indiscriminate expansion of the supply of building labor:

"Some of us know what it is to walk about the streets with nothing to do. What will happen when the boom in building comes to an end? We shall be willing to let people come into our trade if we have proper safeguards; if, in other words, the Government will guarantee them and us continued employment, or alternatively adequate maintenance. If the dread of future unemployment were removed, it would go a long way to remove objections to 'expansion.' We have the opportunity now to make ourselves reasonably safe, and it is only natural that we should take advantage of it. . . . In the past we have worked on a building knowing that as soon as it was finished we should be out of work. . . . Guarantee our employment, and there will be no trouble in getting the houses."

The fear of unemployment is common to these regulations. But in the case of dilution the wage

[6] Interview quoted in the *London Times*, July 4, 1919.

element is even more important than in the case of demarcation. The fear is not only that skilled jobs may become harder to get, the great fear is that all skill will lose its market value. The interest in the dilution problem is not the interest in a new form of control. Dilution is interesting as a symptom of the end of an old form of control. It calls attention to the fact that the current movements in industrial technology are running directly counter to the type of control studied in this section. Apprenticeship and similar regulations are in the main survivals from the handicraft technique or at least from an earlier form of the machine technique. They are not only confined to a small fraction of industry; even there they are giving ground before the standardization of the most typical modern machine production. "Every simplification in the methods of production," says Mr. Murphy in the pamphlet quoted, "every improvement in automatic machine production, every application of machinery in place of hand production means that the way becomes easier for others to enter the trades."

The issues of dilution and particularly the introduction of women labor raise highly interesting problems, but it is unnecessary to consider them further in a study of this kind. That sort of control which merely means keeping other people out of a job may be of high importance as a basis for further extensions of control; in itself it involves little or no direction of industry. It is moreover just this sort of control which is becoming less and less possible with the modernization of industry.

VI

"THE RIGHT TO SACK"

"The control I want is over the employer's right to sack a man."

That remark of a Sheffield shop steward, a remark the more pointed because many of his fellow shop stewards were at the time walking the streets in search of work, expresses a demand for security of tenure, not only against dismissals due to bad trade, but also against disciplinary dismissals and particularly against dismissals for the punishment of men exceptionally active as labor leaders.[1] That is, it is a demand for protection against what the British workers call "victimization"—of defence for the man, "who by reason of continuous activity in forwarding the cause of the Union is dismissed" (rules of Boot and Shoe Operatives), or "who has been victimized, on account of being ever ready to fight for the interests of himself and his fellow members" (rules of Steel Smelters). Victimization, or at least the suspicion of it, is very widespread. "The workmen are ever

[1] In practice, the distinction between dismissals due to bad trade and dismissals for union activity is not a clear one. A time of depression may be made the occasion for a general clearing-out of "agitators."

conscious of the power of the employers to sack them." [2] Even among the miners, for all their industrial power and for all their willingness to use it on a personal issue, there are continual complaints of victimization. A working collier in the Midlands writes of "the invisible insecurity of work," "a kind of victimization which you cannot prove"—"where men stood by their comrades they were soon out of work, not knowing what for."

For our purpose, the interesting thing is not that victimization is practised,[3] or the highly controversial point as to just how much of it there is, but rather the efforts made by the trade unions to prevent it—efforts which have in fact though not in form amounted to a considerable control over the power of dismissal.

The importance of the issue, as felt by the labor extremists, is indicated by a quotation from the *Miners' Next Step:* [4]—

"Grievances are not questions, with us, so much of *numbers* as of *principles*. It might, and probably would be, deemed advisable to have a strike of the whole organization to defend one man from victimization."

The importance of the issue, as expressed in trade union action, is indicated by the number of

[2] J. T. Murphy, *The Workers' Committee,* p. 5.
[3] The American Association of University Professors would testify that it is not unknown in colleges.
[4] See Note on Sources.

strikes called to secure the *reinstatement* of discharged workpeople. In 1913 there were 117 strikes on this issue, directly involving 25,000 workpeople; in 1911 and 1912 approximately 16,000 were involved each year.[5] In the summer of 1918, 20,000 workers took part in a single strike at a London aircraft factory as a protest against the discharge of a woman shop steward and the chairman of shop stewards.[6] An amusing recent instance is the strike of Black Country colliery enginemen that was settled in June, 1919, on the single condition "that the dismissed engineman be reinstated for an hour." An indication of the extent of control over dismissals exercised by the trade unions in this manner, without any sort of agreement, is given in the evidence before the Coal Commission of Mr. Hugh Bramwell, representing the South Wales coal-owners:—

"Minor strikes of workmen on this question are not uncommon. A manager knows he cannot be unjust without risking the stoppage of the mine—consequently when he does act, he does so under a sense of responsibility."[7]

[5] The Government *Report on Strikes and Lockouts* does not give separate figures for reinstatement cases for those years, but estimates that they were "nearly one-half" of the cases under the heading of "Employment of particular classes or persons":—1911, 170 disputes, 32,639 people; 1912, 179 disputes, 34,985 people. See Note on Sources.
[6] Furnishing Trades Association Monthly Report, August, 1918.
[7] *Cd.* 360, p. 874.

There have been a few attempts either to express in written agreement this trade union check over the right of dismissal or to set up some joint body for settling disputed cases. The rules of the conciliation board of the Leicester dyeing trade contain under the head of "Freedom of Workpeople" what is at least a pious expression of opinion against victimization:—

"That all workmen delegates shall be as free as employers to express their opinion without fear or favor; and no workman shall be dismissed from his employment for any action he may take on the Board."

A dispute over the discharge of a shop steward at one of the Vickers munition works was settled through the Ministry of Munitions, on the following terms:—

"(1) The steward to be reinstated and full inquiry into procedure afterwards.

"(2) That in future cases of proposed dismissal of stewards or local trade union officials, notice of appeal shall be given to the management within 48 hours. The management to hear the case within a further 48 hours; failing agreement the question to be dealt with by the trade union officials and the Employers' Association within 7 days if possible."

The Government's Commission on Industrial Unrest (1917) in its report on South Wales recommended:—

"That every employee should be guaranteed what we may call 'security of tenure'—that is, that no workman should be liable to be dismissed except with the consent of his fellow workmen as well as his employer."

The report on *Works Committees* issued by the Ministry of Labor gives several instances in which "alleged unjust dismissals" are discussed by joint committees, although at least two employers who experimented in this direction found that their shop stewards' committees preferred not to discuss beforehand disciplinary discharges, in order that they might avoid responsibility. Messrs. Reuben Gaunt & Sons, Ltd., a firm of Yorkshire worsted spinners, have recently gone beyond the stage of joint discussion to that of actual joint decision on disciplinary dismissals. Any employee has the right of appeal from discharge or punishment to a body composed of equal numbers chosen by the firm and the workers—in a recent case before this tribunal the defendant was a foreman charged with bullying a woman worker.

It will be noticed that the last few instances, and the suggestion of the Commission on Industrial Unrest, run beyond victimization proper— *i.e.* persecution for union activity—to a reference to all cases of disciplinary dismissal. The same is true of the reinstatement strikes. Victimization is only a special case under the issues of supposed personal injustice which the Unions contest.

"Redress for all . . . unjust or captious and un-
lawful dismissals," is given as one of the objects
in the constitution of the British Steel Smelters.
It is in practice fought for by many other unions.
One important dispute, for example, was occa-
sioned by the discharge of a railway guard,
Richardson, for refusing to obey an order that
conflicted with the Company's printed rules—that
is, for refusing to take out a train loaded beyond
the specified capacity; his reinstatement was secured by trade union pressure.[8] A strike of pottery workers secured the reinstatement of a manager who, the men said, had been discharged for
refusing to bully his workmen.

The same principle is naturally extended to reductions in rank as well as outright dismissals.
One of the most famous of all reinstatement cases
was the "Knox Strike" of 1911 when six thousand
men on the North Eastern Railway came out, in
the words of the Government report, "for reinstatement of an engine-driver who had been reduced in rank owing to alleged drunkenness off
duty for which he had been fined in the Police
Court." The papers featured the affair as a strike
for the "right to get drunk." Finally Driver
Knox was "reinstated as a result of Home Office
Enquiry into the case." For our purpose it does

---

[8] G. D. H. Cole and R. Page Arnot, *Trade Unionism on the
Railways*, p. 33.

not matter much whether the Police Court or the Home Office was the better judge of drunkenness. The point is that the men were quick to contest a case of what they considered an unjust punishment.[9]

Trade union control over disciplinary dismissals and reductions in grade—whether for "agitation" or other causes—is, judged by formal agreement, very slight. By the more important test of the effect of the readiness to strike on the issue, the control is much more considerable. The "employer's right to sack a man" is at least exercised with a degree of deference to public opinion in the workshop and to the danger of the "one-man strike."

[9] Mr. Cole and others point to this strike as the first of many recent disputes over "discipline."

VII

PROMOTION

THE trade unions have, as we have seen, taken a share in determining the conditions under which workers are taken on. And in defending their members against injustice, they have taken at least a negative share in determining the conditions under which they are dismissed, disciplined or demoted. Have they exercised any similar control over the conditions under which workers are promoted from one grade to another?

In most cases promotion falls outside the union's business. Trade unionism is first of all concerned with the general standard of the entire group; promotion is the luck of the exceptional individual. But the answer to the question is not an unqualified *"no."*

There are certain industries in which there is what the Webbs call "regulated progression within the trade"—that is, a system under which vacancies within a grade are filled, if there are no men of that grade available, by men from the grade just below. The best example is that of the Boiler-makers in which the holders-up may become platers and rivetters only when no properly-apprenticed

111

members of those branches of the trade are out of work. A similar progression is enforced by the Steel Smelters. The Webbs made the point that, beyond this modified seniority, in which, while the man chosen must be from a certain group, the choice of the most promising individual from that group is left to the employer, the principle of seniority does not enter into trade union policy. "No such idea of seniority [as in the Civil Service] is to be found in the trade union regulations." This is now not strictly true. In the cotton industry there are occasional strikes "against the alleged promotion of a piecer out of his turn." The Railwaymen in 1911 demanded that length of service should "have primary consideration in all cases of promotion." It is quite in line with the Webb statement, however, that it has been a civil service union, that of the Postal and Telegraph Clerks (now a part of the amalgamated Union of Post Office Workers), that has been most insistent in urging the establishment of the seniority rule. Their leaders defend the principle (which they would admit to be "finally indefensible" if they were really controlling the service) on the ground that "you don't need a Napoleon" for each little job.

There have been other demands, not for the establishment of a rigid principle of seniority, but for some sort of joint control. *The Railway Re-*

view, the official organ of the National Union of Railwaymen, argues for joint control by the creation of "staff committees by whom all appointments and promotions should be made." The Postal and Telegraph Clerks had been fighting for the inclusion of promotion among the subjects over which the Postal Joint Industrial Council is to have jurisdiction. In 1917, a resolution was carried at their convention that, "the Association shall have free access to the official records of its members," in order that cases of injustice might be contested; and, in the course of discussion, a member remarked that he "imagined that even now the Executive got in cases of promotion occasionally." Their claim is partly, though very guardedly, met by the Provisional Joint Committee on the Application of the Whitley Report to the Administrative Departments of the Civil Service, which recommended in its report of May 28, 1919, that the question of promotion should be provided for as follows in the constitution of the Joint Industrial Council:—

(1) The National Council should determine the general principles governing promotion, but should not consider individual cases.

(2) The Departmental Councils should be allowed to "discuss any promotion in regard to which it is represented by the staff side that the principles of promotion accepted by or with the sanction of the National Council

have been violated. To ensure satisfactory working or this arrangement steps will have to be taken to acquaint the staff with the nature of the accepted principles of promotion."

(3) The District and Office (or Works) Committee are not to discuss promotion.

The rules of the Federation of Weavers' and Overlookers' Amalgamations (cotton)ᵒattempt to limit promotion to union members by providing, "that no encouragement or permission shall be given to any weaver to learn over-looking who does not belong to his trade union." There are occasional disputes in various industries over the bringing in of "outsiders" to supervisory positions instead of promoting men from the particular shop. Much more interesting is a strike of the Glass Bottle Makers "against appointment of a manager who had not served at the trade" which was settled by allowing the appointment to stand but establishing the principle—"no other non-bottle hand to be employed as manager." A strike of Oldham Tramwaymen in 1911 "against the employment of certain officials," etc. was settled as follows:—

"Officials not to be dismissed, but further vacancies to be open to the men."

A similar feeling in a more important industry is the resentment of "practical" railwaymen against the supervision of men who have not come up through the ranks but have come in from outside with some technical training and are taught practical railwaying by the men over whom they are shortly to be put in authority. I have heard this bitterness come out in a speech by a Railwaymen's official; it may be illustrated by these extracts from the *Railway Review*:— [1]

"The key to advancement in the railway industry service beyond a strictly limited point is not that of knowledge, or ability, or diligence, or a combination of these attributes. It is rather that of relationship to persons in high places; the public school accent; the toney manner; a mental vision frankly and avowedly anti-working class. . . . And since the gentry in the top stories of the building make all the laws for those in the basement and yet have had little or no experience of basement life and conditions, there must necessarily be trouble and unrest." [2]

These examples show a fairly widespread feeling that promotion is, to some extent, the workers'

[1] In quoting these I am concerned, not with the truth of the charges made, but only with the making of the charges, as an indication that the union considers the regulation of promotion as within its field of action.

[2] It is interesting to place alongside this strenuous demand of the railwaymen, " To abolish for ever the inhibition against promotion of wages men to salaried positions," the suggestion, made by an electrical engineer, that this same " principle of upward mobility " of labor would be a shrewd way to " diminish the demand for democratic control." It might easily be argued that the greater upward mobility of labor in the United States, or more accurately the tradition of past mobility and the " log cabin to White House " careers, accounts, in part, for the slower development of control demands on the part of American Labor.

business, but very little in the way of control, except a few negative safeguards against merely arbitrary promotions. The subject is not, however, complete without turning in the next section, to the few but highly interesting cases in which the workers take a positive part in regulating the most significant form of promotion—the choice of foremen.

VIII

THE CHOICE OF FOREMEN

THE general question of promotion counts for little either in present trade union policy or in a study of control; promotion to the position of foreman or to other grades whose duties involve direct supervision is very close to the center of the problem. The immediate issues of control arise in contact with the foreman's authority; the method of his selection is a pivotal issue. The common belief that no employer ever yields or divides authority on this point is not true; it is nearly enough true, especially in large-scale industry, to indicate that this is a question where the control issue might be consciously and keenly fought.

Of the few instances in which the workers play a decisive part in the choice of foreman, the little Stuff Pressers' Society again furnishes the best example, though it is apparently losing its full right of election. "The foreman," says the account already quoted, "is selected by the Society in conjunction with the employers and men. Formerly the men made the selection, this being endorsed by the Society, which then recommended the choice to the firm; but in recent years this method of procedure is to some extent falling into abeyance, due largely to the growth in power of the Bradford Dyers' Association. . . . The relation of the foreman to the firm is mainly to act as contractor in behalf of the men . . . Inside the shop the foreman works at his table like the rest of the men whenever his duties as supervisor allow, his wages being determined on identical grounds to that of the men except that a supplementary income of 5% is paid to him by the men for his services as supervisor. . . . This fusion of the labor forces allows no opportunity for the antagonism so discernible in most industries, where the foreman acts largely as the 'watchdog' of the firm . . . The salient features of the organization are, then, first a democratically controlled workshop, against which principle as I have indicated above, the Trust is threatening attack. It has already introduced a payment to foremen.''

Another small union, that of the Spindle and Flyer Makers, has the privilege of ''nomination'' of foremen which is said really to amount to election; and there are one or two other small monopolistic crafts in which the men have practically their own way in the matter. The Compositors do not choose their own foremen; but the ''father of the chapel,'' their shop steward, performs enough supervisory functions for the firm so that he is in effect an elected sub-foreman; and the "clicker" chosen by a "companionship" or team of compositors to do their bargaining with the firm and to allot piece work might also be thought of as an elected supervisor—in very much the same sense as the stuff pressers' foreman. But these are in reality not more than quite natural extensions of the control easily exercised by skilled gangs engaged in collective work. "When the work is carried on, not by individual craftsmen but by associated groups of highly skilled wage-earners, it is practically within the power of these groups" (to extend a remark of the Webbs) to control the immediate workshop arrangements. This again is not very far from the practice of "co-operative work" which D. F. Schloss defined in 1891 [1] as involving three principles, of which the second is of interest here:—

(1) Workers associated by free choice.

(2) *Workers under a leader elected and removable by themselves.*

(3) Pay divided among members of group on principles recognized by themselves as equitable.

He gave interesting examples of this practice, but they were for the most part only on the very fringes of "the great industry," in such indus-

[1] *Methods of Industrial Remuneration.*

trial pockets as the Cornish tin mines, and the practice has since his time fallen still further into disuse. Both these examples of co-operative work and the examples of election of foremen referred to here are taken from a sort of industry in which it is possible for the foreman to be a fellow-worker with his men and to represent them in bargaining as well as to supervise their work. They amount in effect to a democratic form of subcontract, and together with other forms of subcontract they seem to be giving away before the standardizing process of large-scale modern industry.

There is, then, some body of experience of trade union control over the choice of foremen in a number of the older crafts. Is there any trade union control over the choice of foremen in "the great industry" itself, in the modern large-scale, carefully-regimented industries where the strain of superintendence is the greatest? The answer can be almost a direct "no." I have been able to find no instance in which the workers in modernized industry have either the recognized right of election of foremen or the formal right of vetoing an unpopular selection. Instances even of consultation over the choice are extremely rare, even in cases where the works committees discuss a fairly wide range of subjects. Messrs. Hans Renold, Ltd., chain manufacturers with a large factory just outside Manchester, make a practice of announcing the choice of a foreman to the shop stewards' committee and explaining their reasons for it before publication of the announcement. Messrs. Rowntree & Sons, Ltd., at their cocoa works at York, allow this discussion to take place before the decision is actually reached and (presumably) allow it to influence the decision. Their precise rule on this point, which was adopted by their Works Council in the spring of 1919 after the workers' side had brought in a proposal which came much nearer direct election, is as follows:—

"That before any person is appointed as an overlooker, the name of such person shall be submitted to a Committee of the workers on the Department Council, but the final decision regarding the appointment will continue to rest with the Director of the Department."

These very minor exceptions are perhaps chiefly of importance as showing how definite a principle it is in the constitutional theory of modern industry—if there is any such thing—that the workers are excluded from any control over the choice of their supervisors.

It is impossible, however, to break off the discussion at this point for two reasons:—First, there is already an organized opposition to this theory—the desire for a say in the choice of foremen is a serious factor in the demands of labor.

Second, the theory, like other constitutional theories, in practice does not at all work out to the letter—the workers have now more say in the choice of foremen than any formal agreement suggests. The best evidence on the first point—that the choice of foremen has already become to some extent an open question—is the discussion in the *Works Committees* report of the Ministry of Labor:—

"The appointment of foremen is a question on which there may be said to be three groups of opinions. Many employers hold that it is purely a management question. The opposite extreme to this is the claim made by a considerable section of Trade Unionists that the workmen should choose their own foremen. A position intermediate to these two extremes is taken up by a certain number of employers and by a section of workpeople; the appointment (they feel) should be made by the management, but it should be submitted to the Works Council before it becomes effective. Even this intermediate position, however, is not really a common position; there are differences of opinion as to the conditions under which the appointment should come before the Works Committee—that is to say, whether or not the Works Committee should have power to veto the appointment." (pp. 33-34)

Mr. Cole and other Guild Socialists speak of the election of foremen as "one of the next steps." The principle—or a step towards it—has been embodied in several schemes suggested by groups of workers. One suggestion now being elaborated is that of a panel system—under which the workers' committee should nominate a list of candidates for a vacancy from which the employer should choose one. Messrs. Gallacher & Paton of the Clyde engineering shop stewards, have suggested [2] a system of "collective contracts" under which "the Convenors of the Works Committee and the Departmental Committee would gradually but surely drive out and supplant the Works Manager and Departmental Foreman." Many such proposals make a distinction between officials who are primarily "man-managers," whose chief duty is the supervision of workers, and those who are primarily technicians; and it is with the choice of the former that the schemes are concerned. On the other hand, a detailed set of proposals for the future control of the mines, put forward by the same group of extremists who wrote the *Miners' Next Step*, insists that even the definitely technical officials should be directly elected, with the proviso that candidates must possess the technical certificates of qualification now necessary. "The one essential condition of our plan is the democratic election of all officials." It is not worth while to set out these schemes in detail at this point; they are referred to as an evidence of an articulate

[2] See below, p. 173, and Note on Sources.

opposition to the exclusion of workers from a say in the choice of their supervisors.

It is more important to point out that the workers do often actually exercise more power over the choice of foremen than any agreement suggests. At one Manchester motor works a particularly active shop stewards' committee had been making trouble for a succession of foremen; finally the firm in despair said, "Choose your own foreman, then," and they did. This is only an extreme instance of a sort of control which is not uncommon. At the height of their power during the war, the Clyde shop stewards, while they claimed no right to choose foremen, could "make it impossible" for an unpopular foreman. The extent to which the workers make it impossible for foremen to whom they object—and therefore exercise a clumsy and delayed but real and very important veto over the choice of foremen—will be considered in Section X. It was of veto in their sense rather than of veto by formal right that Mr. Cole spoke in his testimony before the Coal Commission:—

"The extent to which trade unions exercise an amount of control over the selection of foremen negatively by veto is increasing very fast." (Question 13169)

And it is this sort of veto that makes the most important limit to the power of the employer to select supervisors at will.

"Control over employers, foremen, etc. . . . is," said D. F. Schloss, "aimed at by the essential principles of Trade Unionism." Yet workers' control over foremen by direct election is practically non-existent in the great industry. This, however, by no means exhausts all possible forms of control in the field. There are at least two further methods by which the workers exert control over their supervisors,—first, by pressure through the trade union if the supervisor belongs to the same or to a friendly union; and second, by the refusal to work under intolerable supervision or objectionable supervisors. These methods of control will be the subjects of the next two sections.

IX

THE ORGANIZATION OF FOREMEN

THE organization of foremen, like all questions of trade union structure, is of interest for this inquiry only as it affects trade union function in the direction of control. But it is evident that the extent of control by workers over their immediate supervisors depends in part on the answers to the questions:—Are these supervisors organized at all? Are they organized in the same unions as the workers under them? Are they organized in separate unions? And are these last friendly or hostile to the other unions?

Trade union practice in regard to the inclusion of foremen within the same unions as the workers under them is varied and is complicated by a number of motives. The "friendly benefit" side of trade unionism tends to hold a man in his union after he has been promoted to the foreman's job. Conscious trade union policy on the question has been affected by two contradictory principles:—

Don't trust them: Capture them.

The idea behind the former is that the workman by accepting promotion has stepped across a defi-

126

nite line and has become the employer's man.
From that time on he is bargaining for the employer and against the worker; therefore he must
not be trusted with any news of the workers'
plans. He is the "guv'nor's man" and therefore
no longer "safe." The natural outcome of this
feeling is to exclude foremen from the union, or at
least to let them remain only as honorary members or for purposes of friendly benefit, as the
Glass Bottle Workers do by their rule that "a
walking manager may remain a member of the
society, but shall not be allowed to attend any
meetings without being specially summoned."
This attitude has been the general one in the past.
"Foremen, deputies, superintendents, and the
like," writes Mr. Cole,[1] "are naturally for the
most part promoted from the ranks of the Trade
Union Movement. . . It is true that throughout
the history of Trade Unionism a certain number
of such promoted workmen have retained their
connection with their Trade Unions in a more or
less private manner, by being attached to Central Office Branches, and by other similar devices; but even where this has been the case they
have usually lost all share in the government of
their Societies."

The opposing idea is that having your foreman
in your own union is a good way of making sure

[1] G. D. H. Cole, *An Introduction to Trade Unionism*, p. 72.

that he won't treat you unjustly. The public opinion of the union is counted on to enforce upon its supervising numbers a standard of decency in the treatment of subordinates. D. F. Schloss gave the example of the London Stevedores○ where—"If a foreman does not give all the men a fairly equal chance of employment, the trade union committee may punish him by suspension." The Brass Workers have a definite rule for controlling their foreman members:—

"A member who is a journeyman, foreman, charge-hand or piece worker [*i.e.* subcontractor] shall not have under his control or supervision or employ any person above the age of 18 who is not a member of the society, and to whom he does not pay the minimum rate of the district."

A thousand Glasgow Dockers struck in 1911 on the demand that a foreman should join the union, and carried their point. Sub-foremen are included in the compulsory unionism agreements of the Dyers, and, in a number of unions—notably the Dyers and Miners—it is not uncommon for foremen and even a few managers to belong to the men's union.

In this case the object—where there has been a conscious object—has been to "capture" the foremen for quite immediate purposes. Those who are propagandists for extensions of workers' control are much more strongly in favor of the inclusion of foremen within the unions as a step towards full trade union management of industry. A correspondent writing to the *Amalgamated Society of Engineers Journal* puts their argument vigorously:—

"On this point [amalgamation with the other engineering unions and the control of the industry] we are all so cordially unanimous that there seems nothing left to do in the matter except amalgamate and take control. May I suggest that we have a long row to hoe yet, and that we members of the A.S.E. have not yet done all we might to strengthen our own organization. . . . Any member of our society who, because of his ability, is entrusted with a position of responsibility, is no longer to be helped by the A.S.E. . . . The foremen are being induced by employers to join subsidized mutual organizations of one kind or another in order to set them as a class apart from the ordinary working trade unionist. Some of them still realize that they are workers in the best sense of the word and have interests in common with other producers. . . . I would suggest, Sir, that it is of the utmost importance that we should in any measure of control of industry, have the active support of foremen and staff men generally."

The various lines of policy taken by employers on this question have also some bearing on the question of control. An early policy was simply that of forbidding membership in trade unions. This was the attitude of the railway companies in 1907, before the great increase in railway unionism. It is clearly expressed in the memorandum from one of the companies to ·a certain Inspector Rawlinson, transferring him to another position without loss of pay:—

"As a member of the Amalgamated Society of Railway Servants, you cease to be a free agent, and you cannot be permitted to have the control and supervision of men who are not members of the society or members of some other society. You cannot serve two masters. There is no desire to punish you, but the Company's staff and the Company's business must be protected."

Even in 1911, a high official of one of the roads, testifying before a government commission, threatened that "non-unionists would have to be chosen" for the work of some of the supervisory clerks which was "more or less of a confidential nature." Less drastic expressions of this feeling are the agreements secured by the employers to the effect that, "The National Association of Operative Plasterers will not take any steps to compel men regularly employed as foremen or superintendents to become members of the N. A. O. P.;" and, in bookbinding, that the Society will not call out on strike a foreman who has held his position for twelve months.

Another policy of certain employers has been to encourage separate unions for foremen and other supervisors by way of keeping them out of the more dangerous trade unions. This may mean, as it does in the engineering and heavy steel trades, a Foremen's Benefit Society, heavily subsidized by the employers, which the foremen are urged or compelled to join. One object of this is explained by the Vice-President of the Joint Institute of Engineers, Mr. Alex. Richardson, in *The Man-Power of the Nation* (p. 77):—

"So long as foremen continued trade unionists, they could not exhibit independence, and the employers therefore acted wisely in establishing foremen's societies, which conferred on members the superannuation and other benefits they had to forfeit upon severing their connection with the trade unions. That was a move in the direction of inculcating habits of thought different from those of the ordinary workmen."

The same attitude may mean less definite forms of encouragement to a separate union. The Pottery Officials' and Managers' Union came about in this way:—The operatives' society had organized a section of under-managers and foremen, had secured a war bonus for them, and had fought a reinstatement case for one of its manager-members. The employers then announced that they would be glad to recognize a separate officials' union, and the foremen—with the exception of those in the firm affected by the reinstatement strike—left the workers' society and joined the new union. The two unions are now friendly enough; but in the Joint Industrial Council the foremen's union has just been granted two seats, not on the workers' side, as has been suggested in certain other industries, not on an independent "cross bench," as they had asked, but on the employers' side.

The history of these two policies on the part of employers was condensed in the deliberations of the Provisional Joint Committee of the National Industrial Conference, which reported on April 4, 1919. The question of foremen came up as an obstacle to agreement on "full and frank" recognition of trade unions as the basis of negotiation. The first proposal of the employers was that workers "in positions of trust or confidentiality" should be definitely excluded in the recommendation for recognition of unions. Their second proposal was that separate unions of foremen, secretaries, etc. should be recognized but that the right of ordinary trade unions "to speak and act on behalf of" their foremen members should not be conceded. The Committee nearly failed to reach unanimity but finally agreed on the following formula:—

"The machinery [for settling disputes] should also contain provisions for the protection of the employers'

interests where members of trade unions of work people
are engaged in positions of trust or confidentiality, provided the right of such employers to join or remain members of any trade union is not thereby affected.''

It is, of course, by no means true that separate unions of supervisors are always or necessarily hostile to the other trade unions. The National Foremen's Society, recently formed in the
engineering and allied trades in opposition to the
Foremen's Benefit Society, claimed in July, 1919
a membership of 2,000.⁰ Its policy is definitely
trade union and includes the obligation not to
do ''blackleg'' work in case of strikes by the men
working under its members. The South Wales
Colliery Officials' Union is affiliated to the South
Wales Miners' Federation,[2] although in many
districts there has been considerable friction between the Miners' Federation and separate organizations of Under-managers, Deputies, or Master
Hauliers. The Federation of Weavers' and Overlookers'[3] Amalgamations in the cotton industry
has already been mentioned as a genuine labor
alliance. In this case there is an unusual form
of control over supervision; if a woman weaver
complains of a bullying overlooker, the matter is

[2] Coal Commission Evidence. Question 13192.
[3] The overlookers in the textile industries are not strictly comparable to foremen in other industries. They are primarily mechanics and only incidentally supervisors.

adjusted between the two unions concerned. The Power Loom Overlookers are represented on the workers' side of the Joint Industrial Council in the woolen trades, and a London Union of Clerical Workers and Builders' Foremen has applied for representation with the workers in the Building Trades Parliament. The largest of all unions of supervisors and clerical workers, the Railway Clerks' Association, which is rapidly extending its organization into the higher grades [4] works as an ally of the National Union of Railwaymen and has been conspicuous in demanding workers' control.

The organization of foremen, then, involves in some cases an indirect but genuine control by the workers over the conduct of their supervisors. Its extension is clearly in the policy of certain groups of workers who are consciously aiming at control. And certain employers have attempted either to prevent the process of organization or to divert it into separate and exclusive channels in the fear of just that sort of control.

[4] By a recent agreement between the R. C. A. and the Companies there are now only some two hundred of the higher railway officials in the country who are held to be ineligible to be members of and be represented by the railway unions.

X

THE STANDARD OF FOREMANSHIP

WORKERS' choice of foremen is rare; the effect of organization of foremen on workers' control is real but indirect. The most important means by which workers exercise control over their supervisors is simply that of the strike or threat of strike when supervision becomes unbearable. The effective power of this form of control is usually underestimated since it is difficult to detect and define and can hardly be embodied in a formal agreement. But in proportion to the strength of the trade union, it represents a real veto, if not actually over the choice, at least over the retention of foremen—and a real regulation of their actions.

Mr. R. H. Tawney sums up the situation as "autocracy checked by insurgence;" the present point is that there is a great deal of insurgence. Some sense of this may be gained by going through the official *Reports on Strikes and Lockouts*.[1] In 1912 there were thirty-two disputes reported as caused by objections to certain foremen; in 1913, 25 disputes involving 10,500 workers.

[1] See Note on Sources.

The reports of causes read like these:—"alleged harassing conduct of a foreman," "alleged tyrannical conduct of an under-forewoman," "alleged overbearing conduct of officials." The award in a recent arbitration case details the charges against an unpopular under-manager as "indifference to and want of consideration of suggestions made to him by workers in connection with their work and improvements; uncivil, inconsiderate, harsh and autocratic treatment, and neglect to properly consider their claims as regards both employment and remuneration; and the preference of friends and relatives." And among the results of the strikes, along with numerous dismissals and resignations of the officials in question, there are occasional agreements that, "the men must be treated with proper respect and threats and abusive language must not be used," or "tyrannical acts to cease."

The number and the frequent success of these strikes indicates, as was suggested in Section VIII, a considerable trade union veto over the choice of foremen. The "right of rejecting as fellow-workers" may often become the right of rejecting as foremen. This alone, however, does not sufficiently emphasize the amount of trade union pressure effective in setting a standard of decent foremanship. The rules of the British Steel Smelters provide that members leaving on account of "unjustifiable abuse or ill-treatment from employer or foreman" are entitled to dispute pay. The secretary of a union which had never succeeded in securing the dismissal of a bullying foreman was nevertheless sure that its protests were effective as warnings to foremen. And in some trades a definite standard is so much a matter of course that the issue rarely arises. The Compositors, for example, will not stand for what is known as "policing" by foremen and managers and any violation of the code is immediately reported to the union for action. A story was told me by a former miners' agent in Lanarkshire illustrating a similar standard on the part of the Scottish Miners. In a case arising under the Minimum Wage Act, the overman was called upon to testify whether or not a certain workman did his work properly. The examination was as follows (in free translation from the original Scotch):—

Overman: "I never saw him work."

Magistrate: "But isn't it your duty under the Mines Act to visit each working place twice a day?"

"Yes."

"Don't you do it?"

"Yes."

"Then why didn't you ever see him work?"

"They always stop work when they see an overman coming, and sit down and wait till he's gone—even take out their pipes if it's a mine free from gas. They won't let anybody watch them.''

An equally extreme standard was enforced for a part of the war period at a Clyde engineering works. The convenor (chairman) of shop stewards was told one morning that there was a grievance at the smithy. He found one of the blacksmiths in a rage because the managing director, in his ordinary morning's walk through the works, had stopped for five minutes or so and watched this man's fire. After a shop meeting the convenor took up a deputation to the director and secured the promise that it should not happen again. At the next works meeting the convenor reported the incident to the body of workers— with the result that a similar standard came into effect throughout the works, and the director hardly dared stop at all on his morning's walk.

Much of the feeling in struggles for the recognition of unions (long since secured in the better-organized trades and conceded in principle at least for all by the unanimous recommendations of the National Industrial Conference) was due to the workers' desire to have someone outside the control of the immediate employer to represent them on just these questions. This finds very definite expression in the dispute that occasionally arises over the trade union official's claim of the right to enter the works in order to investigate disputes. This has been paralleled during the war by the frequent claim of the shop steward or of the covenor (chairman) of shop stewards or of the chairman of the Works' Committee for freedom to go into any department of the works to investigate a grievance. An amusing story was told me of the way this right was won in one of the Clyde ship-building works:—The convenor had begun to exercise the right—and to go freely from shop to shop as disputes arose—without the permission of the management. The manager then ordered him to stop and to stay at his own machine. The convenor obeyed, but arranged for a grievance to occur the next morning in the shop farthest from his own. The steward from that shop came to him with word of the grievance. "I can't leave my work."— "But it's important."—"How many men involved?"—"200."—" I don't dare leave my machine. Tell them to come to me." And so the 200 men walked the length of the works, gathered round the convenor's machine while he kept on with his work, and discussed the dispute. The result—in the prevailing shortage of labor—was the concession of the privilege. But the fighting of the same issue in another works, with Mr. David Kirkwood as the shop steward in question, led to the deportation of the Clyde strike leaders in 1916.

The shop stewards' agreement of December, 1917, between the engineering employers and certain of the engineering unions provided that:—

"In connection with this agreement shop stewards shall be afforded facilities to deal with questions raised in the shop or portion of a shop in which they are employed. In course of dealing with these questions they may, with the previous consent of the management (such consent not to be unreasonably withheld), visit any other shop or portion of a shop in the establishment. In all other respects shop stewards shall conform to the same working conditions as their fellow-workmen."

The *Works Committees* report of the Ministry of Labor states that, "from the experience of several works . . . it would appear that this freedom of movement is found to be an essential condition of the success of a committee." The various elaborate methods of procedure for the presentation of grievances by trade union officials or shop stewards, whether embodied in long-standing collective agreements or in recent constitutions of works committees (as well as the various provisions for securing for the aggrieved individual the "principle of the open door" to the higher management) are beside the present point. The interesting thing for our purpose is that they involve a recognition that grievances of this sort are within the field of action of the workers' representatives. An editorial in *The Post* (the journal of the Postmen's Federation)○ of March 8, 1918, emphasized as one of the chief functions of the shop steward his duties in "a case of petty spite or constant bullying from an overseer or a foreman." "It would appear," says the *Works Committees report,* "that a Works Committee, if it is to be of any value in ventilating and removing grievances, must be in a position to ventilate grievances arising from the conduct of foremen and overlookers. Such grievances touch the worker most closely in his daily work." The case already referred to at Reuben Gaunt's, Ltd., in which a foreman charged with bullying was tried by a joint body representing the management and the workers, is a definite embodiment of this principle.

These are still only partial indications of the importance of grievances against foremen in trade union activity. The union may try to secure the discharge of an arbitrary foreman; the union may secure consideration of its grievances against him by peaceful means. But frequently the resentment merely smolders and breaks out on other issues. This feeling, whether or not it appears on the face of the workers' demands, is undoubtedly, as the secretary of an employers' association told me, "at the bottom of some of the bitterest strikes." A correspondent writing to the *Times* during the railway dispute of 1907 declared that:—

"The whole cause of these continued disturbances is due to the authority and petty tyranny exercised by the foremen, who are nothing less than despots and slave-drivers."

And the Commission on Industrial Unrest in 1917, in analyzing the unrest in South Wales, said:—

"We must also recognize the fact that the Welsh collier, even though possibly addicted to bluntness of speech in conversation with his fellow-workmen is quick to resent any ebullition of temper or violence of language towards himself on the part of those placed in authority over him. . . . Much avoidable friction is due to lack of self-control in language and temper and want of tact generally on the part of officials, though circumstances may often be such as to test them severely in this respect."

The control exercised by trade unions over the actions of foremen is a real and continuous thing, though it gains public notice only when it is fought for in a strike. It is not of course argued that this control is wholly different from the modicum of control exercised by any body of men under supervision, whether organized or unorganized. The manager who sees that a certain foreman

fails to get the best work out of his men because
he is unpopular and so replaces him is to that
extent "controlled" by the dislikes of the workers.
Moreover, any group of men, no matter how help-
lessly situated, enforces, if only by nagging and
sulkiness, some sort of standard of treatment from
its overseers—a standard which I was made to
feel very definitely in a few days' service as a
prison guard.   The most accurate literary expression of this group-standard, in *The Code* by
Robert Frost, is written of the completely unorganized "hired men" of the New England
farms:—

> "The hand that knows his business won't be told
> To do work faster or better—these two things."

But from the individual hired man, working
alongside the small farmer in the hurry to get in
the hay before a rain and defending his "code"
by simply thrusting his pitchfork into the ground
and marching himself off the field, it is a long
way to the action of the whole body of workers
in a great engineering establishment or in a group
of coal pits scattered up and down a Welsh valley, no individual of whom is of any particular
importance to the employer, nevertheless enforcing by their collective power a certain level of
personal treatment when one foreman has violated the code in respect to one worker.   No one

claims that trade unionism is mere knight erran-
try, that a high recklessness over obscure and
delicate points of honor leads to lack of caution
in regard to trade union funds or the interests of
trade union members. Even the authors of the
Miners' Next Step, for all their insistence on fighting individual grievances that involve principles,
recommend as a point of tactics that:—

"Whenever it is contemplated bringing any body of
men out on strike, demands must be put forward to
improve the status of each section so brought out."

But the extent to which decent foremanship may
be felt to be a matter of union and inter-union concern is suggested by the description, in the annual
report of the Furnishing Trades Association for
1917, of joint action by the metal and woodworking trades in an aircraft factory:—

"A mass-meeting of all sections made it quite clear
that they were determined to insist that any attempt to
treat any group of men without regard to their feelings
or self-respect would be treated as a challenge to all the
unions, and as such would be taken up and replied to by
a general stoppage of work. They demand the right to
work under a manager who will treat them as men inside
the shop."

A standard of foremanship, or at least a standard of manners in foremen, enforced in the more

spectacular cases by striking for the foreman's dismissal but also by other methods of steady pressure, is as real—though less definite and possibly less universal—a subject of trade union regulation as the standard of wages itself.

XI

SPECIAL MANAGERIAL FUNCTIONS

THE last three sections dealt with the relation of labor to its supervisors. This section deals with the relation of labor to certain special functions of supervision, usually thought of as the business of foremen or managers but sometimes exercised by the workers.

The first of these is the enforcement of minor *discipline*. There is, as the Ministry of Labor reports, "a considerable body of experience" of the exercise of disciplinary functions by works committees. The experience to which that report refers falls, however, entirely into two classes,— cases of administering bonus schemes under which deductions are made for various offences, and cases of enforcing special war-time discipline under the power or the threat of the Munitions of War Act. In a typical instance of the first, a joint committee meets monthly to assess the fines incurred for the following offences:—

"a. Insubordination, or use of improper language.

b. Undue carelessness and wilful damage.

c. Neglect to enter goods, advices, time cards, dockets or time sheets."

The war emergency cases are more interesting. The Munitions of War Act of 1915 and the regulations issued under its authority by the Ministry of Munitions put discipline in the "controlled establishments"[1] on a basis totally different from peace conditions. Violations of a firm's posted rules were subject to prosecution in special courts, the munitions tribunals, in which a chairman appointed by the Ministry acted as judge with an equal number of assessors representing the employers and the trade unions. This method was in many cases felt by both parties to be a nuisance, and various experiments in joint discipline were tried. The Whitehead Torpedo Works, in suggesting a joint scheme to its employees, said:—

"There is a class of rules, offences against which are punishable by a fine of half a crown dismissal, or a prosecution under the Munitions Act. None of these penalties is a convenient one. Fines are as much disliked by the firm as by the men; dismissal entails the loss of services which may be badly needed; and prosecutions entail great waste of time and may produce more evils than the original ones they are meant to cure."

[1] "If the Minister of Munitions considers it expedient for the purpose of the successful prosecution of the war that any establishment in which munition work is carried on should be subject to the special provisions as to limitation of employers' profits and control of persons employed and other matters contained in this section, he may make an order declaring that establishment to be a controlled establishment." Munitions of War Act, 1915, Part II, Section 4.

Some committees were reluctant to take on themselves the responsibility and unpopularity of punishing their fellows; those that accepted it probably did so with the feeling that the special war powers of the employer made punishment inevitable and that this was a way of making it reasonable. In one remarkable case a Works Tribunal—not a joint committee but a chairman and a jury of twelve elected wholly by the workers—exercised authority over these matters and is said to have brought about great improvement in discipline and timekeeping.

"Bad timekeeping," by the way—*i.e.* irregular attendance at work—was the most important offence which came under this sort of discipline. Special joint committees to deal with this problem were set up at the suggestion of the Ministry of Munitions in the ironworks of Cleveland and Durham. The duties and powers of the local committees were defined as follows in the Cleveland rules:—

" (a) To inquire fully into every case brought by the Manager of the Works of alleged bad timekeeping on the part of any workman employed at the works under his charge.

(b) To give warning and advice to any workman who may appear to need it.

(c) To inflict subject to the provisions of the Truck Acts, such penalty or fine as in the judgment of the Committee the case shall merit, such fine not to exceed twenty shillings in any one instance.

(d) In the case of repeated offences, to transmit the facts and evidence to the judgment of the Central.

(e) In the event of the Works Committee being equally divided on any case [*which, it may be added, is said to have happened very rarely*] the same shall be submitted to the Central Committee for decision.

(f) Each Works Committee shall have power to reduce or remit altogether any fine imposed by the Committee, if the offender's conduct during the four weeks succeeding the hearing of his case justifies any variation in the original penalty.''

All these cases were under the direct power of the Munitions of War Act, and accepted only for its duration. The only further extension of this principle was in the Absentee Committees of the Miners, which in their development as Output Committees were one of the most interesting by-products of the war and will be discussed in a later chapter. Much the same argument, however, was used while the Miners were discussing the question of assuming responsibility for the attendance of their members. "If we don't accept it, we may be put under the Act. Then there'll be punishment anyway; we had better see that it's done justly." The "appeal to all mine workers" for good timekeeping, issued as a placard by the Yorkshire Miners, read in part:—

"Fellow Workers: This appeal is made to prevent more drastic measures being brought to bear upon our great industry by the Government."

"It is a line of punishment by your own men," said one of the Miners' leaders, "and if the men have no confidence in their own men who have been selected from their own branch, whom can they have confidence in?"

A second of these special managerial functions is that of providing for the *safety* of the workers. Here it is naturally the Miners that have needed and secured the greatest extent of control. The Mines Acts of 1911 and earlier give the workers power to appoint an inspector of their own to make a complete examination of the machinery and workings as often as once a month and also to make examination, in company with a legal adviser or with a mining or electrical engineer, after an accident. How much this privilege means in practice is hard to estimate, and probably varies greatly from district to district. A correspondent writing to the *Colliery Engineman* claims that it means very little in Cumberland:—

"The Act which enables mine-workers to appoint a person to periodically inspect every part of the mine, ventilating apparatus, machinery, etc., has been allowed to remain a dead letter at most of the collieries in this coalfield. One of the chief reasons for this has been that if the persons elected as local inspectors give an adverse report, the management would soon find some means of getting rid of them. . . . It is not uncommon to be told by mine-workers that their mine has not been examined by local inspectors for 10 years. During the inquiry into the Senyhenyd explosion, 1911, in which 439 men and boys lost their lives it came out in evidence that the miners had not inspected the mine for 18 months. The reason the men gave was that no man dared to give a true report.''

On the other hand a South Wales leader declared that:—

"In many parts of the South Wales coalfield, the workmen themselves have appointed practical examiners, and these men are doing very excellent work, in my opinion, preventing accidents.''

but advocated that these examiners be empowered to prosecute the owners for violations. Even as the law stands, however, it implies a definite statutory recognition of the right of the workers to take an active and independent part in the prevention of accident.

The Miners' Federation also claims responsibility for the clauses in the Mines Act which set the qualifications of the firemen, examiners, and deputies—the officials directly entrusted with safety functions. Here again the miners claim that these men have not dared to report faithfully the conditions for fear of the employers. At their 1917 Conference, the Miners' Federation passed the following resolution in order, as they claimed, to secure for the men in these positions a combination of the fearlessness of the government inspector and the knowledge of the practical miner:—

"That it would be conducive to the best interests of the miners that firemen, examiners, and deputies should be appointed by the workmen and paid by the State."

The report of the Commission on Industrial Unrest in South Wales (1917) recommended that the appointment and dismissal of those officials should be entrusted to joint committees. Certain of the Deputies' Associations favored the opposite—state control and appointment—in order to secure freedom from pressure from either side.

The Miners have also exerted a considerable negative control over safety arrangements by refusing to work under conditions they thought dangerous. There are a number of references to these "safety strikes" scattered through the evidence before the Coal Commission. One of the more specific occurs in the testimony of Mr. Winstone of the South Wales Miners' Federation:—

"Q. Was there a stoppage in Monmouthshire recently?

A. Yes.

Q. Do you mind telling us the nature of the stoppage?

A. The stoppage took place at the Risca Colliery in Monmouthshire where 15,000 men were idle for several days owing to a danger arising from gas, a shortage of timber, and the dukie rope cutting into the timber and cutting through the rails.

Q. That is what we could call a safety strike?

A. Yes. Then at the Bedwas Mine the men are out today because of a safety stoppage. The owners declined to stall the place, and the men were fearing that a crush would take place, and so they stopped."

These disputes are not only interesting as indicating a degree of present control but as often furnishing the background for further demands for control. A miner who had been discharged from a Scotch colliery for refusing to work in a place which he considered dangerous explained his case in great detail and with diagrams in a leaflet addressed to his fellow-workers at the colliery and reprinted in *The Worker* (Glasgow) of September 27, 1919. The moral which he drew was this:—

"If I lost, it's you who have lost, for you will have lost the right to decide yourselves about the safety of your own place. My idea is that we should demand that chocks—hard wood chocks—should be put in every loosened place and kept up with the face. That as soon as possible we should appoint pit committees to control the method of working; this would guarantee more safety to the coal getter."

The same feeling was expressed as a part of
the official policy of the Miners' Federation by
Mr. Robert Smillie in the course of a deputation
to the Prime Minister, on October 9, 1919, to demand nationalization and joint control:—

"The miners put forward their claim primarily on the
question of safety."

The Miners, then, have considerable power, both
legal and actual, over the safety of the mines and
are pressing vigorously for further control. There
is in the other industries no case of workers' control over safety to compare with this. It is true
that in many industries there are Factory Act regulations—often secured in part by trade union agitation—and even occasional provisions for inspectors appointed by workpeople; but in practice they
apparently involve little or no trade union action.
There is, however, at least one interesting case of
the beginnings of joint control. A joint sub-
committee of the Builders' Parliament in conjunction with representatives from the Whitley Councils in the other wood-working industries and in
consultation with the manufacturers of wood-
working machines, has made a study of the dan-
gers arising from the use of wood-working machinery. Its report of August 14, 1919, contains
a series of detailed suggestions intended as a basis
for further regulations under the Factory Acts.

A third and less important special function of supervision occasionally exercised by the workers is that of the *allocation of work, i.e.* the distribution within a given group of workers of the particular jobs or working places. The question is of some importance in many piece-work trades, and there is much 'complaint among the miners and others that favoritism in assigning working-places and jobs is used as a covert method of victimization. There are very few cases, however, in which complaint has gone over into control. Lord Gainford, the chief representative of the coal-owners, told the Coal Commission of the system in effect in the Durham coalfield:—

"In our county at the end of every quarter the men ballot amongst themselves for the different positions in the mines. The men as a rule are allowed to select their own working mates, and they go into the place which has been selected by ballot."

The printers furnish the best example of control under this head; a "companionship" (team) of compositors on piece work has the right to appoint its own "clicker" who distributes the work so as to divide equitably "the fat" (*i.e.* work on which good money can be made). It is probable that in many trades there are occasional instances of informal control of this sort, as, for example, at a certain "pot-bank" in which the equalization of work between one team (of jiggerer, turner, and handler) and another is arranged by the men. A writer in the *Railway Review* suggests that "allocations of turns of duty" are a field for joint or workers' control to replace what he calls the "incompetency and want of foresight and arrangement on the part of petty officials," and suggests that "at each depot . . . a representative of the men might be periodically chosen to regulate these turns of duty." The issue is even more important in the case of the street railways, where the real irksomeness of the working day depends not so much on the number of hours actually worked as on the "spread-over time" between the beginning of the first run and the end of the last. The matter depends almost solely upon the care spent in arranging the working schedules, and the tramwaymen in Leeds and other parts of Yorkshire have recently won a substantial concession in securing the right to be consulted in any change of these schedules—a right which at the time of the last change amounted in substance to the actual working-out of the schedules by the union officials and a large increase in the percentage of continuous runs.

The fourth of these special functions of management is that of the *measurement of results*. There are instances of a degree of control by workers over the two matters of *measurement of quantity* (where the pay is based on the amount of output of the individual or the works), and *measurement of quality* (where deductions are made from the pay for spoiled work). The best known and longest established case under the first head is that of the miners' checkweighman. By a law of 1887 (which strengthened a law of 1860) a majority of miners in each pit may appoint a representative to watch the weighing of the coal at the pit's mouth and to keep an accurate check on the recording of each man's work, and the checkweighman's pay is deducted from the wages of all the coal-getters who are paid by weight. A strike of 1200 men in 1913 "against raising and tipping coal after the fixed hour and in absence of checkweighman," is an indication that this right is felt to be an important one; the incidental result of the arrangement, in providing a means of support for Miners' Federation officials, has been exultantly pointed out by the Webbs and others. A bill extending this practice to certain other industries,—iron and steel works, the docks, limestone and chalk quarries, etc.—was introduced by the Labor Party and passed by the present Parliament. This is a case of the right to safeguard the earnings of the individual piece worker. A slightly different situation is that in which the payment depends, not on the output of the individual, but on that of the works. In the Durham coke-ovens the pay is based on the average weight of coke produced by the ovens. The agreement in regard to the "Ascertainment of Yield" is as follows:—

"That for the purpose of correctly ascertaining the average weight of coke produced per oven at any yard either party may require that the coke ᵇ weighed . . . the men to have the liberty to send ᶠ man to inspect and take a copy of the weighings c coke as recorded in the weighman's book."

A check on the judgment of quality is important in a few of the smaller trades, in which deductions are made for spoiled and bad work, though it is obviously a more difficult matter for joint or trade union action than a simple weighing of tons of coal. In pottery the custom of paying only for ware that comes "good from oven" and the lack of any joint means of assessing the fault in cases of breakage is at present a subject of dispute. In nut and bolt making, there is the rough and ready check of putting all rejected work on the scrap heap in the presence of its maker. The value is assessed and agreed upon and deducted from the maker's earnings; the waste is then his property. The elaborate regulations of the Yorkshire Glass Bottle Makers for determining the responsibility for bad work are worth quoting, if only as indicating the old-fashioned nature of the trade:—

"That bottles picked out [rejected] be not broken down until the men have had an opportunity of inspecting them. . . . . In all cases of bad or faulty metal the men shall immediately send for the manager to take the responsibility. . . . Any workman commencing to work knowing the metal to be bad, without skimming it according to the established custom of the trade, or failing to carry out the conditions herein specified, shall not be entitled to payment for the bottles put out."

The Nottingham lace weavers put the determination of the fault entirely in the hands of the shop committee:—

"No stoppage [deduction] shall be made for places caused by the fault of the machine. . . . Where neglect of the workman causes extra mending, places across or spoiled work, and where a workman fails to carry out written instructions in a workmanlike manner a claim for stoppage may be made by the employer, but all claims must be supplied in writing with particulars to the shop committee. Unless the shop committee receive such particulars and consent to the stoppage, no stoppage shall be made and the employer shall be left to such other remedy as may be open to him."

The sum of duties exercised by the representatives of the workers under these special managerial functions is considerable. Their importance in a study of control is lessened by two facts:—the most highly-developed cases of the enforcement of discipline were definitely for the war emergency in fear of worse things, and do not at all represent the responsibilities the greater number of trade unionists are ready to accept under peace conditions; the control under the other heads is almost entirely a mere check on the care or honesty of the employer and involves little independent direction. The exercise of the disciplinary function was then mainly an emergency measure; the other functions might be more accurately spoken of as *check-managerial* than managerial.

XII

METHODS OF PAYMENT

THE last section clearly raises the question of the *methods of payment* of wages. The issue of the amount of wages falls outside our definition; the issue of the method of payment, however "immediate to the wage bargain itself," is too closely bound up with the methods of control to be completely passed by. There is certainly no use in attempting to go over all the ground covered by Mr. D. F. Schloss's *Methods of Industrial Remuneration* (1892, 1894 and 1898) or Mr. G. D. H. Cole's *Payment of Wages* (1918). The object is merely to show how the arguments for and against certain methods of payment are colored by the struggle for control, and how various methods of payment have given rise to particular attempts at workers' control.

The first point is suggested by a comparison of the two books mentioned. Mr. Schloss declared that:—

"In regard to the *method* of industrial remuneration Trade Unionism does not propose to make any change whatever in the arrangements now prevailing."

161

The more recent movements grouped as the "Demand for Control" make such a statement no longer possible. Mr. Cole's book is in fact largely taken up with the arguments for and against various changes which trades unionists (if not Trade Unionism) are anxious either to make or to prevent. It is here worth while merely to mention a few of the issues to indicate the complexity of motives and their bearing on "control" as well as on the amount of wages. The various wood-working trades, for example, have been striking or agitating for the abandonment of the piece work and premium bonus systems which had in some cases been forced upon them during the war. Here the issue of quality of workmanship—which the workers claim is sacrificed under piece work—seems to be more real than in most trades, though it is by no means the only motive. *The Carpenters' and Joiners' Journal* argues :—

"That employers who desire the best class of craftsmanship put into any kind of joinery work, never request joiners to adopt premium bonus or piece work systems, because all men—employers and workmen alike—recognize that either of the above named systems inevitably leads to "rushing" work, therefore necessarily "scamping" work, and consequently the demoralizing effect in the long run hinders instead of assisting in increasing the output of the genuine craftsman's production."

In engineering and other industries a guerrilla warfare is being waged over the introduction and the conditions of introduction of piece work and more especially of premium bonus and "efficiency" systems. The general argument of the employers for the introduction of payment by results is that it is necessary as providing an incentive for greater production—a way to "speed up" the workers. Some of them favor collective payment by results, that is, payment based on the output of the whole shop or works, as a way of getting the workers to "speed each other up"—which recalls the old argument for profit sharing that it "makes every workman an overseer." The motives of the workers who oppose the system are various—a distaste for being speeded up and the past experience and fear of rate-cutting are among the chief. A fairly constant argument against individual piece work in many industries is that it makes collective bargaining harder to enforce and that it divides the workers against themselves instead of making for the "solidarity of labor,"—that is, as the *Ironfounders' Journal* puts it, "That it promotes selfishness in the workshop." On the other hand I heard a printing employer argue on just the same ground against a change to piece-work which his employees wanted—that it would destroy the good team work among his compositors. The Miners' Federation at its 1917 Conference passed a resolution in favor of the abolition of piece work; but a vigorous minority insisted that time work would mean much more irksome supervision, that "you would probably want a doggy or a deputy in every stall to see that the men are working their hardest." Somewhat the same point is occasionally put in the statement that the workers "feel freer" in regard to attendance under piece work. The most conspicuous advocates of workers' control, including Mr. Frank Hodges of the Miners and Mr. G. D. H. Cole, are in favor of time work.[1] With that opinion, as it applies to future policy, it is not the affair of the present study to deal; from the historical point of view, one fact might be set on the other side, that the genuine interest of the miners in the problems of mine-management, as well as the favorable attitude of the cotton operatives toward improvements in machinery, are partly traceable to their piece-work systems. In any case, it is clear that the quarrels over methods of payment cannot be completely disentangled from the general question of the control of industry.

For the present purpose, however, it is more useful to examine the specific forms of control developed or advocated in connection with the methods of payment now in force. Most of the

[1] The qualifications which Cole would attach to this opinion are stated on pp. 111 and 112 of *The Payment of Wages*.

labor arguments for time work are negative, that
is, arguments that piece work is more dangerous
to the standard rate; therefore it is no surprise
to find fewer special forms of control under payment by time. The only case I know of, in fact,
of the exercise by workers of unusual functions
of direction under any sort of time system, is that
of the "grading system" of the Birmingham brass
trades. There the executive of the National Union
of Brass Workers grades each worker according
to his ability and places him in one of seven different classes, for each of which a minimum wage is
set by collective bargaining. If an employer challenges the qualifications of any man, a practical
examination in the processes of the trade is given
him by the managers of the Municipal Brass
Trades School.

Piece work and the more complicated systems
of payment by results naturally show more instances of union activity, if not a greater degree
of control, over the methods of payment. The
difference of course lies, not in the bargaining
for the general standard of wages, but in the application of the standard rate to the setting of particular piece rates (or, under bonus systems, basic
times) for particular jobs or processes. The procedure varies much more widely than can be indicated here, but may be thought of as falling into
two broad classes,—that in which "lists" or agree-

ments reached by formal collective bargaining cover every process in the trade, and that in which the setting of the particular price is more or less entirely a matter between the employer and the individual workman or immediate groups of workmen concerned. The outstanding example of the first class is the cotton industry, where the expert secretaries of the two associations, with no motive for setting a new price in a single mill either above or below the general standard of Lancashire and with a strong professional pride in the correctness of their mathematics, have little difficulty in applying the elaborate agreed lists to any variation of speed, pattern, or process. Their greatest difficulty (aside of course from the general level of wages), has been the "bad spinning" question, *i.e.* disputes arising from the claims of workers that the cotton supplied them was of such bad quality that they could not make the standard rate at list prices. The Brooklands Agreement, which was the chief treaty governing the industry, broke down in 1912 over just this point, the employers being willing to admit that grievances under this head should be promptly discussed, but refusing to accept a formal agreed test.° The same issue occasionally occurs in other industries; in a branch of the woolen trades, it is settled by the following arrangements:—

"Should any dispute arise as to the quality of the wool, a sample shall be submitted to the Bradford Conditioning House by a representative of the workmen. Each body to abide by the decision of the certificate, and the expenses of the test to be paid by the party found to be in error."

A somewhat parallel difficulty is encountered in coal-mining in settling rates for "abnormal places"—working places that are for one reason or another so difficult that a standard wage cannot be earned without special allowance. The Miners' Minimum Wage Act of 1912 was in part intended to meet this problem by assuring each man a wage irrespective of his place; but, since the minimum rates are in all cases well below the normal earnings in a good place, the question still often leads to serious disputes. These are usually fought out between the miners' agents and the employer and involve no special forms of control. One South Wales colliery, however, works on the agreement that:—

"When any variation in the conditions of any working place or places occurs, the person or persons working in such places shall have the right to call in the aid of any two members of the Workmen's Committee, together with two Officers of the Company, in order to agree upon any additional rate or allowance for working such place or places."

The Commission on Industrial Unrest in its report on South Wales recommended, as a subject for discussion in a possible Joint Industrial Council, "the right of the men with the employers to select an equal number of the workers engaged in carrying out tests in new seams before price lists are arranged."

Rate-fixing in the other class of industries, those not covered by lists, may mean anything from purely "take-it-or-leave-it" determination (whether arbitrary or "scientific") by the employer or a strictly individual bargain to fairly complete though informal collective bargaining. Engineering is the storm center among this second class of industries and shows the widest variations. The principle which is supposed to govern it is that of "mutuality":—

"The prices to be paid shall be fixed by mutual arrangement between the employer and workman or workmen who perform the work."

This means at least a bargain; the worker has the right—which may or may not mean the opportunity—to say no; as it stands, it may mean no more than individual bargaining. Doubtless, however, there are always the rudiments of a collective bargain. One man's acceptance of a bad bargain is obviously the other men's loss, and the men doubtless talk over their rates. From this informal understanding there are various stages to full collective bargaining. Certain unions make regulations that their men shall not accept rates below those set "by a majority of members working in the shops." This pricing by shopmates leads naturally to the election of a shop steward or a shop committee to take over the pricing function, a step of great importance as the origin of many of the most active shop committees. This may mean within the shops almost as complete a standardization as in the price-list industries, particularly if the steward or the committee keeps a "book of prices" with which to compare any new prices offered.

The situation is somewhat different in those piece-work and premium bonus systems in which the management employs a special scientific rate-fixer or where the time a job should take is determined in a special time-study office, though a similar range of variations in procedure occurs here. The whole method may be considered merely the firm's business, or the firm may be willing to discuss with a committee the methods by which prices are fixed but not the prices fixed in individual cases. On the other hand it is quite possible for scientific price fixing to co-exist with a considerable extent of joint control. On just this point it is worth while to quote at length from the scheme

and experience of the Phoenix Dynamo Company
of Bradford:—

"One of the greatest objections to present piece-work
systems is that the employer works out the price in
secret, writes down the time on a card, and this settles
the price. Now, the men feel that payment by results
is a bargain and that it is not within the province of
the employer to state arbitrarily what the price is to
be. . . .

On getting out a new job we would calculate the feeds
and speeds which were suitable for the tool on which the
job was to be performed, and then put forward the time
we offer; you are not bound to accept it and can appeal
if you like. In this event you go to the Time Study
Office, where the man who has dealt with the job will go
through the detail of his calculations, and if he has
made a slip will at once put it right.

Our time fixing is not infallible, and the men can
help us by pointing out errors. If, however, we are
unconvinced that the price is unreasonable, and the man
is equally unconvinced that it is reasonable, he can
then say, 'I want this job to go to Committee'. . . .

The Committee consists of 3 of the firm's representatives and 3 workmen's representatives consisting of the
man concerned and 2 workmen selected by him who are
operating the same type of machine or whose work is
closely allied to the work in question. . . . In the event
of the Committee failing to agree it is then up to the
firm to demonstrate in their own works that the time
is fair and that time and a quarter [over the guaranteed time rate] can be made on it. . . .

The surprising part of the scheme over the period

in which it has now been operating is the very small number of Committees which are held. It would appear that a very stupid workman who goes to the Time Study Office to argue with the rate-fixer, or a very thick-headed rate-fixer, are either of them rather afraid of what a Committee would decide about their particular case, and so whichever party feels himself to be technically weakest in the argument appears to give way."

A similar arrangement applies by agreement in the engineering trade at Barrow. This is probably the furthest extent of joint control possible where the specialized skill is still entirely the property of one side. The *Works Committee's* pamphlet already quoted reports the suggestion from a firm's rate-fixer that a desirable next step would be the appointment by the men of a separate rate-fixer of their own—an idea already in operation at a Bristol engineering works in which the firm pays a rate-fixer who is chosen by the men.

All these are cases of individual payment by results. But collective payment by results—where the payment is based on the production of a group or team of workers, or on that of the shop or entire factory—has also its direct and important bearings on the problem of control. The connection between collective piece work and control in the smaller crafts has already been mentioned. Perhaps it is worth while to quote again the rep-

resentative of the Stuff Pressers to illustrate the
type:—

"This principle of collective payment throws the responsibility upon every individual to contribute his
maximum quota to the whole. It has almost completely
crushed out of existence the practice of 'ca-canny,' for
where is the man of sufficient courage to exercise his
genius for shirking when the consequences of his action
would be to bring down on his head the wrath of the
shop?"

At the present time workers in engineering and
other industries show a much greater readiness to
accept collective piece work or a collective (shop
or works) bonus on output than the individual
systems. Nor can the reason be put quite as simply as by the director of a steel works who told
me that the reason for this preference was that
"it didn't show up the rotters as quickly." Another side is put in the resolution in favor of collective piece work passed by the Weymouth Joint
Committee of Allied Engineering Trades on the
ground that, "it restores the old collective spirit,
securing collective effort, collective interest and
harmony, that it produces evenness of earnings in
place of inequality." An elaborately safeguarded
system of collective piece work is that put into
force by the Bradford Dyers' Association in 1913,
which contained the following clauses:—

"The Association may at any branch introduce payment by piece-work rates. *All piece work shall be based on collective work and collective payment. . . .*

The fixing of rates and the arrangements of sets shall be mutually agreed upon in writing by representatives of the Associations and the Unions. Such rates shall be so fixed as to enable a full rated man to earn not less than 7d. per hour. . . .

No rate or set shall be altered without the consent in writing of the Association and the Union or Unions to which the employees affected belong.

Trials of three calendar months' duration shall precede the final settlement of rates."

Under this system the "sets" of workers are said to have taken an increased part in arranging their own work, a development towards control which had been actively in the mind of at least one of the Dyers' leaders who had advocated the scheme.

The cases already quoted perhaps cover most of the range of methods of payment which carry with them degrees of workers' control important in the present industrial system. It is worth while, however, to contrast two other systems, which imply much greater control by the workers, *co-operative work* and *collective contract*. The former was quoted by D. F. Schloss as an archaic dying system on the very edges of modern industry; the latter has been advocated by two Clyde shop stewards as a revolutionary idea for the great industry itself. "The distinctive features of Co-operative Work . . . are that (1) the members of the co-operative group are associated by their own free choice, determining for themselves of how many persons and of what persons that group shall consist, (2) the associated workmen select from amongst themselves their own leader, and (3) arrange the division of the collective wages between the members of the group in such manner as may be mutually agreed upon between these associates as being equitable."[2] Messrs. Gallacher and Paton argue[3] that "the next step" for a shop stewards' committee, after some experience as the "sole medium of contact between the firm and the workers" should be to "undertake in one large contract, or in two or three contracts at most, the entire business of production throughout the establishment. Granted an alliance with the organized office-workers—a development which is assured so soon as the Shop Committees are worthy of confidence and influential enough to give adequate protection—these contracts might include the work of design and purchase of raw material, as well as the operations of manufacture and construction. But to begin with, the undertaking will cover only the manual operations. The contract price, or wages—for

[2] D. F. Schloss, *op. cit.*, 1918 edition, p. 155.
[3] *Towards Industrial Democracy*. See Note on Sources.

it is still wages—will be remitted by the firm to the Works Committee in a lump sum, and distributed to the workers by their own representatives, or their officials, and by whatever system or scale of remuneration they choose to adopt. . . . A specially enlightened union of this sort would, no doubt, elect to pool the earnings of its members and pay to each a regular salary weekly, monthly, or quarterly, exacting, of course, from the recipient a fixed minimum record of work for the period. . . . The functions of management will have passed to the Committees, and it will be their business to see that contract prices amply cover all the costs of these functions.''

It is obvious, then, that the various methods of wage payment raise issues far beyond the immediate bargaining for wages. Methods of payment themselves depend largely on the technique of the industry concerned, but each system of payment has in turn its by-products in particular forms of attempts at control, and one of the most detailed projects put forward by the propagandists for workers' control is based on a proposed change in the method of payment. But it is high time to discuss the questions raised in the last few sections, not only with reference to the relations of man to man in industry, but also more specifically to the relations of man to the technique of production.

XIII

TECHNIQUE: RESTRICTION AND RESTRICTIONS

THE people who write about the things the workers
do and do not control, often use the broad distinction between *conditions of employment* on the
one hand and *methods of production* on the other.
Sometimes they say that the former are rightly
the worker's affair, the latter entirely the employer's. The moral of it is not this book's business, but the distinction is a help in classifying.
The forms of control already studied fall under
the first head; those still to be discussed belong
to the second. But the division is by no means
rigid—the facts do not divide so neatly; no one
of the earlier sections has failed to raise questions
of the technique of production. Nor does it represent a sharply logical demarcation; the process
at which a man works is perhaps the most important condition of his employment. But clearly
in turning to technique, we are coming to a vital
part of our subject. We have discussed some of
the personal relationships in industry—the *politics
of industry;* but how about the work itself? What

control have the organized workers exercised over the actual *technology of industry?*

The newspaper reader is likely to think of workers' control over production, if at all, as either sheer *restriction* of output, or else as a series of *restrictions* which prevent the use and (where the issue really comes to a head) the introduction of the best industrial technique. This section, then, will deal with restriction and restrictions.

Restriction of output—apparently better known as "this damned restriction of output"—is an interesting subject, if only for the passion it arouses. But it is necessary to examine it very closely to see whether it falls within the range of our inquiry. To decide how much is to be produced—the employer's decision whether it is more profitable to increase or restrict his output of a certain commodity—is obviously a main element in the control of industry. But it is not claimed that the workers in restricting output (except in one or two rare instances which will be mentioned under "Trade Policy") have made any conscious attempt to share in that decision. The charge is that the workers—or rather some groups of workers—have been deliberately setting a limit to their own output; deciding for themselves "what amount of output by each operative should be considered a fair day's work, not to be considerably exceeded under penalty of the serious displeasure of the workshop.'' There is no doubt at all that a ca'canny (go slow) policy is a serious problem in many industries—and a ca'canny that cannot be explained as a mere natural difference between the employer's and the worker's idea of a "fair day's work." Very likely the extent of this policy is exaggerated in certain current exhortations to hard work, but its existence is admitted by too many trade union leaders [1] to be a matter of doubt. Besides sheer laziness two motives are usually suggested for the restriction of output. There is first the fear of the rate-cutting that has in the past so often followed increases in output. "Slow down," says Lola Ridge's heroine in *The Ghetto*, "You'll have him cutting us again!" The second is the notion that somehow the less work is done the more there will be to go around. This is the meaning of a catch phrase from the *Ragged Trousered Philanthropists*:—

"Just because we've been working a dam sight too hard, now we've got no work to do."

The use of ca'canny or the "stay-in strike" as a conscious form of militant labor policy—either as a weapon in a particular dispute or with the

---

[1] Some of them even use it as a text for denouncing the present industrial system.

fixed idea of making capitalism impossible by making it unprofitable—is another matter and surely of much rarer occurrence. Its classic expression is in *The Miners' Next Step* published in 1911 by a group of Welsh miners:—

"Lodges should, as far as possible, discard the old method of coming out on strike for any little minor grievance. And adopt the more scientific weapon of the irritation strike by simply remaining at work reducing their output, and so contrive by their general conduct, to make the colliery unremunerative. . . .

Use of the irritation strike

If the men wish to bring effective pressure to bear, they must use methods which tend to reduce profits. One way of doing this is to decrease production, while continuing at work. Quite a number of instances where this method has been successfully adopted in South Wales could be adduced."

But the very fact that the writers felt it necessary to explain at such length, even for South Wales readers, what an irritation strike was, is sufficient indication of its rarity. As a means of winning control, it is advocated by only a tiny minority. From the point of view of this inquiry, the subject may be ruled out of the question. Restricting output as a method of piece-work bargaining introduces no particularly new principle into the wage bargain. Shirking is not controlling industry though, like striking, it may be a means towards it. And the "stay-in strike" is no more, and no less, a means of controlling industry than the ordinary strike and therefore needs no separate treatment here. Restriction of output is more a method of warfare than a form of control and, since this is neither a discussion of the ways of winning control nor of the technique of industrial strife, it is fortunately unnecessary to make any further guesses about the amount of restriction.

But if mere *restriction* of output—for all its interest as an industrial problem and an industrial symptom—has no great bearing on the subject, certain specific *restrictions* are very closely related to control. The Munitions of War Act of 1915 provided (II.4.[3]) that:—

"Any rule, practice, or custom not having the force of law which tends to restrict production or employment shall be suspended" . . . in the controlled establishments.

The Government's pledge was given to the trade unions in the famous Treasury Agreement (see next section) that these regulations would be restored after the war; the same pledge was a part of the Government's contract with the employers; the employers were under obligation to keep a record of all such changes in practice; and the Restoration (of Pre-War Practices) Act has just made the pledge enforceable at law. Evidently, then, there was an extensive body of custom and vested right in regulations that could at least be held to "restrict production or employment" and which were considered by the unions, and recognized by the Government, as of first-rate importance.

It is then important to try to estimate how far this mass of confusing, usually local, and often unwritten custom, involved a real—though negative and restrictive—control over the technique of industry. Certain restrictions that were held to fall within the meaning of this clause may be ruled out at once from the present subject, or have been discussed in earlier sections. Limitations on the amount of overtime, for example, were given up for the war emergency; the question is an important one but surely not primarily one of technique, and its most direct bearing on control has already been discussed under "Unemployment." Regulations forbidding piece work and premium bonus systems were held to come under the Act; they of course affect industrial technique only indirectly, and were sufficiently covered in the last section.

A more important set of these restrictions has to do with the subjects of the "Right to a Trade" —apprenticeship, demarcation, and the opposition to dilution and the employment of women—referred to in the fifth section. These are certainly, when enforced, a direct interference with the "manipulation of the workman by the employer;" they involve saying which machines shall be run by which sorts of workmen and to that extent imply a real restriction on technique. The restrictions against dilution are from the point of view of technique especially significant. Demarcation matters less; a job will be done very much the same way whether it is done by a skilled shipwright or by a skilled boilermaker. But you cannot put a semi-skilled or unskilled man or woman on the work formerly done by a skilled engineer without changing the method of production. You must split up the job into simpler processes, fit the machine with jigs or other fool-proof contrivances, and in general standardize your work so that it can be done on automatic machines. It is just because changes of this sort have been made and found immensely profitable that the issue is so significant. This was the general tendency of "scientific management" even before the war; the war greatly emphasized the tendency by its demand for standardized munition production. "Industrial methods have been changing," writes Mr. J. T. Murphy in *The Workers' Committee*, "until the all-round mechanic, for example, is the exception and not the rule. Specialization has progressed by leaps and bounds. Automatic machine production has vastly increased. Apprenticeship in thousands of cases is a farce, for even the apprentices are kept on repetition work and have become a species of cheap labor. . . . It will be thus clearly perceived that every simplification in the methods of production, every application of machinery in place of hand production, means that the way becomes easier for others to enter the trade." This is taken from an argument against craft unionism; it should be somewhat discounted since it is based on engineering, the one industry most affected by the change, and since it is based on war-time experience, when the demand was more standardized than peace-time demand is likely to be. But there is no question whatever that the general movement of industrial technique is towards specialization, and that the trade union rules against dilution are a restriction on that tendency. This control is purely negative, and purely a defence of old customary rights; the rules were never thought of as implying a right to say what should be done; but it has been suggested that even without the war a demand for positive control would have arisen as a *quid pro quo* for the yielding of these restrictive regulations. The possibility of the removal of all such restrictions on technique is even stated in a pamphlet written in 1919 as sequel to the *Miner's Next Step*—the price for removal being positive workers' control:—

"The disastrous grasping policy of the mine owner has had the result of causing the workmen to erect a code of customs and rules, designed to protect their wages and conditions. These act directly in restraint of production, as well as of the owners' greed. Remove this code by removing its cause, and the management of a mine loses three-fourths of its worries, while it at least doubles its efficiency." (*Industrial Democracy for Miners*, p. 11.)

I suppose few accounts of restrictions on technique have been written without an emphasis on the objection to machinery. Historically of great interest, it is a nearly dead issue now. In the years 1911, 1912 and 1913, there were two strikes against the introduction of machinery (one of Glass Bottle Makers, the other of Dockers) and one against the use of a portable instead of a stationary drill (Boilermakers). Less than a thousand men were directly involved in these three strikes; as against that 6,500 Ironfounders were in 1912 engaged in a dispute which was settled as follows:—

"Employers' Assurances accepted by men as to immediate steps being taken to improve output."

No doubt the restrictions on technique have materially interfered with industrial innovations; Mr. Cole speaks of the trade unions in the past as "extremely bad and partial judges of new industrial processes." But it is a mistake to think of trade union regulation of technique as a series of flat negatives and flat opposition to change. That this is not true—that the issue is more often the conditions of change and the right to be consulted and is even sometimes an insistence by the union on improved technique—it is the business of the next two sections to show.

XIV

TECHNIQUE: CONSULTATION OVER CHANGES

A CHANGE in technique is a change in the conditions of work. It is therefore natural on the general principles of collective bargaining to expect to find the claim and practice of consultation over changes in technique. Bargaining over the conditions of change is far more important in the present labor situation than a mere opposition to change. The real objection is to unregulated change. "The typical dispute is to-day a dispute as to terms," said the Webbs in 1891; certainly it is no less true now. As long ago as 1864, the Executive of the Ironmoulders advised its members:—

"It may go against the grain for us to fraternize with what we consider innovations, but depend upon it, it will be our best policy to lay hold of these improvements and make them subservient to our best interests."

Apparently fraternizing with innovations now goes less against the trade union grain; in many unions is it a long-established commonplace; in most it is no new thing. Even a conservative old union like the Yorkshire Glass Bottle Makers agrees:—

"That the workmen are willing to adopt other methods of working than the Yorkshire method, providing satisfactory terms and conditions be agreed upon between the manufacturers and the workmen through their representatives."

Laying hold of these improvements and making them subservient—or at least not positively harmful—to the workers' interests is a cardinal point in trade union policy.

The unions have used various methods to save their members from the immediate hardships so often connected with changes in technique. The simplest is, of course, merely to secure an undertaking that wages will not be lowered, for example:—

"The owners shall be at liberty to adopt such improved methods of screening and cleaning as they may consider necessary, provided that any methods so adopted shall not in any way prejudicially effect the wages of the workman."

This does not meet the far more serious changes where the fear is that members of the trade will be permanently displaced. An agreement under which the Leek Silk Weavers consented to the introduction of two-loom weaving contained the

"Employers' Undertaking . . . not to discharge any man in order to initiate the two-loom system." Another method is to secure an arrangement by which the workers who would otherwise have been thrown out of work by a new invention or a new process are secured the first chance to learn and do the new job. The best known example of this was the printing trade; the linotype was introduced in 1894 into the offices of London newspapers under the following agreement:—

"All skilled operators . . . shall be members of the London Society of Compositors, preference being given to members of the Companionship into which the machines are introduced. . . .

"A Probationary Period of three months shall be allowed the operator to receive his average weekly earnings for the previous three months."

A strike of Scottish Bookbinders in 1912 secured the principles:—

"Qualified tradesmen to have first claim upon all machinery introduced in future displacing qualified male labor and to be paid standard wages."

Similar, if less formal, arrangements have been made in other changing trades, as for example in pottery when "casting" began to replace "pressing."

The conditions under which the unions during

the war accepted dilution, and the clause already quoted from the Munition Act forbidding restrictive regulations, are interesting not only as embodying particular safeguards, *e.g.* that the "rate for the job" be maintained even if less skilled labor is put on it,[1] but because the Act laid down the general principle of the right to consultation on changes in methods of work. Section 7 of Schedule II reads:—

"Due notice shall be given to the workmen concerned wherever practicable of any changes of working conditions which it is desired to introduce as a result of the establishment becoming a controlled establishment, and opportunity for local consultation with workmen or their representatives shall be given if desired."

The Commissioners on Industrial Unrest (1917) reported that the non-enforcement of this clause —or perhaps the free use of the saving phrase "wherever practicable"—was a cause of unrest. This right to consultation was naturally one of the claims of the shop stewards—a claim evidently enforced while the shortage of labor gave them their opportunity. Their rules at Coventry read as follows on the point:—

[1] It is said that this provision was badly observed, partly because the skilled men were not at all anxious to keep up the dilutees' wages, even though it was for their own after-war interest. The attitude more often adopted by trade union officials, however, was to place on "the rate for the job" an interpretation which made diluted labor expensive, so using the rate as a means of hampering dilution.

"That all proposed changes to existing shop practices and trade union conditions in the shop shall be first notified to the Shop Stewards of that department through the Chief Convenor of Shop Stewards."

The great but unrecorded powers of certain engineering shop stewards during the war in fact represent the highest degree of the practice of consultation. It is true that this consisted largely in fighting over wage questions (as in the case of the Manchester committee that is said to have spent 27 hours of one week in meetings with the management), but it at least involved in practice detailed discussion of technical problems and changes and in theory a recognition of a right to consultation over technique. In an extreme case on the Clyde, the steward in each shop, in consultation with the foreman, practically determined the distribution of work within the shop, and similarly the convenor of shop stewards discussed with the works manager the allocation of work between departments and was even shown the firm's books. It even became in this case the custom for notices posted by the manager announcing a change in working rules to be countersigned by the men's representative; when this was not done, the workmen said:—"It's no signed by MacManus," and disregarded it.

It is only here with the recognition of a right

or principle of consultation over changes in technique that we come really to control in a proper sense of the word. The former instances are, after all, not much more than special cases of bargaining; but an established claim to be consulted in every technical change is at least the basis for considerable control. It is difficult to draw any very valid distinction between consultation and bargaining; yet consultation over changes in technique very often may mean more than a mere chance to bargain over terms of a change before it happens; it often means a real, though not always an important, give-and-take of advice and opinion on the advisability of a change. An illustration of the most rudimentary form of this might be taken from the experience of a somewhat paternalistic forging firm, that had consulted its workmen over some detail of the time-keeping arrangements. The attitude of the men is said to have been this:—"The Directors couldn't even do a little thing like that without consulting us." A foreman in one of the National Factories attributed the success of his factory and the good feeling in it largely to the practice of the management in discussing both with a foremen's and a worker's committee the work ahead and the means of doing it. On a much greater scale the same claim was put forward in the House of Commons by Mr. Brace, one of the Miners' Members, in the important debate on the increase of coal prices (July 14, 1919) :—

"Why were we not taken into consultation? . . . Very nearly on the last day of the Coal Commission the Miners' Federation of Great Britain representatives made an earnest appeal that they should be allowed to co-operate with the Government in finding a way for dealing with the reduction in output, and the reply we had, very much later, was 6/- a ton increase on the price of coal."

The same idea is of course a central one of the whole scheme of the Whitley and *Works Commit-tees* reports, and has perhaps been sufficiently advertised by them. But the right to take a share in the deciding on new industrial processes is a real part of the forward program of an important fraction of the trade union movement.

In order to make concrete the references to the actual and proposed recognitions of the "right to consultation," I think it is worth while to quote in full the Treasury Agreement of 1915—on which the Munitions Act and the official Government policy on changes in technique during the war were based—and, for comparison with it, a com-prehensive scheme drawn up by a committee of workers representing the Clyde engineering and shipbuilding trades to meet the same problem of dilution and the changes necessary for war-time production. The first document was the result of a conference between Mr. Lloyd George, then Chancellor of the Exchequer, and representatives of the chief munition-making unions. It represented the terms—and the degree of consultation—under which most of the official trade union leaders consented to give up for the war their restrictions against dilution. The second scheme was drawn up by Mr. John Muir and other leaders of the shop stewards' movement on the Clyde. It was rejected by the Government—Mr. Lloyd George declaring that he couldn't "carry on an industrial revolution in the middle of a world war"—and several of its authors were shortly in prison as revolutionists. The scheme was a war-time one and therefore did not have to face the problem of unemployment as the background of trade union regulations. It is, however, of great interest in tying together the threads of this and the last section—the network of restrictions and the conditions of and consultations over their removal—and in pointing the way to the next section—on trade union insistences on improvements in technique. It represents a definite attempt on the part of a group of workers to pass from negative to positive, and from obstructive to responsible, control of industry.

THE TREASURY AGREEMENT

"The Workmen's Representatives at the Conference will recommend to their members the following proposals with a view to accelerating the output of munitions and equipments of war:—

(1) During the war period there shall in no case be any stoppage of work upon munitions and equipments of war or other work required for a satisfactory completion of the war.

All differences on wages or conditions of employment arising out of the war shall be dealt with without stoppage in accordance with paragraph (2).

Questions not arising out of the war should not be made the cause of stoppage during the war period.

(2) Subject to any existing agreements or methods now prevailing for the settlement of disputes, differences of a purely individual or local character shall unless mutually arranged be the subject of a deputation to the firm employing the workmen concerned, and differences of a general character affecting wages and conditions of employment arising out of the war shall be the subject of Conferences between the parties.

In all cases of failure to reach a settlement of disputes by the parties directly concerned, or their representatives, or under existing agreements, the matter in dispute shall be dealt with under any one of the three following alternatives as may be mutually agreed, or, in default of agreement, settled by the Board of Trade.

(a) The Committee on Production.

(b) A single arbitrator agreed upon by the parties or appointed by the Board of Trade.

(c) A court of arbitration upon which Labor is represented equally with the employers.

(3) An Advisory Committee representative of the organized workers engaged in production for Government requirements shall be appointed by the Government for the purpose of facilitating the carrying out of these recommendations and for consultation by the Government or by the workmen concerned.

(4) Provided that the conditions set out in paragraph (5) are accepted by the Government as applicable to all contracts for the execution of war munitions and equipments, the workmen's representatives at the Conference are of opinion that during the war period the relaxation of the present trade practices is imperative, and that each Union be recommended to take into favorable consideration such changes in working conditions or trade customs as may be necessary with a view to accelerating the output of war munitions or equipments.

(5) The recommendations contained in paragraph (4) are conditional on the Government requiring all contractors and sub-contractors engaged on munitions and equipments of war or other work required for the satisfactory completion of the war to give an undertaking to the following effect:—

Any departure during the war from the practice ruling in our workshops, shipyards, and other industries prior to the war, shall only be for the period of the war.

No change in practice made during the war shall be allowed to prejudice the position of the work people in our employment or of their Trade Unions in regard to the resumption and maintenance after the war of any rules or customs existing prior to the war.

In any readjustment of staff which may have to be effected after the war, priority of employment will be

given to workmen in our employment at the beginning
of the war who are serving with the colors or who are
now in our employment.

Where the custom of a shop is changed during the
war by the introduction of semi-skilled men to perform
work hitherto performed by a class of workmen of higher
skill, the rates paid shall be the usual rates of the district
for that class of work.

The relaxation of existing demarcation restrictions or
admission of semi-skilled or female labor shall not affect
adversely the rates customarily paid for the job.   In
cases where men who ordinarily do the work are adversely affected thereby, the necessary readjustments
shall be made so that they can maintain their previous
earnings.

A record of the nature of the departures from the
conditions prevailing before the date of this undertaking shall be kept and shall be open for inspection by the
authorized representative of the Government.

Due notice shall be given to the workmen concerned,
wherever practicable, of any changes of working conditions which it is desired to introduce as the result of
this arrangement, and opportunity of local consultation
with the men or their representatives shall be given if
desired.

All differences with our workmen engaged on Government work arising out of changes so introduced, or with
regard to wages or conditions of employment arising
out of the war, shall be settled without stoppage of
work in accordance with the procedure laid down in
paragraph (2).

It is clearly understood that, except as expressly provided in the fourth paragraph of clause 5, nothing in

this undertaking is to prejudice the position of employers or employees after the war.

D. Lloyd George.
Walter Runciman.
Arthur Henderson
(Chairman of Workmen's Representatives).
Wm. Mosses
(Secretary of Workmen's Representatives)^O

March 19, 1915.

THE CLYDE DILUTION SCHEME

"The Clyde District Committee of the Federation of
Engineering and Shipbuilding Trades, which represents all the workers in the industries mentioned, are
ready to co-operate with the Admiralty Shipyard Labor
Committee for the Clyde in accelerating all work
required by that Department, wherever possible, in the
national emergency.

We believe that with greater co-ordination and better
distribution of labor, the present admittedly high standard of output can be further improved upon.

Therefore it is agreed that:—

(1) The existing members of the Unions affiliated to
the Federation will be used to the best advantage.

(2) If at any time the Central Board hereinafter mentioned are satisfied that any rule or custom tends to restrict output, it shall be suspended for the duration of
the war.

(3) Pneumatic, hydraulic, electric, oxy-acetylene and
all other time and labor-saving devices will be adopted
and used to the fullest practicable extent.

(4) There shall be interchangeability of work between
the members of any particular Union affiliated to the

Federation and to effect that purpose all lines of demarcation between members of that Union shall be suspended for the period of the War.

(5) For the period of the War all allocation of work between the different Shipyard Unions will be suspended, and the work performed by the members of the Shipyard Unions will be interchangeable, it being agreed that any work of one Shipyard Union performed by the members of another Shipyard Union shall not form any precedent after the War.

(6) When in any particular trade men are unobtainable, and the work is of such a character, or the conditions such as to enable the labor introduced to perform the work with reasonable efficiency, skilled men from allied trades and semi-skilled and unskilled men and (where the work is appropriate and the conditions and surroundings are suitable to their sex) women may be introduced into the trade of the Unions affiliated to the Federation.

(7) The relaxation of existing demarcation restrictions or admission of semi-skilled or female labor shall not affect adversely the rates customarily paid for job. In cases where men who ordinarily do the work are adversely affected thereby, the necessary readjustment shall be made so that they can maintain their previous earnings.

(8) Labor introduced under Clause 6 to do any work of the Unions affiliated to the Federation shall be under the supervision of the foreman of the work.

(9) Where overtime is required on any job of the members of the Unions affiliated to the Federation, to which labor has been introduced under Clause 6, any members of the Unions affiliated to the Federation employed thereon shall have equality of treatment.

(10) In the event of any member of any particular Union affiliated to the Federation being available for employment at his own occupation he shall have the preference.

(11) A record of the nature of any departure in any shipbuilding, or ship-repairing establishment from the conditions prevailing when the establishment became a controlled establishment shall be kept, and, so far as the departure affects any Unions affiliated to the Federation, copies shall be handed to the Society concerned and the Central Board hereinafter mentioned.

(12) Due notice of any intended change of practice in any shipbuilding or ship-repairing establishment shall be given to the Shop Stewards of the Union concerned with their Union representatives.

(13) Facilities shall be given by the employers to the shop committees to meet when necessary for the purposes of this scheme.

(14) All differences arising out of, or in connection with this agreement shall, without stoppage of work, be promptly referred to and settled between the Central Board and the Shipyard Labor Committee of the Admiralty.

(15) Under the scheme of transfer no workman or workwoman shall suffer any pecuniary loss when transferred from one Admiralty firm to another; they shall receive the standard Trade Union district rate of wages, if on time or piece, plus travelling allowances according to the War Munitions Volunteer scheme; in the event of being transferred to work paid at a lower rate than his or her own rate, the original rate shall be paid; this practice shall also be carried out in cases of transfer from one department to another in an Admiralty firm, or from one district to another.

For the purposes of this scheme the Federation will establish Shop Committees in the various yards and engine shops in the Clyde area, under the direction and control of a Central Board, which will co-operate with the Shipyard Labor Committee of the Admiralty, to co-ordinate all efforts for the acceleration of output.

Shop Committees to consist of Shop Stewards now representing the various Unions in the shops and yards affiliated to the Federation. Where the present number of Shop Stewards in any one yard is inadequate, the Societies concerned will immediately instruct their members to appoint a representative by election in the shop or yard where there is a deficiency, for the purposes of this scheme.

The duties of Shop Committees shall be to report where:—

(1) An unnecessary supply of labor prevails;

(2) In the department labor can be more effectively employed by distribution, transfer, or otherwise;

(3) Machinery can be more usefully employed;

(4) Machinery can be usefully introduced;

(5) Any other proposals regarded as being conducive to the acceleration of output;

(6) The Committees will each appoint a representative steward, who will notify the Secretary of the Central Board immediately it is thought that increased output can be secured in any direction.

The duties of the Central Board, which will be appointed by and be responsible to the Federation, shall be to investigate all cases and suggestions submitted to them by the authorized Shop Committee, and to co-operate with the Admiralty Board, with a view to the more effective employment of labor and machinery in any manner deemed necessary.

The Central Board shall also be the Board to whom complaint shall be made with regard to grievances arising out of the application of the foregoing scheme.''

XV

TECHNIQUE: INSISTENCE ON IMPROVEMENTS

THE unions have blocked certain changes in technique which they thought would injure their interests. The unions have laid down conditions under which changes in technique might be made without injuring their interests. These are real forms of control over technique but of negative control. At the end of the last section there was a suggestion—in the demands for consultation for its own sake and in the proposals of the Clyde Committee—of a positive interest in planning the technique of industry. We have discussed the workers' negative interference in technique and their claim to consultation over technique; it is the business of this section to study the cases of workers' insistence on improvements in technique.

Some interest in good technique is a natural outcome of a highly-developed system of piece rates in which rate-cutting is prevented. If the piece workers' earnings depend on the efficiency of the machines or the quality of the material supplied or the arrangement of the factory, the worker's "facilities" may naturally become a part of the bargain and the union secretary may even find himself acting as a semi-official efficiency inspector. This was the origin of the long-standing "benevolence" of the cotton unions toward new machinery of which the Webbs wrote as follows:—

"In Lancashire it quickly becomes a grievance in the Cotton Trade Unions, if any one employer, or any one district, falls behind the rest. . . . . No employer takes the trouble to induce the laggards in his own industry to keep up with the march of invention. Their falling behind is indeed an immediate advantage to himself. But to the Trade Unions, representing all the operatives, the sluggishness of the poor or stupid employers is a serious danger. The old-fashioned master spinners, with slow-going family concerns, complain bitterly of the harshness with which the Trade Union officials refuse to make any allowance for their relatively imperfect machinery, and even insist, as we have seen, on their paying positively a higher piece-work rate if they do not work their mills as efficiently as their best-equipped competitors. Thus, the Amalgamated Association of Operative Cotton-spinners, instead of obstructing new machinery, actually penalizes the employer who fails to introduce it."

"Penalizes" is a word that may suggest too much; the situation is that the unions allow a reduction in piece-work price for the introduction of more efficient machinery, the effect is to encourage improvements. It thus becomes the business of the union secretary to investigate claims of bad ma-

chinery or bad material (the "bad spinning" disputes) or, in fact, any inefficiencies in management
that affect the worker's output, and to get them set
right or paid for. Somewhat similar principles
govern the piece-work arrangements of the Boilermakers. Their first national agreement admitted
that the employer was "entitled to a revision of
rates on account of labor-saving devices" and for
"improved arrangements in yards." On the other
hand, the present arrangements provide for the
settlement of complaints from the side of the men
"with respect to insufficiency of pressure, character of tools, inefficiency of plant, or obstructed
or odd jobs."

A number of strikes have turned on this relation
of industrial technique to piece-rate earnings. One
of the terms of a settlement in a strike of nearly
10,000 workers in the Paisley thread mills, in 1907,
was as follows:—

"Improvements made in arrangements of machinery
enabling higher wages to be earned."

The similar effect of an Ironfounders' strike—
in enforcing better technique—has already been
mentioned.

The Miners illustrate several of the steps between complaints over facilities and actual responsibility for the organization of industry. The is-

sue again starts with piece work. The hewer is paid for the amount of coal that gets to the surface; that depends in large part on the supply of tubs and the arrangements for haulage. Time spent underground waiting for tubs and the number of days the pit is closed for lack of the necessary facilities,[1] are of direct bearing on the miners' wage. These are by no means new complaints—a fact worth remembering now that the output of coal is a subject of public passion and Parliament is debating pit-props. Sir Richard Redmayne, His Majesty's Chief Inspector of Mines, reminded the Coal Commission that complaints by the workers of lack of tubs, trams, etc. had been coming in to his department for years. These complaints were by no means ended by the passing of the Minimum Wage Act of 1912. The management can still turn the workers back at the pithead when there is no work, and the minimum rates are set below what a man would naturally earn with good facilities, although one Miners' agent quotes an official's remark—"What do you care? You're on the 'min'!"—to a workman complaining of some defect in management.

For the sake of concreteness, it is worth while to list some of the specific complaints made by the Miners' leaders, national and local:—too little

[1] *Cf.* the claims of the United Mine Workers of America in their recent strike.

coal-cutting machinery; too little mechanical haulage; shortage of trains, tubs, rails, horses, and of timber for pit-props; bad condition of roads; wagons too big to go through the passageways; bad distribution of tubs and wagons; bad distribution of rolling stock.

Charges of this sort were frequently referred to in the course of the hearings before the Coal Commission.[2] Mr. Herbert Smith gave figures of the results of an inquiry into shortage of tubs, etc. in 300 Yorkshire pits (Q.27759), and Mr. Hodges spoke of the "thousands of instances" of faulty transport facilities " that were submitted to the Executive Committee of the South Wales Miners' Federation when they were putting up their scheme for increased output" (Q. 7178). Three references are well worth quoting:—

"*Mr. Smillie.* Hardly a day passes but what we get letters signed from one or other colliery complaining that the men have been sent home day after day or are in the pit and are only doing half work, and in some collieries there would be 400 or 500 tons more a day if there could be a clearance. . . .

Sir Richard Redmayne. I have not the least doubt in the world you are getting such letters; I get such letters. . . . I have here case after case of detailed enquiry into such cases. Sometimes I found there was no shadow of truth in them, sometimes I found there

[2] Especially Questions 7168, 7178, 7183, 26994, 26995, 27469, 27472, 27759-27790.

was. . . . I cannot think that is the whole truth, namely, that the cause of the decline in output is attributable to want of clearance—partially, yes." (Q. 27007.)

"*Mr. Hodges.* This is the report of the check weigher to his Committee [at a Lancashire colliery]:—

'For the last three months I have been continually bombarding the management for reasons as to the shortage of tubs, etc., which the men are constantly complaining about. During my investigation I found there have been stoppages of the main haulage roads through having day-work men working on the haulage getting the roof down and stopping gangs whilst the tubs were filled with dirt. On May 15th [1919] four men came out of the Trencherbone Mine as a protest for the manner in which they were being treated in regard to empty tubs. It was 12 o'clock noon when they got to the surface, and they had not had any empty tub from 11 o'clock of the previous day. Their tally number is 63. For the last few weeks the men in the Cranberry Mine have been having a bad time of it owing to the shortage of tubs. . . . I have spoken to the firemen. They say they are ashamed to go among the men who have to get their time over the best way possible.'!" (Q. 27472.)

"*Mr Hodges.* Do you know the Nine Mile Point Colliery?

Mr. Winstone [President South Wales Miners' Federation]. Very well.

Mr. Hodges. Do you remember the workmen at that colliery had to embark on a strike at one time because the management were developing the worst seams in the colliery and leaving the best seams until the market conditions were better and the control lifted?

Mr. Winstone. Yes, they urged the colliery company to develop a piece of coal which was nearer to the colliery, and admitted to be better coal, and which could not be developed on account of the opposition of the royalty owner.'' (Q. 23677-23678.)

The present point is not how far these charges are justified or how far they explain reduced output. Their real significance for this inquiry is in showing to what extent the actual problems of management and business discretion have been made subjects of trade union demands.

The Miners, then, have a long record of insistences on detailed improvements in the method of working. One by-product of the war was to give these complaints something of a responsible status. The Miners' Federation was asked by the Government to set up Absentee Committees, such as those already mentioned, to punish the men who stayed away from work. In most districts the Miners refused to do so except on condition that these committees should also have power to criticize the management when it was at fault in not providing facilities: if the worker is to be punished for staying away from work, their argument ran, why not the officials for keeping the men idle by mismanagement? The agreement of May 16, 1916, between the Executive Committee of the Miners' Federation and the Parliamentary Committee of the Mining Association, under which the committees were set up, recognized this dual function:—

"That in regard to absenteeism this meeting agrees to the matter being referred to the districts, on the distinct understanding that Committees will at once be set up in each district to devise and put into operation effective machinery to secure the attendance of all the workmen employed to the fullest extent, and to inquire into the circumstances of workmen employed at the mine not being provided with work when they have presented themselves at the mine, the intention being to secure, as far as possible, the output of coal necessary for the country's needs."

The local application of this principle is well illustrated by a miner's account of a large meeting of coal-owners and Miners' delegates at Stoke-on-Trent:—

"The meeting of representatives of employers and employed soon became lively and it showed the intense interest that was taken in the Government suggestions, and the men pointed out to the Coal Owners that there were other causes which caused a reduced output of coal besides absenteeism:—the faults of the management in allowing the miners to wait for timber, no facilities in taking men to their work and bringing them back, the waiting for tubs through scarcity and uneven distribution of the same. If they were going to work this scheme and draw up rules, they must bring the management in as well as the men.''

A specimen of the provisions for enforcing this side of the agreement may be taken from the rules of the North Staffordshire Output Committees :—

"It shall be open to the Pit Committee to consider the facilities for output, and for the provision of material necessary for the proper performance of their work by the workmen, and to report thereon. If the report of the Committee imputes negligence on the part of any official of the mine, a written copy shall be forwarded to the manager, who shall take such steps as he shall deem necessary, in the circumstances, and shall inform the Committee in writing of the action he has taken, it being understood that it is the intention for the manager and his officials to afford all possible reasonable facilities for output. If the Committee shall not be in agreement that the steps taken by the manager are satisfactory, it shall then deal with the case as if the alleged negligence were a breach of the Rules, and failing agreement the matter should be reported to the Central Committee for decision. . . .

The Central Committee shall consider and advise upon steps to be taken to the further improvement of output and of maintaining an increased attendance.''

The provisions for imposing fines for bad attendance and for working out fines by subsequent good attendance were similar to those quoted from the Cleveland ironworks.

So much for the scheme on paper; it repre-

sents at least a definite and admitted claim (if only
for the period of the war) on the part of the
Miners to the right to insist on technical efficiency.
It is harder to say how much it meant in practice.
The attempt to set up the committees was general
on the part of the Miners' leaders; at a number of
pits they were unsuccessful. Moreover, the ef-
fectiveness of the committees' work varied greatly,
though there is no doubt that on the whole attendance was considerably increased. Nor did the
committees in all cases undertake all the functions
suggested above; Lancashire, for example, would
not take the responsibility of finding. Of more
importance for the present point is the fact that
many of the committees failed to carry into force
the insistence on improved facilities. It is true
that Yorkshire reached the point of fining negligent
officials and that many committees reported improvements "which affected the output of coal
and increased the wages of the men" or a greater
keenness on the part of the mines officials to make
sure that no time was lost. Perhaps the most striking case in which positive responsibility for technique was assumed by the Miners was at a Yorkshire pit, in which the men appointed a controller
to supervise the distribution of tubs underground
and paid half his wages. Mr. Herbert Smith, the
Vice-President of the Miners' Federation, put the
case before the Coal Commission:—

"The Mitchel Main employs 1,750 men. I have a letter from a man who was appointed coal controller, down the pit. I will read you this letter . . . 'Our members have been below the district's day's work and some below the minimum on account of the shortage of tubs. We can prove this statement and our management cannot deny it. . . . We have gone to the lengths of appointing a controller and paid half his wages from our check, and Mr. Edward J. Peace was appointed to that position and during the time he was down the mine organizing the distribution of coal and everything, the output was a good deal better.' . . . Men were rather anxious when they paid a man out of their own pockets to organize?"   (Q. 27788.)

But on the other hand many committees were met with solid opposition in their attempts to consider problems of management. In South Wales the scheme fell through entirely because of disagreement over the scope of the inquiry. The story and the disputed clause in the men's scheme came out before the Coal Commission in the discussion between Mr. Hodges of the South Wales Miners' Federation and Mr. Hugh Bramwell representing the South Wales coal-owners:—

"*Mr. Hodges.* I also had the privilege of drafting a scheme for the establishment of Joint Committees in South Wales, to which I referred when you were in the box last, and I remember very distinctly the scheme coming before you, and you rejected it. You agreed to several clauses. When it came to this clause you rejected it?

Mr. Bramwell. Yes; we went to the Coal Controller about that.

Mr. Hodges. Here the workmen made certain propositions to you which they thought would be really helpful?

Mr. Bramwell. Yes; they interfered with the management.

Mr. Hodges. I will read them. 'The Committee shall receive reports from the Management and Workmen on matters affecting output, such as:

(a) Shortage of trams and road materials.

(b) Shortage of, or unsuitable, timber.

(c) Bad haulage roads and inadequate haulage.

(d) And any other cause which in their opinion is likely to interfere with the smooth working of the mine or interfere with the production of the largest output.'

You rejected the scheme because it contained that clause?

Mr. Bramwell. That was, I think, one clause we objected to. We went to the Coal Controller with you about it. The Coal Controller offered us the scheme which was accepted by the bulk of the other coalfields. It was you who rejected that.

Mr. Hodges. Certainly. I remember it and I confess it because the Coal Controller's scheme was felt by the South Wales Miners that it did not give them——?

Mr. Bramwell. Because it did not give them power to interfere with the management.

Mr. Hodges. That is so. Not to interfere with the manager in his work, but it did not give them power to make suggestions as to how the work should be carried on successfully?

Mr. Bramwell. It was not a question of suggestions.''
(Q. 21186-21190.)

Moreover the principle of the right to make technical criticisms was not always enforced even where formally conceded. In some cases the workers' side did not dare bring up the question or else simply let their opportunities pass. And a large number of committees definitely broke down in disputes over this issue.

This experience is worth setting out in such detail, because it brings us again to a consciously felt "frontier of control." The quality of the innovation that this trade union insistence on technique implied may be indicated by the grounds on which it was opposed by a minority of miners and a number of managers. Some of the former called it *doing the employer's work.* "When the miners' leaders began to draw the miners' attention to the loss of turns and pointed out to them that, if they only increased their attendance a little, it would increase the output by 13 million tons of coal, they soon told their leaders that it was the business of the employer to talk like that." Trade union officials were not paid for "advocating increased output which would only affect the coal-owner." On the other hand, as shown in Mr. Bramwell's testimony, managers felt that it was interfering with management and *taking the management out of their hands.* When a trade union is found vigorously doing the employer's work and taking it out of the management's hands, the case comes very near the center of the problem of control.

It is this background of quarrels and responsibilities regarding problems of actual production that makes somewhat less astonishing the part played by the Miners' Federation in the Coal Commission's inquiry. Their claim was not merely that the mine-workers should have higher wages and shorter hours; but that these demands could be met by improving the organization of the industry; and that the Miners were prepared both to suggest and to help carry out the necessary improvements. Detailed evidence of the technical defects of the industry was a more important part of the Miners' case than even the reports of the conditions of their housing.[3] "I want the mines nationalized," said Mr. Smillie on the occasion of a recent deputation to the Prime Minister, "in order that, by the fullest possible development on intelligent lines, with the assistance of the engineering power which we know we possess and the inventions which we know we possess, we might largely develop the mines and increase the output. That is one of our first claims."

[3] *E.g.,* Coal Commission Evidence, vol. I, pp. 321-322.

These cases in which the organized pressure of the trade unions is on the side of improvements in technique are emphasized, not as of frequent occurrence outside the industries named, but as the furthest extensions of constructive control. There are other instances of suggestions for improvement made by groups of workers still to be considered; the present section deals only with those in which improved technique has been definitely something for the trade union to fight for.

XVI

TECHNIQUE: SUGGESTIONS AND INVENTIONS

THE positive interferences in technique already mentioned had their beginnings, at least, in the demand for facilities for piece-work earnings. I do not mean that this is the only factor; the significant transition in motives from wages to workmanship has already been suggested. Still the beginnings were piece work, and the interferences were backed by the organized force of the unions. There are, however, other cases of an interest on the part of groups of workers in the betterment of technique which are not so immediately bound up with piece-work earnings and which are not to the same extent enforced by the unions. They are not, then, *insistences* on improvements; they are better classed as *suggestions and inventions*. Not as significant from the point of view of control as those just mentioned, they are, nevertheless, interesting as indicating some degree of joint action in the development of industrial technique.

The work of the individual inventor is beside our point, except as he is encouraged and protected by collective action. I heard a group of Midland working-class students debating with great interest the encouragement and protection of inventors and the state of the patent laws; they made no suggestion that it might be a subject for trade union and works committee action. Similarly the various schemes of individual firms for encouraging inventions and suggestions,—from the mere provision of "suggestion boxes" to the long-standing and successful systems of awards for inventions in force at William Denny's shipbuilding yard at Dumbarton and at Barr and Stroud's engineering works at Glasgow and the similar scheme introduced in March, 1919, at Cadbury's cocoa works at Bourneville which produced 759 suggestions in the first seven months—are not cases of workers' control; though it is hardly a coincidence that the first firm mentioned was, as pointed out by D. F. Schloss, a pioneer in devolution of responsibility to groups of workers and that all three have highly developed works committees.

A works committee is of course hardly likely to make inventions; that is not a political function. It may, as the Ministry of Labor's report on *Works Committees* suggests, do two things:—(1) create an atmosphere which will encourage the making of suggestions and (2) provide the machinery, by sub-committee or otherwise, for stimulating an interest in and for considering and testing inventions. As an illustration of the need for the first, the former labor superintendent of an engineering firm told me of a man who had been victimized by his foreman for suggesting to the manager an improvement in process. A sub-committee with a part of the latter function has just (October, 1919) been set up at Cadbury's at the suggestion of the workers' side of the Works Council. It is called the "Brains Committee" and its object is to hunt for promising talent among the employees. The works manager describes it as the "most talked-of thing in the works." The encouragement of inventions was clearly intended as an important part of the Whitley scheme. The following is a typical clause from the list of functions of a Joint Industrial Council:—

"The provision of facilities for the full consideration and utilization of inventions and improvements designed by work people and for the adequate safeguarding of the rights of the designers of such improvements." (Paint Color and varnish Industry.)

So much for inventions proper; there is still the field of suggestions in regard to meeting the various practical problems of organization and the planning of work. This is obviously a more natural subject for group action than the former; of this sort were the suggestions made by the Output Committees referred to in the last section.

Many works committees have discussed the actual arrangement of work; the report by the Ministry of Labor says that "testimony to the value of suggestions [made by them] . . . has been received from employers." The suggestions reported were usually on minor matters of detail; in one interesting case, however, a committee of pattern-makers suggested, as an alternative to dilution, the purchase of certain tools and brought about a 50% increase of output.[1] A recent instance is even more striking. The British Westinghouse Co. was considering closing down its foundry on account of the high cost of production. The works manager put the proposal before his shop stewards' committee. The committee objected and asked for two weeks in which to collect statistics of wages in other foundries in order to show that the high cost of production was not due to high wages. These figures were presented and indicated that the wages in the foundry were, if anything, lower than in competing ones. The committee argued that this showed that the trouble was one of organization and asked for another two weeks in which to prepare suggestions. At the end of that time the committee presented a memorandum on foundry organization—which the works manager described as the ablest he had

[1] P. 30, *Works Committees,* Industrial Report No. 2, Ministry of Labor.

ever seen, and the firm has decided to keep the foundry going and to spend hundreds of pounds in carrying out the committee's suggestions. The encouragement of suggestions is of course an integral part of the Whitley idea. The third report of the Whitley committee says of the works committees:—

"They should always keep in the forefront the idea of constructive co-operation in the improvement of the industry to which they belong. Suggestions of all kinds tending to improvement should be frankly welcomed and freely discussed. Practical proposals should be examined from all points of view. There is an undeveloped asset of constructive ability—valuable alike to the industry and to the State—awaiting the means of realization."

These read like merely pious and peace-loving phrases; the argument from the waste of ability in a system which discourages suggestions, however, I have heard from both sides,—from the head of the labor department of a manufacturers' association; from a foreman in one of the National Factories where suggestions had been taken from both the foremen's and the workmen's committees, and, most strikingly, in Mr. William Straker's evidently sincere reference before the Coal Commission to the "coal-owners' huge blunder" in neglecting to use the practical ability of the men. "For a generation," says the first

Sankey report (signed by the Chairman and three employer members of the Coal Commission), "the colliery worker has been educated socially and technically. The result is a great national asset. Why not use it?"

These are mainly arguments for what might be; the actual instances of workers' activity under this head amount to comparatively little. The organization of the facilities for invention and suggestions may become an important function of joint committees. It implies a direct assumption of a degree of interest in and responsibility for technique. At the moment, however, it is a much less significant form of workers' control than that collective enforcing of industrial efficiency mentioned under the "Insistence on Improvements."

XVII

TRADE POLICY: JOINT ACTION

THERE are still other people who write about control who make a .distinction similar to that used in the transition from discipline to technique Their argument runs like this:—The workers should have much to say about the immediate processes of production, which are the stuff of their daily life; but general trade policy—buying and selling, exchange, the market, the adjustment of supply and demand, large-scale research and planning—is obviously not their business. Again the moral may be disregarded and the distinction used for classification. Again, however, it must be recognized that it is not a rigid one:—unemployment, for example, is clearly a matter of general trade policy; there is no sharply logical line that sets off the invention of a device invented for use in a particular shop, from the organization of research for a great industry. And it will again be seen, in this and the following section, that the unions have not kept neatly to one side of the demarcation laid down in the theory. The present section will consider cases in which the unions have acted jointly with the employers in these matters; the next with cases of independent action or demands on the part of the workers.

A loose sort of joint action between employers' and workmen's organizations for the common purposes of their industries is of course no new thing. A rudimentary provision for it—now superseded by a Joint Industrial Council—is found in the rules of the conciliation boards in the building trades:—

"Although the principal objects of the Conciliation Boards are the settlement of disputes . . ., it shall also be within their province to meet and discuss any question of trade interest at the request of any of the parties to the agreement."

Apparently legislation was one of the trade questions intended. The Plumbers' board made this object more specific:—

"To consider any question affecting the Plumbing trade and to procure the improvement of any existing laws, usages and customs, which the Board may consider to be prejudicial to the trade, and to amend or oppose legislation or other measures or the establishment of any usages or customs which in the opinion of the Board might prejudicially affect our Craft."

The cotton industry gives the best examples of this sort of joint action. The Oldham agreement reads:—

"It is agreed that in respect to the opening of new markets abroad, the alteration of restrictive foreign tariffs and other similar matters which may benefit or injure the cotton trade, the same shall be dealt with by a Committee of three or more from each Federation, all the Associations agreeing to bring the whole weight of their influence to bear in furthering the general interests of the cotton industry in this country."

This clause has not been at all a dead letter; as witness the recent project of a trip to India and the United States by a party of cotton manufacturers and union leaders, and the well-known readiness with which both sides of the cotton industry will rally against Government interference —or answer the cry of Lancashire against London.

The logical, though infrequent, extension of the sort of co-operation suggested in the agreement mentioned is definite combination to fix prices "thereby securing better profits to manufacturers and better profits to work people" at the consumer's expense or to secure tariff or other preferential advantages. The former is evidently aimed at in the rules of the conciliation board for china manufacture:—

"*Mutual Trade Alliance*. . . . No Member of the Manufacturers' Association shall employ any workman who is not a Member of the Operatives' Association, and no workman shall take employment under any manufacturer who is not a Member of the Manufacturers'

Association, *or who is selling his goods at lower prices than those which from time to time are decided upon.*" (Italics mine.)

The "Birmingham Alliances," in six branches of the light metal trades, contain the same arrangement and the definite stipulation that prices are to be set by a "Wages Board, to be formed of an equal number of employers and employed."° The latter object—combination for trade war purposes —is sometimes said to be a main part of the Whitley scheme. "His (the Minister of Labor's) idea," said a trade union journal, "appears to be that joint bodies of employers and employed will be excellent institutions to conduct a trade war after the war." Some color is given to this view by the activity of one or two of the Joint Councils in asking for tariff advantages[1] and " anti-dumping" laws.

It is not fair, however, to suggest this as the only motive behind the Whitley scheme or even its chief outlet for joint action on trade policy. The first stated object of a Joint Industrial Council usually reads something like this:—

[1] *Cf.*, the sneer in one of the *Daily Herald's* " Hymns of Reconstruction,"—

> "Whitley Councils.
> Two opposite sides,
> Two opposite sides,
> See how they agree,
> See how they agree!
> They both are after Protection for trade
> That is the way that profits are made:
> No better example of mutual aid
> Than two opposite sides."

"To secure the largest possible measure of joint action between the employers and work people for the safe-guarding and development of the industry as a part of national life." (Bobbin and Shuttle Making Industry.)

The proposal by Mr. Malcolm Sparkes, a London master builder, which led to the formation of the Joint Industrial Council for the building trades began as follows:—

"The interests of employers and employed are in many respects opposed; but they have a common interest in promoting the efficiency and status of the service in which they are engaged and in advancing the well-being of its personnel."

And the phrase—"the industry as a national service"—has at least got from the building trades constitution into the conversation of local leaders. How much all this means in practice it is too early to say.

It is worth while, however, to look at some of the specific functions suggested under the head of this broad generalization. "The consideration of measures for regularizing production and employment" and the provisions for encouraging and protecting inventors have been mentioned in earlier sections. The Council for the Silk Industry (among others) provides for:—

"The regular consideration of, and the compilation of, available statistics as to wages, working costs, fluctuations in the cost of materials and Customs tariffs, and the study and promotion of scientific and practical systems of account keeping.''

A number of constitutions have clauses such as the following:—

"The encouragement of study and research with a view to the improvement and perfection of the quality of the product, and of machinery and methods of economical manufacture in all branches of the industry.'' (Match Manufacturing Industry.)

The program for the building trades council already quoted was even more specific in stating a similar object:—

"Continuous and Progressive Improvement—To provide a Clearing House for ideas, and to investigate, in conjunction with experts, every suggested line of improvement including, for example, such questions as:—
Industrial Control and Status of Labor.
Scientific Management and Increase of Output.
Welfare Methods.
Closer association between commercial and aesthetic requirements.''

It is again too early to say how much these projects mean. A sub-committee of the Building Trades Parliament is making an attempt to provide the basis for a complete reorganization of the industry. Its interim report on Organized Public Service in the Building Industry,[2] known as the

² See Note on Sources.

"Foster Report," has already been referred to under "Unemployment." Its recommendations, however, go much further than was there indicated. In addition to the provisions for making unemployment a charge on the industry and for the regularization of employment, the report recommends a regulation of the Wages of Management (on lines admittedly not yet worked out), a limitation and guarantee by the industry as a whole of the rate of interest on capital, and the disposal of the surplus earnings of the industry at the discretion of the Council. The detailed provisions under the last two heads are as follows:—

"The Hiring of Capital.

36. We recommend that approved capital, invested in the Building Industry, and registered annually after audit, shall receive a limited but guaranteed rate of interest, bearing a definite relation to the average yield of the most remunerative Government Stock. The fixing of the ratio will have to be worked out by further investigation, but we recommend that once determined upon, the guarantee shall apply to all firms in the Industry, except where failure to earn the aforesaid rate is declared by the Committee on the advice of the auditors to be due to incompetent management. . . .

The Surplus Earnings of the Industry.

40. . . . We, therefore, recommend:

(a) That the amount of the surplus earnings of the Industry shall be publicly declared every year, and accompanied by a schedule of the services to which the money has been voted.

    (b) That it shall be held in trust by a National Joint Committee of the Building Trades Industrial Council, and shall be applied to the following common services, which will be developed under the control of the Industry as a whole:—

1. Guarantee of Interest on approved capital, as outlined in paragraph 36.
2. Loans to firms in the Industry for purposes of development.
3. Education and research in various directions for improvement of the Industry, both independently and in co-operation with other industries.
4. Superannuation scheme for the whole registered personnel of the Industry.
5. Replacement of approved capital lost through no fault of the management.
6. Such other purposes as may be thought advisable.''

This project was vigorously and seriously debated at one meeting of the Building Trades Parliament and has been referred back to the same Committee for further consideration.

All these things mean the possibility of joint action, though in most cases they mean little activity on the part of the rank and file of workers, on a wide field of questions. For a review of the present situation in regard to control, however, they must be heavily discounted. In the older forms of joint action, those that are more purely for the sake of protection or prices, there is little evidence of labor acting as anything but a very junior partner; the newer forms are still almost entirely on paper.

This does not at all exhaust the account of cases of joint action on matters of business policy. As has already been suggested in earlier sections—for example in the account of the Westinghouse works committee's advice on foundry organization—certain individual firms have given opportunities for discussion at least on questions that would surely be classed under the heading of trade policy. A number of firms make the practice of telling their works committees about their prospective contracts, etc., and in some cases report considerable keenness on the part of their committees in discussing them. There was during the war a very striking experiment of real workers' control in this and in every field at a Newcastle aircraft factory—John Dawson and Co., Ltd. A joint body representing management and workers exercised almost the full powers of an ordinary board of directors. "The business of the Works Council," says the pamphlet edited by its secretary and published in March, 1919 under the title of *Democratic Control the Key to Industrial Progress,* "is to control matters of policy, consider and decide upon extension or contraction of business, and to provide for the maintenance of output.

The Workers' Representatives are elected by ballot, and have an equal voice with the Management Representatives in all decisions. There being no casting vote it is essential that both sides agree by a majority upon any question that may arise. In the absence of an agreement the subject would remain in abeyance until a common ground of action could be arrived at . . . . Broadly speaking, the functions of the Works Council may be defined as those of a Management Council which issues its decisions to the Executive Staff for that Staff to carry into effect.

The decisions of the Works Council on matters of policy are of necessity subject in all cases to the control of the Directors in regard to finance . . . The Directors have the responsibility of controlling the finance and sales organization of the Company, and the general work of the Staff. Whilst they are unfettered in regard to the exercise of their powers, the Works Council may call for, and in fact receives, all information in regard to the policy of the management, expansion of business and results of operations undertaken.'' The exclusion of the Works Council from financial control was explained by Mr. G. H. Humphrey, the Proprietor and originator of the scheme, as a matter of banking accommodation:—

"Dependent as we are on loans and the Banks, we have to maintain a Capitalist front to the world and a

Democratic one to the workers. As we are financed by loans we have to give personal guarantees, and our personal guarantees have no weight unless we own half the organization. I have, therefore, given away only one half of the voting stock of the Company, retaining the other half which I use as my ballast for my personal guarantees.''

This must of course be understood as one man's experiment, and not as an illustration of a large body of experience, and it is an experiment that is no longer in operation, since John Dawson's, though highly successful in war-time production, was unable to finance the readjustment to peace conditions. It is, however, of great interest as marking the most definite devolution of an employer's authority.

Of almost equal interest, and perhaps of greater importance, was the joint action on trade policy that was a by-product of State control during the war. It is true that trade union and employers' association representation on bodies charged with public functions was not quite unknown before the war; there was a minority of two labor members, for example, on the Port of London Authority. State action for war purposes made the practice of real importance. The State took over, in various degrees, the control over the most important industries in the country; in certain industries, this control was largely administered—after early attempts to do everything by State action—through bodies composed in part of representatives of employers and employed. This principle, it is true, did not extend to shipping; the National Maritime Board was a joint body, but its functions were merely conciliatory. The railways were and are administered under the Board of Trade by a Railway Executive Committee of railway presidents. The National Union of Railwaymen asked repeatedly for representation on this committee; the request was denied, but the following clause was inserted in the 1919 agreement:—

"When the new Ministry of Ways and Communications is set up it is the intention of the Government to provide in the organization for and to avail itself fully of the advantage of assistance, co-operation, and advice from the workers in the transportation industry."

Negotiations on this point are now (November, 1919) proceeding between the Government and the Railwaymen. Mr. J. H. Thomas announced at Bristol on November 16 that the Government had made an offer to the unions of three seats on the Railway Executive Committee.

In the other branches of the transport industry, road transport was administered without labor representation; but local consultative committees, on which the Transport Workers' Federation was represented, exercised certain functions in reference to both dock and canal traffic. The coal industry was much under State supervision from the outbreak of the war; by February, 1917, the Government had assumed complete control. At that time the Coal Mining Organization Committee, which included representatives of the Miners (Smillie, Hartshorn,$^{\circ}$ and Walsh)$^{\circ}$ and the mine-owners, and which had played an important part not only in conducting output campaigns but in suggesting economies of distribution was made into an Advisory Board to the Coal Controller, with equal representation from the two sides. The Miners' Federation was not satisfied with the limited and purely advisory powers of this Board, and at its 1918 Conference passed the following resolution:—

"In the opinion of this Conference the present form of Governmental control of the mines tends to develop into pure bureaucratic administration, which is in itself as equally inimical to the interests of the workmen and the industry as was the uncontrolled form of private ownership. We, therefore, propose that, pending the complete nationalization of the mines with joint control by the State and the workers, the present Joint Advisory Committee of the Coal Controller should be vested with directive power jointly with the Coal Controller."

In South Wales a Joint Allocation Committee was set up to meet the problem of distributing orders for the various grades of coal to the different collieries in order to bring about uniformity of employment throughout the coalfield. Mr. Hodges described this as "a taste of effective control in the allocation of trade," though Mr. Evan Williams of the coal-owners insisted that while, "you gave us valuable information," the scheme itself "was not put into operation." [3]

In the engineering and allied industries and particularly the production of munitions, the control exercised by the State was perhaps most direct and there was very little devolution of authority (except to the Munitions Tribunals already mentioned). In certain districts, however, notably the Northeast Coast and the Clyde, local Munitions of War Committees were set up with seven employers, seven union representatives and a number of State nominees. These were directly charged with the function of accelerating production. Mr. Cole wrote [4] of this as a step of great importance :—

"It will go down to history as the first definite and official recognition of the right of the workers to a say in the management of their own industries. Here for the first time the nominees of the workers meet those of the masters on equal terms, to discuss not merely wages, hours, or conditions of labor, but the actual business of production."

The real control exercised by these committees, however, varied widely with the degree of interest

[3] Coal Commission Evidence, Questions 23705-23714.
[4] *Labor in War Time*, p. 198.

shown by the workers in the different localities.

The most striking examples of joint administration by employers and employed were the Wool and Cotton Control Boards. The Government was the chief consumer of wool during the war. Early in 1916 it took considerable power under the Defence of the Realm Act to direct production, and in the same year bought almost the entire supply of raw material in order to establish priorities for war work. In April, 1917, an Advisory Committee, on which the unions had five members as against twenty-four representing the employers and merchants, was set up and immediately extended the system of priorities and drastically restricted the hours to be worked by mills employed in the civilian trade. During August and September, after considerable unrest in the industry, the Wool Control Board—eleven representatives of the unions, eleven of the employers, and eleven of the War Office Contracts Department— was set up with extensive powers in organizing the civilian trade and full power to ration raw material to the various branches of the industry and to the particular firms engaged. "Clearly," says the *Labor Year Book* (1919), "the principle of equal representation of Trade Unions with the employers on a body possessing such powers creates a precedent of the greatest possible importance, and one which is still strongly resented by some employers in the industry.''

The Cotton Control Board—which in its final form consisted of seven employers and merchants, seven union leaders, and two nominees of the Board of Trade—exercised even more important administrative powers.º The problem in the case of cotton was the shortage of raw material; many of the ships that had formerly brought cotton were either sunk or diverted to other purposes. The object of control was to regulate the price of the raw material and to conserve the supply. The Control Board was set up on June 28, 1917; its first acts were to regulate purchases by a system of licenses and to take a complete census of cotton stocks. It was soon given full powers to fix the price of the raw material and to allocate it among the different firms. The latter function was performed by restricting the percentage of spindles that could be run on other than Government work. An important extension of the Board's duties resulted from the effects of the shortage and the consequent restriction. Some provision had to be made for those unemployed. The arrangement made was this: firms were to be allowed to exceed the specified percentage of spindles on payment of a levy for all spindles in excess; this levy became an unemployment fund which was administered, on agreed principles, wholly by the trade unions. This was discussed in Section IV as an application of the principle that unemployment should be a charge on the industry and as a definite delegation of responsibility to the trade unions for administering benefit.

The case of the Cotton Control Board has been taken—by Mr. Penty, for example, in his *Industrial Crisis and the Way Out*—as a striking instance of trade union direction of industry. It is easy to make out the case. Here were a group of union leaders on a Board which was charged with the responsibility of meeting the problems of a great industry in a great emergency and which was given almost unlimited powers to say what work should or should not be done and what machines should or should not be kept running. These were great and executive powers—certainly an opportunity for positive control. The best evidence, however, seems to be that, except as regards the unemployment benefit which they administered independently and with little friction, the control exercised by the union leaders was more negative than positive. They were there to see that no harm was done to the unions; the constructive planning was left almost entirely to a few of the employers and civil servants. This was not because the union leaders, being in a minority, were voted down; it was because they attended only the formal weekly meetings—the real planning

was done between them. It is true that the employers at the end of the war hastened to secure the
abolition of the board for fear the union leaders
would through it learn to run the industry; there
is no evidence, however, that they even thought of
taking their position as an opportunity for learning control.

Joint action for commercial purposes is then
not unheard of. The Whitley proposals are of
some importance in offering a possibility of widen-
ing the range of subjects. Joint acceptance of
public responsibility for the conduct of industry
was a significant war development. The next section will discuss the few trade union attempts at
independent action in these fields.

XVIII

TRADE POLICY: WORKERS' DEMANDS

THE previous section dealt with joint action on trade policy—action rarely initiated from the labor side and carried on for joint purposes. The present section deals with attempts by the workers to manipulate trade policy for their own purposes, with their independent suggestions for improvement in trade policy, and with their demands for trade and financial information. The actual instances are less frequent; the fact that the initiative comes from the workers, however, makes them of interest for a study of control.

The last section discussed the "Birmingham Alliances," a rare instance of trade unions joining with their employers to rig prices. There are also rare instances of trade unions trying to rig prices on their own account by limitation of output, or of trade unions disagreeing with their employers as to the best means of rigging prices. The classic illustration of the latter is the cotton dispute of 1878 described by the Webbs. The owners announced a ten per cent reduction of wages to meet a depression due to a glut in the market. The unions argued that the way to meet a glut in the market was to stop overproduction, and offered to accept the reduction in wages on condition that the factories should work only four days a week. "One hundred thousand factory workers," said the Weavers' Manifesto, "are waging war with their employers as to the best possible way to remove the glut from an overstocked market, and at the same time reduce the difficulties arising from an insufficient supply of raw cotton. To remedy this state of things the employers propose a reduction of wages. . . . We contend that a reduction in the rate of wages cannot either remove the glut in the cloth market or assist to tide us over the difficulty arising from the limited supply of raw material." The ten weeks' strike over economic policy finally ended in the complete defeat of the workers.

The cotton unions have on this and other occasions claimed, unsuccessfully, a right to force upon the employers their notions of the way to adjust output to demand in order to maintain prices and wages. The Miners alone have once or twice attempted to do the adjusting on their own account. Two facts may partly explain this. For a long period of years the coal-owners in certain districts, notably Northumberland, had agreed to a limitation of output—"the limitation of the vend"—for the purpose of keeping up the price of coal; of this the workers were, of course, aware and in Lancashire had even been at times parties to the agreement. In the second place, the miners' wages in many districts were governed, either under formal *sliding scale* agreement or according to the general practice of arbitrators, by the selling price of coal; manipulation of the selling price by the owners or dealers was thus felt by the miners to be "gambling with men's wages." It is not then surprising that the Miners have in a few instances insisted that, "supply and demand should be adjusted rather by diminishing the output than by forcing coal upon unwilling buyers." In 1892 the Miners saved themselves from a reduction in wages, threatened on account of the great surplus stocks of coal [1] which the coal-owners could not sell, by arbitrarily taking a week's holiday. A similar issue arose just before the outbreak of war in 1914. The Scottish Miners were threatened with a reduction which would have brought their wages below the national minimum agreed on by the Miners' Federation; yet they were under agreement to submit to arbitration, and the lowered price of coal, due to overproduction, would be used as the chief argument against them. The Scottish union, apparently following an expedient sometimes practiced in Lanarkshire, decided to work only four days a week in order to

[1] It is very difficult in 1919 to think back to a time when there could have been "great surplus stocks of coal" in England.

reduce the surplus and to force up the price. The matter was vigorously debated at a conference of the Miners' Federation of Great Britain. "When they were last before the neutral chairman," said a Scottish delegate, "one of the grounds put forward for the reduction of 25% was that some of the collieries were only working two or three days a week, and because of the glut of coal in the market prices were going down. The four-days policy would enable all their men to get an equal share of work, and would also take in hand the insane competition amongst the sellers of coal." The question was argued at length. For the policy it was urged that:—

"If the employers will not so regulate the working of the mines as to prevent the overproduction and bring wages up to a decent living wage, then the workers themselves are entitled to take the matters into their own hands."

On the other hand there was a strong feeling against "the acceptance of the principle of the policy of restriction." The Conference finally decided not to approve the four-days policy, but to support the Scottish Miners in case their wages fell below the agreed minimum. Within two weeks the Great War had broken out; and in the "industrial truce" that followed immediately, and with the increased demand for coal which was a more lasting effect of the war, the issue was not pressed.

These direct attempts to regulate the amount of production for the sake of wages are unusual even in the two industries named and practically unknown outside. There are, however, cases of suggestions for changes in trade policy less immediately connected with wages. The Miners' demand that "small coal" should be brought to the surface and used and paid for is perhaps a border case. The demand begins with wages; it is supported by arguments of the danger of "gob fires" when the coal is stowed in the workings and of the national waste involved. The 1916 Conference resolved:—

"That the Miners' Federation of Great Britain be urged to take immediate steps to bring before the Coal Control Board the enormous national loss caused by the practice of stowing small coal in the workings, with a view of making the necessary arrangements for securing that all coal produced in the mines should be sent to the surface."

A long-standing argument of the Miners for nationalization that on the ground of *conservation,* is clearly a demand for an improvement in the policy of the industry:—

"Unless we press for the nationalization of mines at once there will be nothing but the worst seams left for the nation to work."

A very large part of the Miners' case before the Coal Commission was taken up with the argument on technical grounds that unification by national-ization would make possible a number of improve-ments [2]—the pooling of privately-owned railway trucks, for example—in trade policy.

The most conspicuous instance of a trade union suggesting schemes for the improvement of its industry is that of the Postal and Telegraph Clerks' Association. Some years ago its parent society (United Kingdom Postal Clerks' Associa-tion) printed a pamphlet containing a scheme for extending the service by the institution of a postal banking scheme. Its foreword read:—

"With a view to bringing before the public the pos-sibilities of the British Postal Service as a means of pro-viding the business community and the general public with the facilities for the transaction of business, the United Kingdom Postal Clerks' Association has been tabulating evidence and information concerning the Postal Services of other countries.

This pamphlet outlines the most remarkable feature of Post Office activity which has taken place during the last five years, viz., the development of the Post Office Bank-ing Business for the transmission of moneys, known as the Postal Cheque and Transfer Service.

The importance of the subject from a business stand-

[2] These suggestions are listed in two of the first set of reports issued by the Coal Commission—that of Justice Sankey and three employers and that of the six labor representatives. Cmd. 87 and 85.

point has impelled the Postal Clerks' Association to place this matter before the public with a view to directing attention to Postal affairs, so that the Post Office Authorities may be induced to improve and develop the Service on the lines indicated."

With either the details or the merits of the project, this inquiry is, of course, not concerned; the point is that it represents the expenditure of trade union money and energy in attempting to force what is believed to be an improvement of the service in which its members are engaged. Apparently this intention is still of importance to the Postal and Telegraph Clerks. A resolution passed at their 1916 Conference declared:—

"This Conference is convinced that . . . the most effective work which the Executive Committee can accomplish during the period immediately before us will be by applying itself to consideration of the problem of development of the Service, having in mind the needs of the community, the possibility of increased services to the community . . ." and the betterment of conditions for the staff.

Another resolution passed at the same Conference shows the direct bearing of this sort of interest in industry on the problem of control:—

"Having in view the possibility of the Association assuming in the future more direct and active participation in the administration of the Postal Service, this Conference recommends the organization within the branches of circles for 'craft' study and discussion. Members of the Association only to be admitted to such circles."

The Branch moving the resolution had already started such a study group. Similarly the Executive Committee urged the rank and file to educate themselves to apply the Whitley report and in turn to use the Whitley scheme as an education in control: [3]—

"Members should begin to study minutely the conditions of their offices and the history of trade and industry, so that when the time comes they are prepared to administer the principle with a statesmanship worthy of a great trade union."

In more than one union the preaching of the study of the industry as a step toward control has been part of recent propaganda by the leaders.[4] The fear of just this was a reason for the employers' objection to the Cotton Control Board already referred to— the fear that the union leaders would learn too much about finance,[5] perhaps by hearing

[3] In a speech condemning the Whitley report as offering no real workers' control, I heard one of the ablest of the younger advocates of control taking this attitude toward the labor sympathizers on the Whitley committee:—don't blame them; they were trying to provide a training ground.

[4] One of them declared, however that, "you might as well talk to wooden dummies."

[5] The cotton union secretaries had long had the reputation of knowing a great deal about the financial position of their industry.

the merchants and manufacturers accuse each other of profiteering. The labor side of the Wool Control Board was more conscious of this possibility, and several of the leaders regret bitterly the chance lost by not putting a representative on the full-time staff of the Board.

This desire for a general knowledge of the workings of industry and finance with a direct eye to learning control is confined to a very few. The demand for *publicity of profits* is a widespread one. Oh yes, said a trade union leader to me, the employers will discuss anything with us *"except perhaps costing and profits."* Here is another keenly-felt frontier of control. It was touched on by a Scottish miner in the debate on the Miners' Four Days in 1914:—

"If any such increase in the cost of production has taken place, they [the employers] will have to open their books and prove it, and further, we want to know what profits have been during these periods on the price obtained. They say they will never open their books to us and show their profits, as in their opinion we have nothing to do with profits; that is a question for them."

By 1919 the coal-owners were in fact opening their books to show their profits to the Coal Commission.

D. F. Schloss quoted one of them as follows:—" We know . . the general rate of profits, depreciation, costs, etc., . . . and we know that after we have got our wages out of it, and we leave the balance to the employer, he has nothing to make a great noise about."

It is hard to overestimate the importance of the
Commission in this connection, first, because of
the actual profits revealed, second, because of the
Commission's practically unanimous recommendation in favor of future publicity of profits, and
third, because of its effect in encouraging a similar
demand in other trades. The first result is of no
concern for the present inquiry. The second is
of importance and has been given comparatively
little public attention for the very reason that it
was an agreed recommendation. The Chairman's
report and Sir Arthur Duckham's are on this matter identical in substance. The latter reads as
follows:—

"It is essential that there should be complete publicity as to the operations and financial results of the
coal industry. The Ministry of Mines should be expressly charged with the duty of publishing, not less
than once a year, figures showing the cost of getting coal
in each of the districts of the country, and the proportion chargeable to materials, wages, general expenses,
interest, profits, and other general items."

The other five employers do not touch definitely
upon this point in their recommendations, but they
quote with evident approval the even more emphatic opinion expressed in the evidence and
scheme submitted by the Mining Association of
Great Britain:—

"The authors [of the coal-owners' project] *contend that want of knowledge with respect to prices, costs and profits, and the absence of machinery conferring upon the workers opportunities for obtaining information* and influencing the conditions under which they work have been to a great extent the cause of the existing discontent.

The authors propose that, in future, fluctuations of the wages of the workers in each mining district, over and above the minimum rates, should, instead of being regulated solely as in the past by selling prices, be regulated by reference also to costs and profits in that district.

For this purpose, *average prices, costs and profits* in each district *are to be jointly ascertained, so that the workers may be able in future to discuss questions of wages with a complete knowledge of the results of the industry* in that district.'' (Italics mine.)

On the third point—the influence which the great publicity of the Commission's work has had in encouraging similar demands in other industries it is too early to gather much evidence. One expression of it, from a prominent building trades official, was something like this:—we'll never again accept the plea that they can't afford an advance until they show us the books!

These trade union demands on the subject of trade policy are neither many nor of frequent occurrence, but the range they cover is significantly wide. In a few cases the unions have tried to alter their employers' trade policy in adjusting output to demand. In others they have suggested specific improvements in trade policy. And finally they have made some claim to be shown the inner workings of the business direction of industry.

XIX

THE EXTENT OF CONTROL

THE attempt has been made in the preceding sections to indicate the specific sorts of control of industry now exercised by organized workers in Great Britain. I know no way of adding these and making a neat sum. How much control have the workers got? There is no use in making general answers, like "very little" or "a good deal." But in weighing and judging the extent of control, certain distinctions which have been implicit in the previous discussion are worth making explicit.

"*Agreeable* control is better than *enforced* control," I heard a Birmingham toolmaker say. "Invasion, not admission, should be the trade unionist's watchword," said one of the prominent Guild Socialists. The distinction is of some importance. Which is better depends on what you want, and on economy of effort in getting it; but, from the point of view of definition, enforced control is control in a more real sense. There is a significant psychological difference between "admission" and "invasion," between control presented to and control seized by a trade union. The distinction may be made clearer by illustration. When "Bedstead Smith" organized the first of the "Birmingham Alliances" and let the trade unions come in on the deal, the sort of workers' "control" over price-fixing that resulted was a very different thing from the sort of control that would have resulted, say, if the "Miners' Four Days" policy in 1914 had been applied and had raised the price of coal. Control implies initiative; for that reason, forms of control entirely initiated from above must be ruled out unless or until they are shown to involve workers' *activity* as well as *acquiescence*. On that ground co-partnership and similar bits of "control" offered to workers in connection with profit-sharing schemes have been left out of consideration. This same distinction accounts for the paradox of a refusal of control pointed out with such surprise in the chairman's statement of the Ebbw Vale Steel, Iron, and Coal Co. (July 2, 1919) :—

"After very mature consideration your directors decided to extend an invitation to one of the great trade unions to nominate one of their number to occupy a seat on this board. We felt that the presence of a representative of labor on this board, with all the privileges, with all the responsibilities of an ordinary director, would perhaps give him the opportunity of realizing the many difficulties which from time to time confront those men whose duty it is to control the destinies of our great industrial companies. We felt that in realizing and appreciating our difficulties he might possibly be able to take a broader view of the many questions which have from time to time to be settled between capital and labor; we felt that the presence of a representative of labor on this board would have given an opportunity to myself and to my colleagues to have learned the views of labor at first hand.

"I regret to say our invitation to labor has been refused. In that I am somewhat surprised and considerably disappointed. If labor seeks to control industry, then labor should be prepared to serve its apprenticeship side by side with men who have made it their lifelong study."

Real control of industry cannot be presented like a Christmas-box.

Certain of the advocates of "control" push this distinction even to the point of saying that joint control cannot be in any sense workers' control. Mr. J. T. Murphy, the spokesman of the Shop Stewards' Movement, publishes an attack on the Whitley proposals with the significant title, "Compromise or Independence," in which he says that:—

"A 'joint' committee can only be a committee of employers and employees formed to prevent any encroachment on the power of the dominant body, in this case the employers."

But this is surely an overstatement. The Building Trades Council's committee on "Organized

Public Service" hardly fits Mr. Murphy's definition; and it is impossible to imagine Mr. Smillie,
for example, losing his independence by sitting
on a joint body like the Coal Mining Organization
Committee. It is impossible to rule out all forms
of joint control; the test must be whether in the
particular instance of joint control the workers'
side is independently active. Joint control when
the lead is entirely from the employing side—as
in co-partnership and the "Birmingham Alliances"—may be disregarded. But the Whitley
Councils must be studied and judged by their actions; the classification of each council depends
not on its constitution but on the purely empirical
question whether the chief function of the workers'
side is to be that of junior partnership in petition-
ing for Protection and similar favors from the
Government or whether, as is already the case in
the Building Trades Council, the workers' side is
to play an active part in shaping policy. "One
point, however, must be made clear," says Mr.
Malcolm Sparkes, the chief founder of that council,
in an article maintaining that the Industrial Council Movement is going in the same direction as the
Shop Stewards' Movement. "In itself the Industrial Council is no solution for the problem of control. It is, however, an instrument that can produce the solution." The same test of actual independence of function applies also to joint bodies

exercising state-given powers. This was the basis of the questions asked in Section XVII about the Cotton Control Board. So with the various schemes of voluntary "devolution of managerial functions." The initiative here is clearly from the top. Mr. Humphrey of John Dawson's makes the distinction in the pamphlet already cited:—

"There is a likelihood of a great educative movement amongst the working classes as a result of which they will *take* a large measure of control, and their obstructive employers will wish they had given joint control in their own works when they had the chance to do it gracefully."

Until such schemes are actively taken up by the workers, they amount to nothing in the way of control, however much they cover on paper. But when or if they are so taken up, they should not be ruled out because of their origin; what begins as a gift may become a right. The line between "agreeable" and "enforced" control, or better between *dependent* and *independent* control, must be drawn not on the ground of the origin of control or even of the extent of control, but solely by the test of whether or not the workers' side does actually exert an independent force.

A similar distinction, and one more frequently drawn, is that between *negative* and *positive* con-

trol. It is a commonplace that the control now
exercised by the workers is mainly negative—that
they may sometimes say "no," or say that work
must not be done, or changes must not be introduced, except under certain conditions, but they
can very rarely say that this or that must be done.
They are in the position, as Mr. Tawney says, of
"an Opposition that never becomes a Government." It is easy to confirm this from the instances given; most of the "trade union conditions"—of hiring, apprenticeship, demarcation,
and the rest—are clearly negative. It is much
shorter to enumerate the instances of positive control. In the staffing of shops and in the selection
of foremen, the Stuff Pressers exercise positive
choice. There are other cases of independent administration by the workers within sharply limited
fields, for example by the printers' "clicker" in
allocating work and by the miners' safety inspectors. The workmen directors at Dawson's were
charged with positive functions; certain shop
stewards actually—though not in name—exercised
directive powers during the war. And finally there
are the "Insistences on Changes in Technique"
by the Miners' output committees and others,
which were emphasized because of the great current significance of this distinction. Positive control covers then only a very small proportion of
the cases even of that independent control defined

in the preceding paragraph. On the other hand, a number of the newer demands are put forward with just this sort of control in mind. The Clyde committee, whose proposals were quoted in Section XV, wanted the right to say not *under what conditions* machinery *might* be introduced but actually *where it should* be introduced. The object of the scheme of collective contract put forward is to "take over a whole province" of industrial direction from the employers. In fact the essence of the new demand of labor, as was stated by Mr. Henry Clay in the *Observer,* is for "participation in the direction and not merely in the regulation of industry." Insistence on this distinction does not imply that regulation and negative control are not real control or that they are not of great importance. The standard of foremanship, for example, is maintained almost entirely by the highly negative process of insurgence. And the right to say *yes* or *no* shades very easily into the right to say *which* or *what*. But the distinction is worth emphasizing, as indicating the new Frontier of Control—over which the conscious struggle is marked on the one hand by Mr. Frank Hodges' demand on behalf of the workers for "the daily exercise of directive ability" and on the other by Lord Gainford's testimony before the Coal Commission:—

"I am authorized to say on behalf of the Mining Association that if owners are not to be left complete executive control they will decline to accept the responsibility of carrying on the industry."

A third distinction—and one that I have nowhere seen definitely stated—is that between what might be called *old craft* or *customary* control on the one hand and *conscious* or *contagious* control on the other. This is based not on the greater or less degree of "reality" of control exercised but on the nature and policy of the union exercising it. It is a distinction of no importance if the object of inquiry is merely the static one of presenting the sum of instances of control. But for any study in terms of process, for any study that pretends to estimate moving tendencies, it seems to me of the highest importance. The more striking instances of control already mentioned fall quite clearly into two main classes:—on the one hand control long exercised as a customary right by conservative, exclusive, and usually small unions in old skilled crafts, fighting if at all only to resist "encroachments" on their ancient privileges; and on the other hand control newly and consciously won by aggressive, propagandist, usually industrial, unions in the great organized industries, fighting not to resist encroachments but to make them. The Stuff Pressers, the Hand Papermakers, the Glass Bottle Makers,[1] the Calico Printers and, less typically, the Compositors are instances of the former class of unions. The Miners and the Railwaymen are the most highly-developed examples of the latter. Cases of these two sorts of control, or of the first sort and of the demand for the second, have been set down side by side in almost every section:—full control over employment exercised by the Stuff Pressers and full control over employment demanded by certain industrial unionists among the Engineers; sharing of work long practised by the Yorkshire Glass Bottle Makers and rationing of employment demanded by the Clyde Engineers; the Hand Papermakers long guaranteed "six days' custom" and the Railwaymen this year securing a guaranteed weekly wage; the Stuff Pressers choosing their own foremen and the activists among Engineers, Miners, Railwaymen, and Postal Workers pushing for the right; Compositors and Miners alike enforcing a standard of foremanship and preventing "policing"; the printers' clicker allocating work by long custom and certain Tramwaymen securing it as a new right; co-operative work in the Cornish tin mines and collective contract a new demand of Glasgow engineers; and so on. The difference then is not primarily in the actual bits of control exercised, nor is it merely a matter of the date

[1] See above, p. 158.

of acquisition of power. If the latter difference
did not carry with it a totally different attitude of
mind and if, for example, an official of the Stuff
Pressers toured the country with Mr. Frank
Hodges of the Miners and seconded the latter's
speeches on behalf of "Workers' Control" by
stating that his union had had some workers' control and had found it good, the distinction might
very well be ignored. But in point of fact, nothing
like this does or could happen. In the first place,
the old crafts have no theories of the value of control for control's sake. Just for this reason the
Stuff Pressers are giving up their right to elect
foremen almost without protest, since the change
is going on with no immediate practical loss.
Similarly the old crafts are thoroughly conservative; they are engaged in defending "established
expectations"[2] just as definitely as the advocates

[2] The old craft type of mind is best described on p. 571 of
Industrial Democracy:—" The Doctrine of Vested Interests. . . .
is naturally strongest in the remnants of the time-honored ancient
handicrafts. Those who have troubled to explore the nooks and
crannies of the industrial world, which have hitherto escaped the
full intensity of the commercial struggle, will have found in them
a peculiar type of Trade Union character. Wherever the Doctrine of Vested Interests is still maintained by the workmen, and
admitted by the employers—where, that is to say, the conditions
of employment are consciously based, not on the competitive
battle but on the established expectations of the different classes
—we find an unusual prevalence, among the rank and file, of what
we may call the 'gentle' nature—that conjunction of quiet dignity, grave courtesy, and consideration of other people's rights
and feelings, which is usually connected with old family and long-
established position. But this type of character becomes every
day rarer in the Trade Union world." No contract could be
sharper than that between this "gentleness" and the aggressive-

of the newer control are in the broad sense revolutionary and out to attack "established expectations." The father of a compositors' chapel talks of the London "Scale" with much the same reverence that a thoroughgoing engineers' shop steward saves for the Social Revolution. And as a natural corollary, the old crafts are exclusive and aristocratic and play little part in the labor movement; the advocates of the newer control are widely propagandist. The Stuff Pressers keep themselves to themselves and hug their monopoly; the authors of the *Miners' Next Step* are propagandists for control on the expressed ground that:—

"We cannot get rid of employers and slave-driving in the mining industry, until all other industries have organized for and progressed towards the same objective. Their rate of progress conditions ours; all we can do is to set an example and the pace."

This difference in intention clearly makes a difference in results. Nobody supposes that the Railwaymen demanded a guaranteed week because the Hand Papermakers had one; on the other hand,

ness of the modern advocate of the Doctrine of Workers' Control. The latter temper at its extreme may be indicated by a few sentences from one of J. T. Murphy's pamphlets:—" They [the employers] struggled through the centuries to obtain their power. We also of the working-class have come through the long years of strife and have suffered their batterings and their spite. We do not squeal. Struggle is the law of life. As we see they rose on the backs of our class we see and feel now the gathering power of the labor hosts."

the publicity of profits which the Miners secured through the Coal Commission almost immediately becomes a demand in other trades. This distinction is of great importance in estimating the potential significance of these forms of workers' control. *Old craft* control is traditional and clings on but does not spread. On the other hand, news of each "invasion" made by the theorists and propagandists of the newer control is carried to other trades and made the basis of agitation there. It is for this reason that the word "contagious" seems a significant one for describing this newer and more conscious control. The two things are not the same:—*old craft control* almost necessarily implies small groups of skilled workers; the advocates of *contagious control* are for the most part either members of industrial unions or strong advocates of industrial unionism; the temper of the old crafts is monopolistic and conservative; that of the latter, propagandist and revolutionary. Undoubtedly there is some slight degree of cross-influence, just as the various attempts at independent associations of producers have no doubt had some influence on the present and very different demand for control. The printing unions are by no means isolated from the general tendencies of the labor movement,[3] and of course there are

---

[3] The printing unions were among the first to offer their help to the Railwaymen during the recent strike.

many unions of various sorts between the two extreme types indicated here. But the types are widely and fundamentally different, and it seems to me almost futile to argue from the experience of one to the other:—equally futile, for example, to argue that direct election of foremen would be a good thing for all industry because it worked for a long time with the Stuff Pressers, or to argue that the right to elect foremen is proved of no use to other workmen because the Stuff Pressers are giving it up without protest. And for the purpose of attempting to forecast future developments, the distinction is of the highest importance. It raises the entire question of the historical relation between the type of industrial technique and the type of industrial government. You cannot base a theory of modern industry on the tin mines of Cornwall. *Old craft* control is a survival from an earlier technology and is clearly dying out with the industrial conditions that made it possible. *Contagious* control is a demand made in view of the newer industrial technique; the judgment as to whether or not it is to grow must be made independently of the decay of the other.

The answer to the question, *How much control?* depends, then, on whether or not the question itself is qualified in any of the three senses indicated above. If it is not qualified, the nearest answer that can be given is:—all the control indicated in the earlier sections and whatever more may be thought of under co-partnership or other devices of "industrial peace." If the question is *how much independent control?*—and this seems to me the broadest sense in which the term "control" can be used with any significance—the few cases mentioned in which the initiative lies entirely with the employers must be ruled out, and all instances of joint control must be narrowly examined to see whether they involve workers' activity or merely workers' acquiescence. If the question is *how much positive control?*—and this question is of importance as marking the newest Frontier of Control—the answer can be given in a very few instances,—of which the staffing of shops and choice of foremen by the Stuff Pressers, the work of the labor-directors at Dawson's, and the insistences by a few Miners' output committees on specific improvements in management, are the most conspicuous. If the question is *how much contagious control?*—and this question is important for any guesses about the future—nearly half the cases mentioned, including some of the more striking forms of positive control and the greater part of the negative control covered by the phrase "the right to a trade," must be ruled out as having little bearing on the moving tendencies in the great industry.

NOTE ON SOURCES

The following is a brief list of the more valuable sources of material on workers' control—of those, that is, that can be obtained outside the Labour Research Department or Scotland Yard.

I. BRITISH GOVERNMENT PUBLICATIONS.

(H. M. Stationery Office, Imperial House, Kingsway, London W. C. 2.)

Report on Collective Agreements. 1910, Cd. 5,366.

The most comprehensive cross-section picture of the extent and variety of trade union agreements.

Annual *Reports on Strikes and Lockouts.* 1910, Cd. 5,850. 1911, Cd. 6,472. 1912, Cd. 7,089. 1913, Cd. 7,658.

A valuable indication of the magnitude and, less accurately, the causes of strikes. The sections on the specific issues of strikes are especially suggestive. The classification of causes is, however, inconvenient for the purposes of the student of control.

Report of the Commissioners on Industrial Unrest. 1917.

The section on South Wales discusses the demand for control.

Works Committees. Ministry of Labour. Industrial Report No. 2. (Reprinted in America by the Bureau of Industrial Research, New York.)

The most useful single official document on workers' control. Ably written and packed with invaluable factual material. Further material is being collected for a second edition.

The Whitley Report. Ministry of Labour. Industrial Report No. 1.

Industrial Councils. Ministry of Labour. Industrial Report No. 4.

Sample provisions from the constitutions of Whitley Councils.

Recommendations of the Provisional Joint Committee of the Industrial Conference. 1919, Cmd. 139.

A somewhat startling indication of the things on which British employers and workers agree.

Coal Industry Commission. Interim Reports. 1919, Cmd. 84, 85, 86.

Coal Industry Commission. Reports of Second Stage. 1919, Cmd. 210.

The famous "Sankey Report" recommending nationalization of the mines with a considerable measure of workers' control.

Coal Industry Commission. Minutes of Evidence. Cmd. 359, 360.

The record of a great public clinic in the economics and psychology of modern industry. Control is a leading theme throughout. A great mine of valuable material on this and other subjects that has not yet been worked over by students.

II. SOURCE MATERIALS ON WORKERS' CONTROL.

A. THE PROPAGANDA OF "COMPLETE CONTROL."

The Miners' Next Step. Unofficial Reform Committee. Tonypandy, South Wales. 1912.

Industrial Democracy for Miners. A Plan for the Democratic Control of the Mining Industry. The Industrial Committee of the South Wales Socialist Society, Porth, Rhondda Valley, South Wales, 1919.

The contrast between these two pamphlets, the work of the same group of rank-and-file extremists, is a striking indication of the increasing hopefulness with which the claim for control is urged. *The Miners' Next Step* is bitter and purely destructive, advocating the irritation strike, and is still publicly referred to with bated breath as the type of all that is criminal in syndicalism. Its sequel is hopeful and entirely concerned with constructive, though equally "impossibilist," plans of organizing control.

J. T. Murphy. *The Workers' Committee.* Sheffield Workers' Committee, 56 Rushdale Road, Meersbrook, Sheffield. 1918.

By the chief spokesman for the Shop Stewards Movement. Claimed a sale of 30,000 copies up to May, 1919.

J. T. Murphy. *Compromise or Independence? An Examination of the Whitley Report.* Sheffield Workers' Committee.

W. Gallecher and J. Paton. *Towards Industrial Democracy: A Memorandum on Workshop Control.* Trades and Labour Council, Paisley, Scotland. 1917.

A scheme of "collective contract" devised by two of the Clyde shop stewards. Taken up in the propaganda of the National Guild League.

B. The Miners' Case for Control.

> R. Page Arnot. *Facts from the Coal Commission* and *Further Facts from the Coal Commission.* Miners' Federation, Russell Square, London. 1919.
>
> A skillful abridgment of the most telling evidence for the Miners' case. The second pamphlet contains the text of the Miners' Bill for Nationalization.

> Frank Hodges. *The Nationalisation of the Mines.* Parsons. London. 1920.
>
> By the Secretary of the Miners' Federation, who of all prominent labor leaders has most consistently thought of himself as a student of the control problem.

C. "Joint Control" in the Building Trades.

> *Organized Public Service in the Building Industry.* The Industrial Council for the Building Industry. 48 Bedford Square, London. 1919.
>
> The far-reaching "Foster Report" presented by a sub-committee of the Building Trades Parliament.

> Thos. Foster. *Masters and Men.* Headley. London.
>
> Mr. Foster is a prominent building trades employer, a Guild Socialist, and chairman of the committee that drafted the "Foster Report."

> *History of the Building Trades Parliament.* Garton Foundation. London. 1919.
>
> First-hand. Somewhat sentimental.

D. Employers' Experiments with Control.

> C. G. Renold. *Workshop Committees. Suggested Lines of Development.* Hans Renold, Ltd., Manchester. 1917. (Reprinted in America by the Survey.)
>
> Mr. Renold is a Cornell graduate and the managing director of a highly successful and somewhat "Americanized" chain factory outside of Manchester.

> *Democratic Control the Key to Industrial Progress.* John Dawson, Ltd., Newcastle-on-Tyne. 1919.
>
> An account of the boldest attempt on the part of an employer (Mr. G. H. Humphreys) to give control to the workers. The firm flourished during the war but failed to survive the peace.

E. An Engineer's Counterblast Against Control. Alex. Richardson. *The Man-Power of the Nation.* Reprinted from *Engineering,* 35 Bedford St., Strand, London. 1916.

III. BOOKS ON BRITISH TRADE UNIONISM.

Sidney and Beatrice Webb. *History of Trade Unionism.* Longmans, Green. London, New York. 1894.

Sidney and Beatrice Webb. *Industrial Democracy*. Longmans, Green. London, New York. 1897.

The two great classics of trade unionism. I have drawn heavily on their material throughout, perhaps most obviously in the earlier part of Section IV and in Section V. It is interesting to note, however, that their material is arranged without specific reference to the control problem. The Doctrine of Workers' Control had not yet been invented.

Sidney Webb. *The Restoration of Trade Union Conditions*. Huebsch. 1917.

Sidney and Beatrice Webb. *The History of Trade Unionism*. Longmans, Green. London, New York. 1920.

A new edition, revised and brought up to date.

G. D. H. Cole. *An Introduction to Trade Unionism*. Bell. London. 1918.

The best brief statement of current trade union problems. Valuable statistical appendices on trade union membership.

G. D. H. Cole. *Labour in War Time*. Bell. London. 1915.

G. D. H. Cole and R. Page Arnot. *Trade Unionism on the Railways*. Allen and Unwin. London. 1917.

G. D. H. Cole. *The World of Labour*. Bell. London. 1915.

American students should not judge this by its chapter on American Labor, which is not a fair sample.

G. D. H. Cole. *Self-Government in Industry*. Bell. London. 1917.

G. D. H. Cole. *Labour in the Commonwealth*. Headley. London. 1919.

Mr. Cole's work is almost as indispensable to the study of current trade unionism as is that of the Webbs for the earlier period. The last two books are less concerned with trade unionism as it is than with trade unionism as a Guild Socialist would like to make it, but they also contain information not accessible elsewhere. All the books are written with the control problem in the very forefront.

Labour Year Book, 1916. Labour Party, 33 Eccleston Square, London.

Labour Year Book, 1919. Labour Party, London.

Useful catalogues of and by the labor movement.

The Industrial Situation After the War. Garton Foundation. London. 1918, 1919.

IV. BOOKS ON SPECIAL PROBLEMS.

A. UNEMPLOYMENT.

W. H. Beveridge. *Unemployment: A Problem of Industry*. Longmans. London. 1910.

R. Williams. *The First Year's Working of the Liverpool Docks Scheme.* London. 1914.

B. METHODS OF PAYMENT.

D. F. Schloss. *Methods of Industrial Remuneration.* Williams and Newgate. London. 1892, 1894, 1898.

G. D. H. Cole. *The Payment of Wages.* Allen and Unwin. London. 1918.

V. AMERICAN BOOKS ON BRITISH LABOR.

Paul U. Kellogg and Arthur Gleason. *British Labor and the War.* Boni and Liveright. New York. 1919.

Arthur Gleason. *What the Workers Want.* Harcourt, Brace and Howe. New York. 1920.

Mr. Gleason is by far the best informed American journalist on British Labor. The earlier book is mainly concerned with political questions, but Part VI and a number of the appendices are useful in the present connection. The latter book makes industry its main business and contains very valuable material. The first-hand description of the human side of the Coal Commission, and the statements secured from the leaders of the Miners and the Shop Stewards, are especially useful.

Additional Notes to the Text
by Richard Hyman

References to these notes are marked by a circle in the text

p.3: **William Straker** (1855–1941) was General Secretary of the Northumberland Miners' Association from 1905 to 1935, a member of the Executive of the national Federation from 1911 to 1925, and one of its main spokesmen at the Sankey Commission.

p.14: **Albert Bellamy** (1871–1931) was President of the Amalgamated Society of Railway Servants (ASRS) and (after the latter amalgamated with two smaller unions in 1913) the National Union of Railwaymen until 1917.

p.14: **The Railway Executive Committee,** composed of eleven general managers of the leading railway companies, was set up by the government at the outbreak of war in 1914 in order to administer the railways. As in many other industries, wartime 'state control' was in fact in the hands of the existing private managers; while the government undertook to guarantee the level of profits achieved in 1913, a record year.

p.15: **John Bromley** (1876–1945) was General Secretary of the Associated Society of Locomotive Enginemen and Firemen from 1914 to 1936. The resolution which he moved at the 1919 TUC read as follows: 'that this Congress instructs the Parliamentary Committee [the forerunner of the present General Council] to draft a practical and effective policy for the control of industry, whereby the trade union movement can secure for democracy complete emancipation from wage slavery.' This was carried with no speeches against and only one dissentient – and then totally ignored.

p.17: **'The great cotton unions':** From the second half of the nineteenth century, the Lancashire cotton industry was strongly unionised. The pattern was for local occupational unions to unite in industry-wide federations (misleadingly entitled 'amalgamations'); the three largest of these, the Cardroom, Spinners' and Weavers' Amalgamations, had memberships in 1920 of 80,000, 55,000 and 225,000 respectively. For many years round the turn of the century the combination of coal and cotton unions had dominated the TUC, often ensuring conservative policies; but by 1920 their ascendancy had been challenged by the rise of new industries and unions. The membership of the cotton unions slumped badly as the industry declined between the wars. For an account of textile trade unionism see H.A.Turner, **'Trade Union Growth, Structure and Policy'**, Allen and Unwin, 1962.

p.22: **R.F.Hoxie** was an American student of labour history and industrial relations, best known for his **'Trade Unionism in the United States',** published in 1917.

p.25: **The National Sailors' and Firemen's Union** (later the National Union of Seamen) was led by J. Havelock Wilson (1858–1929) from its formation in 1887 until his death. In the face of extreme hostility from the ship-owners he won a militant reputation; but after 1914 his fervent pro-war attitudes led him to the far right of the labour movement. The Stockholm Conference of the Socialist International was called by the Russian socialists in 1917, as a forum for the workers of the warring nations to discuss peace terms. The Labour Party conference of August 1917 agreed to send delegates, but Wilson instructed his members not to carry them to Stockholm, and the government then refused them passports.

p.25: **The Russian Campaign:** After the Bolshevik revolution of November 1917, the western governments imposed an economic blockade on the Soviet Republic and gave considerable military support to counter-revolutionary forces. In 1919 the British labour movement launched a 'hands off Russia' movement. Events came to a head during the war between Poland and Russia in 1920. In May, London dockers refused to load the *Jolly George* which was to deliver arms to Poland; in August, when direct British intervention in support of Poland seemed possible, the TUC and Labour Party agreed to set up Councils of Action and to resist the war danger by a general strike if necessary. The government backed down in the face of this unprecedented official support for 'direct action'; but indirect harrassment of the Soviet Union continued.

p.28: **The Friendly Society of Ironfounders** was the main component of the Amalgamated Union of Foundry Workers, formed in 1946, which in turn merged with the Amalgamated Engineering Union in 1967.

p.36: **D.F.Schloss** was author of one of the earliest detailed studies of British industrial relations, **'Methods of Industrial Remuneration',** Williams and Norgate, 1892.

p.42: **Graham Wallas** (1858–1932) was a leading member of the Fabian Society from 1886 (shortly after its foundation) until 1904.

p.48: **Ben Turner** (1863–1942) was President of the National Union of Textile Workers, the main union in the woollen industry, from 1902 to 1933. As Chairman of the TUC General Council in 1927–8 he led the union side in the Mond-Turner talks aimed at union-employer collaboration.

p.53: **J.R. Commons** was an American labour historian, best known for the four-volume **'History of Labor in the United States'**.

p.57: **The engineering dispute of 1897–8,** which Goodrich terms 'a great and unsuccessful strike', was a national lock-out of the Amalgamated Society of Engineers and several smaller unions by the newly-formed Employers' Federation. The immediate issue was a strike in London for shorter hours; but the background cause was the unions' resistance in several bitter local disputes to the introduction of semi-automatic machines worked by non-skilled labour. After six months the unions surrendered, accepting the humiliating 'Terms of Settlement' which endorsed the sanctity of managerial prerogatives. The same agreement set up the notorious disputes procedure, with a protracted series of stages culminating in a Central Conference between employer and union representatives.

p.59: **The 'all-grades' movement on the railways** in 1907 was promoted by the Amalgamated Society of Railway Servants (ASRS). The aim was to unify the various grades of labour by presenting a common programme of improvements, and to compel recognition by the vehemently anti-union railway companies. In the face of a national strike threat the government intervened, and persuaded the companies to introduce a system of conciliation boards to which union officials might be elected. The unions accepted this form of partial and indirect recognition, but the system never worked satisfactorily. See H.A.Clegg, Alan Fox and A.F.Thompson, **'A History of British Trade Unions'**, Vol.I, Clarendon Press, 1964, pp.423–8.

p.59: **Richard** (*not* Robert) **Bell** (1859–1930) was General Secretary of the ASRS from 1897 to 1910.

p.60: **James H. Thomas** (1874–1949) was General Secretary of the NUR from 1917 to 1931. A minister in both inter-war Labour governments, he was notorious for his right-wing views and for aping the life-style of the upper class. With Ramsay MacDonald he joined the Tory 'National' government in 1931.

p.61: **The 'Railway Review'** was the journal of the NUR, the **'Railway Gazette'** a management journal.

p.65: **The Railway Clerks' Association,** one of the strongest of the early white-collar unions, changed its title to Transport Salaried Staffs' Association in 1951.

65: **Huddersfield Dyers:** One of the numerous local and sectional societies in the woollen textile industry, many of which merged into the National Union of Dyers, Bleachers and Textile Workers in 1936.

Bradford Woolcombers: A small craft organisation, amalgamated with the National Union of General and Municipal Workers in 1936.

p.65: Yorkshire Glass Bottle Makers: A close-knit craft union, formed in 1860. **Flint Glass Makers' Friendly Society:** A powerful craft union, formed in the 1840s, exercising tight control over occupational entry and labour supply. **Hand Papermakers:** The 'Original' Society of Papermakers, formed in 1800 (thus one of the earliest British trade unions), declined under the impact of mechanisation and wound up in 1948.

p.65: Yorkshire Stuff Pressers: Traditional craft society with strict apprenticeship regulations. **Amalgamated Society of Lithographic Printers:** Sectional craft union, merged with the National Graphical Association in 1969. **Calico Printers:** Closed craft union of machine-printers which adopted many of the traditions of the earlier hand-printers' societies. **Tape Sizers:** Strongly craft-oriented union of key workers in the preparatory processes of cotton-weaving.

p.66: The London Society of Compositors, an old-established craft organisation, changed its name to the London Typographical Society in 1955 and merged with the Typographical Association in 1964 to form the National Graphical Association.

p.67: The National Maritime Board was a joint union-employer body set up in 1917 (*not* 1914). The employers finally conceded recognition of the Seamen's Union, and introduced a closed shop, in return for collaborationist policies: a response to the rightward turn in the attitudes of the union's leaders.

p.69: The National Society of Dyers and Finishers merged into the National Union of Textile Workers in 1922; this in turn became part of the NUDBTW in 1936.

p.70: The Association of Engineering and Shipbuilding Draughtsmen, later the Draughtsmen's and Allied Technicians' Association, merged with the AUEW in 1972 to form its Technical and Supervisory Section (TASS).

p.72: William Thompson (d.1833) was one of the earliest British socialists, whose ideas had some influence on Marx. His views developed from a critique of orthodox political economy, strongly argued in his **'Labour Rewarded'** (1827). He was also a persistent advocate of women's rights.

p.73: The London Corn Porters were a section of the Labour Protection League, which formed part of the Transport and General Workers' Union in 1922.

p.74: Garment Workers: Various sectional and local clothing unions merged to form the Tailors' and Garment Workers' Union in 1920.

p.75: **A.L.Bowley,** a prominent academic statistician, was particularly well known for his studies of wages and the cost of living.

p.78: **The National Transport Workers' Federation** was formed during the struggles of 1911 in order to co-ordinate the numerous sectional organisations of dockers and road transport workers. The merger of most of these unions to form the TGWU in 1922 removed its main function, and it was wound up in 1927.

p.83: **William H. Beveridge** (1879–1963) was a senior civil servant in the Ministry of Munitions during the war. Later he wrote extensively on labour questions, and prepared a highly influential government report on social policy in 1943.

p.83: **'The hideous scramble for work at the London Docks'** was a consequence of the traditional system of casual employment. At the beginning of each day's shift, dockers were forced to fight for the privilege of getting work. The abolition of this system was from the outset a central trade union demand.

p.84: **Ernest Bevin** (1881–1951) became an organiser for the Dockers' Union in Bristol in 1911, and was made a national official in 1913; he achieved great prominence in presenting the dockers' case to the Shaw Court of Inquiry in 1920. He played a key part in the formation of the TGWU and was its General Secretary until 1946. In his early years a member of the Social-Democratic Federation, he became the mainstay of right-wing policies in the TUC between the wars, and in the Labour Party as Foreign Secretary between 1945 and 1951. See Alan Bullock, **'The Life and Times of Ernest Bevin'**, Vol.I, Heinemann, 1960.

p.95: **Yorkshire Association of Power Loom Overlookers:** Organisation of supervisors in the woollen industry, still in existence.

p.98: For details of the comparison in the Engineers' constitution between the apprenticed craftsman and the qualified doctor see Sidney and Beatrice Webb, **'History of Trade Unionism'**, Longmans, 1920, p.218.

p.99: **George N. Barnes** (1859–1940) was General Secretary of the ASE from 1896 to 1908; from 1916 he was a minister in the Lloyd George coalition government.

p.101: **William Bradshaw** (d.1920) was an official of the Operative Stone Masons, and became first Secretary of the National Federation of Building Trade Operatives (formed in 1918 on the basis of a previous weaker federation).

p.104: **The National Union of Boot and Shoe Operatives** was the main component of the National Union of Footwear, Leather and Allied Trades, formed in 1971.

p.104: **The Amalgamated Association of British Steel Smelters** was the main component of the British Iron, Steel and Kindred Trades Association, formed in 1917.

p.114: **Federation of Weavers' and Overlookers' Amalgamations:** the reference is presumably to the Northern Counties Textile Trades Federation, formed in 1906.

p.118: **United Operative Spindle and Flyer Makers' Society:** a small union which merged with the AEU in 1962.

p.128: **The Amalgamated Stevedores' Labour Protection League** was formed in 1872, the earliest stable union in the London Docks. It voted against the merger which formed the TGWU, and in 1923 it accepted a section of members who broke away from the larger union after a major unofficial strike, at the same time changing its name to National Amalgamated Stevedores and Dockers (the 'blue' union). This was the first of a series of conflicts between the two organisations.

p.128: **The National Society of Amalgamated Brass Workers,** now the National Society of Metal Mechanics, was a Birmingham-based union involved in the 'Birmingham Alliances' with employers in the 1890s (see p.226).

p.130: **The National Association of Operative Plasterers,** formed in 1860, joined the TGWU in 1968.

p.133: **The National Foremen's Society,** later the Association of Supervisory Staffs, Executives and Technicians, merged with the Scientific Workers in 1968 to form the Association of Scientific, Technical and Managerial Staffs.

p.139: **David Kirkwood** (1872–1955) was convenor of shop stewards at the Parkhead Forge in Glasgow, a member of the ILP, and one of those deported in 1916. He ended his career as a Labour peer.

p.141: **The Postmen's Federation** was the main component of the Union of Post Office Workers, formed in 1920.

p.152: **James Winstone** (1863–1921) was one of the syndicalist militants in the South Wales coalfield before the war, and President of the local Labour College. He was elected Vice-President of the South Wales Miners' Federation in 1912, and President in 1915.

p.153: **'The Worker'** was launched in January 1916 as the weekly paper of the Clyde Workers' Committee, was quickly banned by the government, and later became the organ of the National Administrative Committee of the Shop Stewards' and Workers' Committee Movement. In 1925 it was taken over as the official paper of the National Minority Movement.

p.162: **The 'Carpenters' and Joiners' Journal'** was the paper of the Amalgamated Society of Carpenters and Joiners, the main precursor of the Amalgamated Society of Woodworkers (formed in 1921) which was in turn the principal component of the Union of Construction, Allied Trades and Technicians (1972).

p.166: **The Brooklands Agreement** terminated a protracted lock-out of cotton spinners in 1893, and created a centralised bargaining procedure – the first in any major British industry.

p.178: **'The Ragged Trousered Philanthropists'**, the classic socialist novel by Robert Tressell, was first published in 1914. Reprinted by Panther in 1965.

p.190: **Arthur MacManus** (1889–1927) was a leading member of the Clyde Workers' Committee and the Socialist Labour Party, President of the Shop Stewards' and Workers' Committee Movement, and first Chairman of the CP.

p.191: **William Brace** (1865–1947) was one of the 'old guard' of the South Wales Miners' Federation; he lost his place on its Executive to a syndicalist in 1911, but was elected its President in 1912. He was a minister in the coalition government between 1915 and 1918.

p.197: **David Lloyd George** (1863–1945), Liberal politician, Minister of Munitions 1915–6, Prime Minister 1916–22. **Walter Runciman** (1870–1949), Liberal politician, President of the Board of Trade 1914–6. **Arthur Henderson** (1863–1935), official of the Ironfounders, MP from 1903, Secretary of the Labour Party 1911–34, leading Labour member of the Lloyd George coalition government. **William Mosses** (1858–1943) was General Secretary of the United Patternmakers' Association from 1884 to 1917 and of the Federation of Engineering and Shipbuilding Trades from its formation in 1891 until 1917. The Federation was broadened into the Confederation of Shipbuilding and Engineering Unions in 1936.

p.226: **The Birmingham Alliances** were joint union-employer committees formed in the brass-working trades in the 1890s in order to regulate both wages and selling prices.

p.235: **Vernon Hartshorn** (1872–1931) was one of the leaders of the non-syndicalist left in the pre-war South Wales Miners' Federation, and among those who defeated the established leadership in the Executive elections of 1911. Subsequently he gave strong support to the war and moved to the right of the union; he was local President from 1921 to 1924.

p.235: **Stephen Walsh** (1879–1929) was a Lancashire miners' official and MP from 1906 until his death; he was Vice-President of the national Federation from 1922 to 1924.

p.238: **The Cotton Control Board:** though Goodrich rejects the argument that this Board represented a form of positive workers' control, his own account is somewhat uncritical. A more candid assessment is given by Hubert D. Henderson, secretary of the Board between 1917 and 1919, in **'The Cotton Control Board'**, Clarendon Press, 1922. For most of its existence the employers were in a majority on the Board; moreover its activities were dominated by the chairman who 'was an employer, with an employer's outlook and ideas... His unquestioned assumption of the initiative thus meant in effect that the initiative rested with the employers. The operatives' leaders fulfilled essentially the role of a friendly opposition, now pleading for concessions, now issuing warnings, but at no time playing an equal part in the determination of policy' (p.11). Moreover the unemployment relief scheme, described with some enthusiasm by Goodrich (pp.80–1) was blatantly used as a bargaining counter by the employers: they threatened to withdraw the scheme unless the unions kept their wage demands well below the rise in living costs. Up to the middle of 1918, wage rates were only a third above the pre-war level, whereas the official cost-of-living index (which in fact *under*stated the increase in working-class living costs) had doubled. An official Tribunal of Inquiry, set up after a strike of spinners in September 1918, reported that 'the profits made are satisfactory, and indeed high... [but] relatively to the cost of living the operatives are substantially worse off than before the war and by comparison with other trades are bearing a disproportionate share of the burden arising from increased prices' (Henderson, p.63).

p.239: **A.J.Penty** was an architect strongly influenced by the views of William Morris on art and society. His **'Restoration of the Guild System'**, published in 1906, provided the mediaevalist element in Guild Socialist theory. Shortly before his death in 1936 he became involved with fascism.

Index

'Abnormal places,' 167

Absentee Committees, 149

Absenteeism, 209

Agreement, Bradford Dyers' Association, 68, 80, 118; Brooklands, 166; Engineering Trades, 57; Leek Silk Weavers', 187; Linotype Operators', 188; Liverpool Dockers', 58; Oldham, 224–225; Pottery, 58; Scottish Bookbinders', 188, Sliding Scale, 243; Steel Dressers', 61; 'Treasury,' 171, 194–197

Agreements, collective, 56–58

Allocation of Work, 58, 61, 155–156, 190

Amalgamated Society of Engineers, 21, 98–99, 275

'Amicable discipline,' 35

Apprentices, limitation of, 58

Apprenticeship, 21, 92–98, 181; Britannia Metal Smiths, rules of, 95

Authority, of Employers, 56–57; opposition to, 30–31

Barnes, George, 99, 277

Barr and Stroud's, 218

Bell, Robert, 59, 275

Beveridge, W. H., 83, 277

Bevin, Ernest, 84, 277

Birmingham Alliances, 241–242, 279

Birmingham brass trades' grading system, 165

Bowley, Professor, 75–76, 86, 277

Bradford Dyers' Association Agreement, 1914, 68, 80, 118; payment system of, 172–173

Bradshaw, Secretary, on building-trades-labor supply, 101, 277

'Brains Committee,' 219

Bramwell, Hugh, testimony of, 106, 212–214

British Westinghouse Co., 220

Brooklands Agreement, 166, 279

Building Trades Parliament, *see under* Joint Industrial Council

Ca'canny policy, IX, 172, 178

Cadbury's, 218, 219

Cannan, Edwin, testimony of, 28–29

Cecil, Lord Robert, quoted, 28

Central Labor College, X, 5

Clay, Henry, XXXVIII, 27, 259

Cleveland Rules, the, 148–149

Clyde Dilution Scheme, XXXVIII, 10, 197–201

Clyde Shop Steward's case, 32

Clyde Workers' Committee, XII, 8, 259

Coal Commission, XVII–XVIII, 1, 46, 51, *and see under* Miners

Coal Miners, *see under* Miners

Cole, G. D. H., XXXVI, 6, 161–162, 164, 168, 236

Collective Agreements, 56–58

Collective bargaining, 53, 62, 165, 166, 168

Collective Contract payment, XVI, 173

Compulsory Unionism, 128

Conciliation Boards, 14, 224–226

Control, 'agreeable,' 253; a political word, 36–38; 'contagious,' 266; 'complete executive,' 51–52; demand for, 3–50; degree of, 54–55; Derbyshire Miners and, 44; extent of, 253–266; favored by Trade Unionists, 17, 18; Frontier of, 56–71; Guild Socialists and, 5–6; independent, 257, 266; irksomeness of present system of, 35; Marxian Industrial Unionists and, 5; Miners' Federation and, 12; National Union of Railwaymen and, 13–14; negative, 202, 217, 257; Old Craft, 264–265; over choice of foremen, 120; political factors of, 38; positive, 257, 264, 266; resentment against, 30–35; striking instances of, 260–261; State, 233; technical factors of, 39; wage element dominant factor in, 21; workers', 4 *et seq.*, 56

Co-operative work, 173–175

Cotton Control Board, 237–239, 248; policy concerning unemployment, 80–81, 279–80

Craftsmanship, 39–42

Dawson's, John, 231–233, 258

De-casualization Policy, 83

Defence of the Realm Act, 237

Demand for control, 1–50; organized demand, 4–18; by propagandist bodies, 5–7; shop stewards, 7–11; trade unions, 11–18; unorganized demand, 18–50

Demarcation issue, 99–100, 181

Denny's, Wm., 218

Dilution, 100–103, 181–182, 189; Clyde scheme of, 10, 197–201

Direct Representation from Workshops, 9

Discipline and management, 61–62

Duckham, Sir Arthur, 250

Education in control, 248

Employers, authority of, 56, 60; limitation on, 63, 77; policy relative to foremen, 129–132

Employment, 63 *et seq.*; joint control of, 68; 'rationing,' 73; regularizing, 82–85; restrictions on, 92 *et seq.*; union membership a condition of, 64–66

Engineering and Shipbuilding Draughtsmen, 70, 276

Engineering Trades Agreement, 1898, 57, 275

Factory Act regulations, 154

Fines, 210

Foremanship, standard of, 135–145

Foremen, choice of, 117–125; National Industrial Conference report on, 132–133; organization of, 126–134; separate unions for, 130; workers' choice of, 120–121, 135

Foremen's Benefit Society, 131, 133

'Forty-hour Movement,' XV, 76

Foster Report, 6, 25, 86–91, 229–230

Foster, Thomas, XXXVIII, 86

Gainford, Lord, 155, 259–260

Gallacher-Paton memorandum, XVI, 10, 70–71, 123, 174

Garton Foundation, report of, 19

Gaunt's, Reuben, 108

Glasgow Trades Union Congress, 15–18, 273

Gleason, Arthur, XXX, 41

Guaranteed Time, 78–79, 91

Guild Socialists, XV–XVII, 5, 122

Hamilton, Lord Claud, 59

Hodges, Frank, XXXVII, 12, 22, 23, 35, 164, 206–207, 212–213, 259

Humphrey, G. H., 232

Improvements, insistence on, 202–216; miners' demand for, 204–215

Industrial Crisis and the Way Out, 239

Industrial Democracy, 91

'Industrial Truce,' 7

Industrial Unionists, and contagious control, 264; Marxian, 5; shop stewards, 9

Industry, workers' control of, 15–18; joint control of, 224–240

Interests in industry, worker's, 19–50; what he gets, 20–25; what it's for, 25–27; how he's treated, 27–38; what he does, 38–50

Inventions, 218–219

Irritation strike, 179

Joint action, *see under* Trade policy

Joint control and price fixing, 169–171

Joint discipline, 147–150

Joint Industrial Council, for the Building Industry, XXXVIII, 86, 113, 224, 227–228, 230; for the Silk Industry, 227–228

Juvenile Employment Committee, 97

Labor Party, 157

Labor Unions, attitude toward innovations, 186–191; *see also under* Trade Unions and separate titles

Liverpool Docks Scheme, First Year's Working of, 79

Lloyd George, David, 60, 193, 279

London Society of Compositors, 67; report of, 97, 276

Machine industry, 39; production, 102

Managerial functions, 146–160; allocation of work, 155–156; measurement of results, 156–159; safety of workers, 150, 154; wartime regulations, 147–149

Mann, Tom, XXIV, 16, 76

Man Power of the Nation, the, 29–30

Marxian Industrial Unionists, 5

Measurement of results, quantity, 157; quality, 158–159

Mining Association of Great Britain, scheme of, 250–251

Miners' Federation, of Great Britain, XVII, 1, 12–13, 42, 151–152, 154, 163–164, 192, 208, 209, 235, 244–245; of South Wales, 6, 152–156, 212–214, 235–236

'Miners' Four Days' policy, 254

Miners' Minimum Wage Act, XXXV, 137, 167

Miners' Next Step, XXXV, 105, 123, 144, 183, 263

Miners, complaints of, 205–206; improvements demanded by, 204–215

Miners' Nationalization Bill, 12–13

Ministry of Labor's Report on Works Committees, 40, 85, 108, 122, 140–141

Muir, John, 193

Munitions of War Act, XI, 147–150

Murphy, J. T., XXV, 100, 102, 182, 255

National Guilds League, XVI, 6

National Industrial Conference, XX, 132

Nationalization and Joint Control, 26; miners' bill for, 6, 12, 13

National Union of Railwaymen, 2–6, 4–5; policy of, 13–14, 42, 61, 78

Northumberland miners, 49, 50

Officialism, revolt against, 8

Oldham agreement, 224–225

Output Committees, 149

Output, 210; restriction of, 177–185

Overtime, Union restrictions against, 74–75

Payment, and control, 164–165; collective, 163, 170–173; by results, 165; Bradford's Dyers' Association's system, 172–173; for work in abnormal places, 167; methods of, 161–175; South Wales Colliery Agreement for, 167; Woolen Trades' plan for, 167

Personal freedom, 34

Piece work, 162–163, 205; Bradford Dyers' Association's system of, 172–173; Phoenix Dynamo Company's objections to, 170; Woodworking Trades opposed to, 162

Phoenix Dynamo Co., 170–171

Pitfalls of the Promoted, the, 29, 30

'Policing,' 31, 137, 261

'Politics of industry,' 176

Poor Law Commission Report, 86

Postal and Telegraph Clerks, 15, 112

Post Office Workers, 46

Power Loom Overlookers, 95, 277

Premium bonus, 162–163

Production, regulation of, 243–245

Promotion, 111–116; Federation of Weavers' rules for, 114; Joint Industrial Council's rules for, 112–113; Seniority rule for, 112; the workers' prerogative, 115

Publicity of profits, 249–251

'Rank and File Movement,' 8

Rate fixing, 168–171

Redmayne, Sir Richard, testimony of, 205–206

Renold's, Hans, 120–121

Restriction and restrictions, 176–185

Richardson, Alexander, 131

Rowntree's, 121

'Sack,' the right to, 102 *et seq.*

Safety, 150–154; strikes, 152–154

Sankey, Justice, quoted, 46

Sankey Report, XVIII, 13, 222

Schloss, D. F., 36, 110, 125, 161–162, 218, 274

Scottish Master Tailors' statement, 73–74

Sharing of work, 73–74

Sheffield Workers' Committee, 9

Shop Committees and duties, 200–201

Shop Stewards' Manual, 8–9, 140; movement, XI–XIII, 7, 9–11, 255
Short time, 73–77
Sliding Scale, 243
Smillie, Robert, XXXVII, 154, 206, 215
Smith, Herbert, XXXVII, 24, 206
Socialism, State, IX, 25–27
Socialist Labor Party, XII–XIII, 5
Sparkes, Malcolm, XXXVIII, 227, 256
Specialization, 182, 183
Stay-in strike, 178–179
Steel Dressers' Agreement, 61
Stockholm International Labor Conference, 25, 274
Straker, William, quoted, 3, 22, 27, 38, 221; testimony before Coal Commission, 33, 47, 273
Strikes, against objectionable promotions, 114; against objectionable supervision, 135–137; against use of machinery, 184; because of a woman shop steward, 184; for reinstatement of operatives, 106–107, 109; for safety, 152; Glasgow Dockers', 128; Iron Founders', 204
Stuff Pressers' Society, 69, 94, 117, 172, 263, 265
'Suggestion Boxes,' 218
Suggestions, right to make, 43–46
Syndicalism, IX, 4

Tawney, R. H., XXXVII, 135, 258
Technique, consultation over changes, 186–201; insistence on improvements, 202–216; restriction and restrictions, 176–185; suggestions and inventions, 217–222
Thomas, J. H., 60, 275
Thompson, William, 72, 276
Trade Policy, joint action regarding, 223–240; Joint Industrial Councils, 226–227; Oldham Agreement, 224–225; publicity of profits, 249–251; scheme of Postal Telegraph Clerks' Association, 223–240; workers' demands, 241–252
Trade, the right to a, 92–103
Trades Union Congress, Glasgow, 1919, 15–16, 18, 273
Trade Union movement, 36
Trade Unions, and overtime, 14–75; and

short time, 75–77; as employment agencies, 66; attitude toward promotions, 111; guaranteed time, 78–79; membership of, 92–93; policy regarding foremen, 126–129, 142
Treasury Agreement, the, XI, 171, 194–197
'Tuppenny Strike,' 8
Turner, Ben, 47–48, 274

Unemployment, 72 et seq.; a charge on the industry, 86; a matter of trade policy, 223; fear of restricts output, 87; prevention of, 86–91; schemes for lessening, 80–86; security against, 23
Unionized industry, 64–66
Unions as employment agencies, 66–70

Victimization, 104, 107–108

Wages, 20; and hours, 20–23, 53; collective contract, 173–174; collective payment, 171–173; methods of payment, 161 et seq.; piece work, 162–173
'Wage Slavery,' 38
Weavers' Manifesto, 242
Webb, Sidney and Beatrice, XXXVII, 36, 86, 91, 93, 112, 157, 203
Wedgwood's, 43
Whitehead Torpedo Works, 147
Whitley Councils, XIX–XX, 5–6, 154, 226, 240; report of, 113–114, 192, 221, 248
Williams, R., 79
Woods, Frank, 97–98
Wool Control Board, 237, 249
Women labor, 102
Work, equalization of, 73–74
Workers, grievances of, 140–142; interests in industry, 19–20, 38; methods of payment of, 161 et seq.; objection to being watched, 137–138; resentment of, 29–35; safety of, 150–154; sensitiveness of, 32; servility of, 33; treatment of, 27–29
Workers' Control, see under Control
Working Schedules, 156
Workmanship, 46–49; collective, 43
Works' Council, 231–233

Yorkshire Glass Bottle Workers, 74, 276